Military and Media

Military and Media

Dr. Rajesh Kumar

PRASHANT PUBLISHING HOUSE
DELHI-110094

Published by :
Prashant Publishing House
C-34, 28 Foota Road, Gali-3,
West Karwal Nagar, Delhi-110094
Phone : 011-22963970, Mob. : 9810396373
e-mail.: prashantpublishinghouse@gmail.com

Military and Media

First Published 2013

ISBN 978-93-80565-39-2

PRINTED IN INDIA
Published by Mr. R.K. Jha M/s Prashant Publishing House and Published at H.S. Offset House Press, Delhi.

Preface

The relationship between the United States military and the media has been a complex one for years. Like any relationship, it can be characterized by ebbs and flows, good times and bad from the perspective of both institutions. From Vietnam to Operation Iraqi Freedom (OIF), the military/media relationship's complexity has been the result of a clash of cultures.

The military funding of science has had a powerful transformative effect on the practice and products of scientific research since the early 20th century. Particularly since World War I, advanced science-based technologies have been viewed as essential elements of a successful military.

The expansion of the number of news outlets over the past 20 years ensures that military action by Western countries is accompanied by massive continuous coverage and commentary. Most analysis of the relationship between war and the media focuses either on the contentious nature of the relationship between journalists and armed forces or on the disruptive impact of news coverage on military operations. This paper argues that the relationship between developments in the media and the military should be conceptualized in a more comprehensive way. Such an approach suggests that the impact of media developments on the conduct of military operations is more radical and than is normally suggested.

Today's scope of military operations often encompass areas of consideration outside of the military such as the economic and political impacts. This calls for high levels of coordination, consultation and interaction among all actors involved. We are of opinion that this comprehensive approach to operations may benefit from social media. We define social media as internet-based applications that allow groups of users to create, share, and gather information with the intention to facilitate overall command communications strategy.

The book deeply highlights the Military and Media work and relationship.

—Editor

Contents

1

Use of News and Perception of the Military

"Army, Marines miss recruiting goals again: More cash and appeals to parents, patriotism haven't reversed trend." This was the headline for NBC news correspondent Jim Miklaszewski's story concerning the problems facing recruiting May 2005. Many similar headlines appeared during the third year of the war in Iraq. April 2005, the Army had missed its recruiting goal for the third month in a row. The recruiters were short by 2,800 recruits, missing their mark by 42%. And for the first time in 10 years, the Marine Corps was unable to meet their goal for four months in a row.

Miklaszewski (2005) reports part of the recruiting problem is related to fear from parents about sending their child into the military and the prospect they will be sent to war. This report is just one example illustrating how the media has managed to cultivate fear by making images of death and casualties resulting on both sides salient during their intense coverage of the war. "Journalism's images of war disturb. Among the most powerful visuals known to humankind, they are haunted by the stubborn inevitability and proximity of death". After September 11, 2001, the number of war images nearly doubled the typical amount of published images. This increase in war images has the potential to cultivate perceptions and feelings toward the military and also has the ability to directly impact recruiting.

Recruiting difficulties have been well documented over the course of the past two to three years dating back to the Army National Guard first missing its monthly goals in 2003. That trend led to the Army Guard missing their fiscal year 2004 goal for the first time in 10 years, falling 7,000 enlistees short of their goal of 56,000, and further causing the Guard to increase its recruiting force more than 50% (Moniz, 2004).

The *New York Times* first reported about Army Recruiting Command's changes regarding lowering goals of recruiters and recruit standards in October 2004. According to the report, one main reason was the Army's inability to enter the 2005 fiscal year with 35% of its yearly goal already achieved. Instead the Army projected its goal as 25%, before officially achieving a goal of 18% – almost half of the original intended target.

Even with lower standards for enlistment, the Army fell 7,000 enlistees short of its target of 80,000. The difficulties of recruiting are also being felt within the Marine Corps, although they continue to meet yearly goals. General Michael W. Hagee, the Marine Corps commandant, has said that with the war in Iraq still raging, many parents were advising their children to wait before signing up for the Marines. "They're saying, 'It's not, maybe, a bad idea to join the Marine Corps, but why don't you consider it a year from now or two years from now,'" he said. "So the recruiters are having to work much harder out there right now".

The war in Iraq made death and the inherent dangers of being in the military salient to the military's audiences. The military was riding the wave of post-September 11th patriotism and seen as upholding a noble and patriotic duty to the country. As the war progressed into the summer of 2005, and more of the nation's service members lives were lost, pressure came from members of both parties in Congress for the White House to create a strategy for withdrawal from Iraq (Klein, 2005).

In regard to the recruiting difficulty, the military branches say they have no way to directly measure the effect that war injuries and deaths are having on each service's recruiting (Moniz, 2005). "There is no way to quantify it, no block on an application that you can check for that," says Maj. Dave Griesmer, a Marine Corps spokesman.

However, there are numbers that show the desirability of military service has not necessarily dropped – just the desirability of serving in the Army and Marine Corps. The Navy and Air Force are reportedly turning away thousands of recruits, and the Air Force has a backlog of nearly 9,000 enlistees (Moniz, 2005). According to the Department of Defense military casualty information (2006), nearly 96% of the deaths during Operation Iraqi Freedom have been members of the Army or Marine Corps making a strong case for the correlation between media messages and the desirability to serve in either of these two services.

Shah, McLeod, and Yoon (2001) conclude "people seek information from whatever media sources are most accessible and normative in their social networks" with older generations using print and broadcast media supplemented by the Internet and the reverse being the case for younger generations. Because the effectiveness of the variety of media messages is not known, the purpose of this study is to examine which, and to what extent, of various communication forms cultivate and affect perception and/or beliefs about the military in high school youth and their parents. In regard to recruiting, the military can use this information to add to, correct, or even influence attitudes of those audiences.

USE OF NEWS AND PERCEPTION OF THE MILITARY

The effect that concerns this research is the perception of the military– how news effect that perception. News can be delivered through television, print, radio, and the Internet. In news, an example of cultivation effects showing statistical significance with heavy exposure to newspaper stories containing negative reports about ethnic crimes leads people to perceive ethnic minorities as being more of a threat than they would if they had read newspapers without negative ethnic reports. When measuring cultivation effects from the news, it is important to know that news or "real" media, especially programs containing violence, have a greater influence upon beliefs than fictional media. An example of this was depicted by embedded media during Operation Iraqi Freedom. Due to unprecedented access by embedded media in bringing the public direct imagery from Iraq, the public's perceptions about the daily life of a soldier in war have become "real" to the audience. News images allow the public to see what is real but in a way that only partly reflects what is actually happening. Images from the war in Iraq may show how horrible life is only through pictures that extremely exaggerate the quality of life during war time and the time frame in which hardship must be endured. Those images are not formed in a vacuum.

The link between negative media and shortfalls in recruiting has been made by several Senators as they denounced other lawmakers and the news media for unfavourable depictions of the Iraq war (Allen, 2005). At a U.S. Senate Armed Services Committee hearing, Sen. James Inhofe, an Oklahoma Republican, said families are discouraging young men and women from enlisting "because of all the negative media that's out there". According to the theory of cultivation, constantly portraying news of death in Iraq could change audiences' perceptions of the actual amount of death occurring. This leads to the following prediction:

H1: Those who rely more on the news for information about the military will have negative attitudes about a) the military and about b) serving in the military.

USE OF ENTERTAINMENT AND PERCEPTION OF THE MILITARY

For most viewers, new types of delivery systems (e.g., cable, satellite, and cassette) represent even further penetration and integration of established viewing patterns into everyday life. Teenagers, as well as adults, now have more sources, such as the Internet, video games, and talk radio, to gather information on the world around them to supplement television use. Depictions or assumptions based on television programming and genres can be applied to genres of video games and where interests lie when searching the Internet. Entertainment media is just another form for audiences to gather information. Although it may seem as though what is watched, read, or heard may be done so purely for entertainment, serious and real life situations are being depicted to audiences (Baum, 2003). Examples of these would be entertainment news, talk shows, and movies. Most television shows and movies regarding the military portray the military in a glamorous light by selecting attractive and popular stars to play the leads and stamping them with the label of the hero that saves the day.

In the past year, movies like *Jarhead*, *Annapolis*, and *Stealth* have been released depicting and glamorizing life in the military. On their opening weekends alone these movies grossed nearly $50 million. The popularity of military portrayal in film has also spread to television shows such as *Over There*, a show depicting current life of war in the Middle East. Even through popular television soap operas like *Days of our Lives* include a plotline of a Marine deployed to fight in the war on terrorism.

In video games such as SOCOM: U.S. Navy SEALs, a player is allowed to become immersed in the military experience by speaking commands to your fellow "teammates" through a headset and giving a person of the actual sense of what it is like to be on a military mission. Whether it is in video games, movies, or television, entertainment media glamorize service in the military in contrast to what a viewer would see in on the news. While entertainment may also deal with the reality of death in military service, we must take into account the way in which the two genres regard death. News rarely demonstrates the ability for valiant efforts of service members to be encapsulated into an entertaining story; instead, it focuses mainly on numbers of dead rather than heroic circumstances behind their sacrifice. Through the entertainment media, death of a service member is rarely in vain. Therefore this study posits that:

H2: Those who rely more on entertainment for information about the military will have positive attitudes about a) the military and about b) serving in the military. Video gaming systems with the ability to produce extremely lifelike images are a relatively recent addition to the media environment. Like movies, these games offer new and often times quite realistic worlds that have the ability to depict violence, sexuality, and other real life situations. As technology grows and these games become more and more prevalent in the daily lives of teenagers who have never been without the influences of these alternate forms of entertainment, it is likely cultivation will have an impact similar to that of television. Due to the fact even perceived realism has shown to play a role in linking exposure to social perceptions, it may be that these alternative media could soon prove to be just as effective upon perception as real television images.

One study found nearly a third of boys and girls reported playing video games at home for one to two hours per week. Video games are also the most popular form of entertainment for boys and men between 12 and 25 years of age and are increasingly popular for parents of children. According to a recent survey of more than 500 households in 2005 regarding video game use, nearly 35% of parents play video games, 80% of which play video games with their children and 66% reportedly do so to bring their family closer together. However the number of parents playing games is relatively small when compared to the 81% of 15-18 year olds who have a video game player in the home, and another half has one in their own room, accessible at any time of the day.

Van Mierlo and Van de Bulck (2003) found players of violent video games predicted higher estimates of the prevalence of violent crime as well as the number of policemen in the total workforce, an indication of the influence the cultivation effect has through video games.

In the past year, at least 10 video games on Microsoft's Xbox video game console have been released portraying depictions of life in the military as a "tactical shooter." The most notable is the release of *America's Army: Rise of a Soldier*, a game originally released via computer download and was further refined for release on the Xbox due to a response of 17 million online downloads. This game was actually developed by the Army to attempt to portray life as a soldier in Iraq as realistically as possible. On the video game website Gamespot.com, users have the ability to give their own rating of the game and more than 70% have given it a rating of 8 or higher on a 10-point scale.

Today, With the Armed Forces clearly recognizing the importance of providing an entertaining experience of life in the military through video games, and with gaming proving to be a much larger role in the lives of adolescents than parents, it only widens the gap between the importance of entertainment in the lives of children in comparison to the significance of news for adults.

Entertainment shows like *The Daily Show with John Stewart* are talking about serious issues through humor, and the effects of these shows on public perception should not be taken lightly, especially for adolescents. For children 15-18 years old, only 10% of their television time is spent watching news, a mere seven minutes reading the newspaper, and the rest dedicated to entertainment media. Those slightly older, in the 18-24 year old category, report they devote 35 minutes per day to news; the attention given to news on a given day nearly doubles for those 35 and older. Because more audiences are tuning in to get the news from different avenues, such as entertainment (Kurtz, 1999), these findings could be very important in understanding how little youth rely on news while learning more from entertainment. Therefore this gives parents the ability to have cultivated more beliefs about negative repercussions of military service through hard news.

H3: Compared to parents, young adults manifest positive attitudes about a) the military and about b) serving in the military.

Media and Power

Images in media can be powerful, and for those who know how to use images in mass media have the ability to shape the perception of the masses. Media provide audiences a chance to view situations and events that they would otherwise never be able to experience. The media are able to do this through detailed and dramatic storytelling, photography, video, film and much more. However, those images relayed to audiences only portray a narrow view of a specific viewpoint. According to cultivation theory, perceptions are affected through cumulative exposure to media images.

In the age of "new media," television still dominates the other forms of media. As of 2003, the television and the telephone were the only two media devices utilized by nearly every household in the United States (U.S. Census Bureau, 2006). The average person will spend more than 1,800 hours this year alone watching television programming – greater than the use of radio, Internet, video games, newspapers, books, and magazines combined. Throughout an entire year, more than 20% of an average person's time is spent watching television. Compare that to eight hours of sleep a night taking up another 33% of the entire year and that leaves slightly less than 50% of the year for work and any other activities. This information provides a profound look into the viewing habits of the average American.

The notion that media images and television viewing are related to people's perceptions of social reality is virtually undisputed in the social sciences (Shrum, 2001), which is normally demonstrated by a positive correlation between the amount of television a person watches and the extent to which that person's real-world perceptions are congruent with the world as it appears in the media.

Using the cultivation theory to direct the study of media effects on parents' and young adults' regarding the desirability of military service, it would be expected that those parents who have a positive attitude about the military cultivated through media will be more likely to support their child entering the military. Correspondingly, those young adults with a positive attitude about the military cultivated through media will also be more likely to consider military service.

Cultivation

According to Gerbner and Gross' (1976) study on cultural indicators, common rituals and mythologies are methods of symbolic socialization and control. They demonstrate how society works by dramatizing its norms and values. They are the necessary parts of interaction that influence our outlook on society, our culture, and help to regulate social relationships. In essence, these stories helped to define past cultures through symbolic means, and today we use a variety of media forms such as television, movies, and books as opposed to basic story telling in the past.

Gerbner and his colleagues began to see a pattern emerge confirming their ideas that television was a much different medium from others at the time and required a new approach to study. Printed media require literacy for utilization, radio only tells information and requires an auditory comprehension to create a picture in a person's mind, and prior to the television any sort of visual media required a person to actually travel some sort of distance to become consumed in that visual experience. Because its accessibility is relatively unlimited, television has the ability to be with us throughout our lives, from even before we are able to read until our older years where it can be used to keep us company. However, this does not dismiss the effects of other forms of mass media as related to cultivation.

Cultivation is not easily understood. Two different types of effects are considered when using cultivation theory, first-order effects and second-order effects. First-order effects refer to estimations of frequency and probability of aspects of social reality that are empirically observable and verifiable in the real world, while second-order effects refer to opinions, beliefs, and attitudes toward an aspect of social reality. In the case of violence, the first-order effect would be for a heavy viewer of television to overstate the amount of crime in the world compared to a light viewer, and the second-order effect would be the heavier viewer believing the world is a scarier place. Gerbner (1998) refers to this as "mean world syndrome."

Quantitative studies on the cultivation effect have shown effects are generally found to be small, but longitudinal studies have shown there are consistent effects, and the fact there are effects, no matter how minute, is significant when dealing with our perceptions.

Although Gerbner (1998) states the cultivation theory should only be used in the case of television, using the theory with other media is not unprecedented. Lubbers and Scheepers (2000) used cultivation and found significant effects in newspaper readers, Van Mierlo and Van de Bulck (2003) found significant cultivation effects in the video game arena, and Hawkins and Pingree (1981) found significant evidence showing differential cultivation effects based upon television genres viewed. Additionally, Pfau, Moy, and Kahlor (1999) used a modified version of the cultivation theory which combined the use of a variety of media and their effects on confidence of democratic institutions. It is upon Hawkins and Pingree's (1981) implications of genre-specific cultivation effects, as well as Pfau and colleagues' (1999) uses of different media, that we base our study upon and categorize various media into the area of news, entertainment, advertising, and conversation.

Because market research has shown our country's youth to constantly change what messages they will be most susceptible to and the generational difference of dominant media use between adults and adolescents, military recruiting must constantly look for new, inventive ways to deliver their message to their target audiences. The ability to provide more information for the military's recruitment campaign on where teenagers receive the strongest influence would allow for a better concentration of assets and resources.

Each of the aforementioned may be considered by both young adults and their parents before a decision can be made to enlist in military service. However, the direct importance of each media form and the direct affect those forms have on either parents or young adults are not known. To study the cultivation effects of information regarding the military, the only way to know where they are receiving their information is by recognizing where and to what frequency young adults go to actively seek knowledge about the military. Knowledge of where young adults seek their information and being able to further predict the impact on attitudes of the target audience, would be vital to military recruiting efforts. However, with today's technology, ways in which both teenagers and parents gather information has become increasingly more diverse due to the Internet, video games, and satellite news coverage.

USE OF DISCUSSIONS AND PERCEPTION OF THE MILITARY

Family communication patterns can also influence the transmission of political attitudes, such as views about the military, from parent to child. Meadowcroft (1986) posited family communication is an important influence on children and young adults' perceptions of social reality because these communication patterns are a framework for interpreting the environment.

Family communication about politics is a complex process. Gemelli (1996) suggests young adults assert their own views, and parents are less likely to transmit their ideas directly to their children. Evolving perspectives can also affect family communication patterns. McDevitt & Chaffee (2002b) argue parental preparation for political communication may actually be meager. However, more parents are watching hard news and receiving information about the military through news media as opposed to entertainment media, a negative affect is likely to be projected.

Beyond typologies of family communication, researchers have noted a lack of political discussion between parents and children. "The impact of media, primarily television, is in some measure a function of parental interest and the likelihood that television news will be watched and discussed in the home". Drew and Reeves (1980) found that only 10% of the children in their samples discussed television with their parents, friends, or in classrooms. Making the correlation between politics and military, it can be expected when youth are having more conversations at home or school about the military, they will have a stronger attitude about the military. However, there can be a multitude of factors contributing to either a young adult's of parent's perception of the military, such as prior military service or the current service of a parent or sibling. With military background in the immediate family it is more likely for parents and their children to have more informed conversations about military service. Those with less direct experience are more likely to have their attitudes affected by the media. Thus, this study posits:

H5: Those who rely more on conversations for information about the military will have negative attitudes toward a) the military and about b) serving in the military.

H6: Both parents and young adults, who have military experience within the immediate family, will have positive attitudes about a) the military and about b) serving in the military.

USE OF ADVERTISING AND PERCEPTION OF THE MILITARY

Advertisements today do not always come in the form of neatly-packaged 30-second spots in between television programs; there are more subtle and direct forms of influence such as Internet chat rooms and blogs, Internet pop-ups, and product placement within television and radio programming.

To illustrate the number of people flocking to the Internet as a source for information, MySpace.com, a blog site, has grown in popularity from zero to nearly 50 million users in two years. It is possible that military blogs, or milblogs, could be an important source for disseminating information about the military, or advertising in this case. However, Internet chat has already caught onto the point where the Army's recruiting website GoArmy.com now includes a link to enter a chat room where Army recruiters are available to answer any questions even until 2 a.m. Sunday through Thursday.

The Internet is not the only place recruiting efforts are currently leaning toward to attract its youth demographic. Product placement has also found a place for recruiting in the form of NASCAR sponsorship for the military services. The Marine Corps spends approximately $3.5 million on its Busch Series sponsorship, while the Army spends "less than $10 million" on its Nextel Cup sponsorship.

While there are no studies directly measuring the persuasiveness of recruiting advertisements, there is significant evidence showing how advertising in general can be an extremely effective tool. The television documentary *Merchants of Cool* illustrates the power of advertising and the rise of Sprite from relative anonymity in the beverage industry to its relationship with hip-hop culture today. By advertising on MTV, linking the product to cultural icons and hip-hop concerts, and even paying "cool" kids to show up to these concerts to have a good time, Sprite was able to successfully launch itself into an association with cultural identity.

By marketing "cheap and easy content" to appeal to our nation's youth through, what the program calls, "mooks" (the guy who even in his late 20s and early 30s continues to act like a teenager) and "midriffs" (the narcissistic teenager who strives to look and act much older than she really is) who adolescents can identify as "cool," and then implying the products teens buy will allow them admission to these desirable groups helps make MTV $1 billion a year in advertising revenue.

Admittedly, this strategy is not about delivering youth with what they want to see on television, it is about figuring out through which kinds of programming to best pitch what marketers want to deliver to the young consumer.

If the Army and Marine Corps have truly found a way to market their product through some sort of "brand recognition," through areas such as their NASCAR advertisements – it could have an even greater impact in terms of parental influence. Moore, Wilkie, and Lutz (2002) used multiple measures to demonstrate how brands transcend by generation through parental influence. Likewise, if parents are able to associate these advertisements with a positive affect, it is likely those perceptions will be passed on. This study predicts:

H4: Those who rely more on advertisements for information about the military will have positive attitudes about joining the military.

PARENTAL INFLUENCE AND PERCEPTION OF THE MILITARY

While a past U.S. Army Research Institute study regarding parental influence has shown a correlation with the decision of adolescents to join the military, there is also significant evidence that youth perception of parental beliefs are often different from the parent's self-reported belief. These differences show there may be either a lack of communication between child and parent or the outside influence on adolescents from parental figures in media.

Data used in the Army's report were taken from surveys collected in 1987, and due to the differences in the change in the household media environment, and the fact this past study did not take place during a time of war when attitudes about death and war are much more salient, more information needs to be gathered to help determine parental influence in an adolescent's decision to enlist.

As the Legree et al. (2000) study points out, the number of parents with direct knowledge about the military is dropping and suggested targeting parents in the services' recruitment strategies. With the recent ads targeting parents, it is reasonably expected that such information would provide them with more positive attitudes about the military thus reinforcing the early studies' findings that parental reports of positive attitudes are associated with adolescent enlistment behavior.

This study posits:

H7: – Parents who manifest positive attitudes toward the military will be more likely to support their young adults joining the military.

H8: – Young adults who manifest positive attitudes toward the military will be more likely to express an interest in joining the military.

Methods

The purpose of this study was to examine the extent to which various communication forms cultivate and affect perception and/or beliefs about the military in high school youth and their parents. Via recruiting, the military can use this information to add to, correct, or even influence attitudes of those audiences.

Telephone Survey

To assess the research questions and the predicted organizational model, a one-panel telephone survey was conducted by the students in the Department of Defense Joint Course in Communication. The telephone surveys were conducted the last week in February (*N*= 119). The sample was drawn from households in the states of Arkansas, Kansas and Oklahoma. The sample was obtained from the Department of Defense. The sample was randomly divided into 'Parents' (*N*=71) and 'Young Adults' (*N*=48) categories. Participants were screened by asking if they were 16 to 18 years old or if they were the parents of 16 – 18 year-olds before they took part in the survey. Participants had to be 16 to 18 years of age or be a parent of a young adult between the ages of 16 to 18. They also had to agree to participate in the study. Each phone survey was between 12 to 20 minutes in duration.

All instruments in the telephone surveys featured multiple-item indicators and were assessed for internal consistency using Cronbach's coefficient alpha.

Sociodemographics

Respondents' sociodemographic characteristics, including gender (Males=64, Females=55), race, age, household income, marital status (Married=52%), number of children, and military service were measured.

Respondents' gender was determined without asking and was operationalized as male or female. Race was assessed by asking if they were: Caucasian (79%), African-American (8%), Hispanic (6.7%), Native-American/Pacific Islander (2.5%), or other (3.8%). Age was assessed by asking the respondents' age. Household income was operationalized as: below $25,000 (5%), between $25,000 and $34,999 (7.6%), between $35,000 and $44,999 (4.2%), between $45,000 and $54,999 (6.7%), between $55,000 and $74,999 (13.4%), and $75,000 and $89,999 (7.6%), and above $90,000 (8.4%). Marital status was assessed by asking if they are married or single (62 married, 57 single), and presence of children was answered yes/no to a question asking if they had children.

Military service was determined by asking if the parents had ever served in the military. We also asked them what their primary source of information about the military was, how many days in the past week they watched national or local television news, how many days in the past week they read the news section of the paper, and how many days during the past week they sought out information about the military on the world wide web.

Independent Measures

Media use and attention served as the independent variables. The study operationalized media use as exposure to and attention paid to specific communication media. This approach is recommended by McLeod and McDonald (1985) and Chafee and Schleuder (1986) who maintain that both exposure and attention paid scales are required in order to compare communications use. This investigation employed two ten-point scales to assess people's exposure to and attention paid to different communication forms.

Media items were broken down into four dimensions: news (national television news programs, local television news programs, newspapers, magazines, radio news programs, television news magazines); entertainment (radio talk shows, television talk shows, television shows, movies, video games, the internet, movies depicting military personnel, video gamed depicting military personnel); advertising (televised military advertising, print military advertising, printed materials about joining the military), and conversations (with parents, friend, and in school settings).

Dependent Measures

Overall attitudes about the U.S. Marine Corps and the Army were assessed with a global attitude measure across media forms adapted from Burgoon, Cohen, Miller, and Montgomery (1978). The measures are based on the operationalization of media use. The measure's seven-point bipolar adjective scale includes: unacceptable/acceptable, foolish/wise, unfavourable/favorable, negative/positive, bad/good, and wrong/right (Marines: a =.96, *M*=6.57, *s.d.*=1.52; Army: a =.96, *M*=6.33, *s.d.*=1.53). Next, the individual's overall attitudes about a young person joining the U.S. Marine Corps or the Army was assessed using the same global attitude measure (Marines: a =.98, *M*=6.35, *s.d.*=1.75; Army a =.94, *M*=6.24, *s.d.*=1.71).

Overall attitude about U.S. military presence in Iraq was assessed with a global attitude measure adapted from Burgoon, Cohen, Miller, and Montgomery (1978). The measure's six-point bipolar adjective scale included: unacceptable/acceptable, foolish/wise, unfavourable/favorable, negative/positive, bad/good, and wrong/right (a =.98).

Thermometer scales (1 to 100) were used to measure the likelihood of young adults serving in the military, as well as a parent's likelihood of encouraging their child to join the military. The participants were asked, "On a scale of 0 to 100 (0 being not at all, and 100 being extremely likely) how likely are you to encourage your child to join the military?" (*M*=46.76, *s.d.*=36.17). The wording of this item was patterned after an item used in past studies of public confidence conducted by, among others, the Institute for Social Research/Center for Political Studies (Asher, 1988) and Harris, Gallup, and NORC.

Parents and young adults were asked how often they had discussions with parents, friends, or in class/work about the military. This was a 0 (never have these types of discussions) to 7 (discuss this a lot) scale.

Results

The communication use of potential recruits and their parents influence their attitudes toward the United States

Army and Marine Corps, and the likelihood of these electing to serve in the Army or Marine Corps.

Regression Analyses

Hierarchical regression analysis was employed to assess the influence of communication use of young adults and parents on potential for military service. This broad issue is embodied in Hypothesis 1, 2, 5, 6, and 7. The first predictor block consisted of sociodemographic variables: ethnicity, age, income, and gender. The next block consisted of a wide array of communication forms.

Each embodied a unique source of information about the military, including: talk radio, network television news, conversations with others, print newspapers, general video game use, video games depicting military personnel, entertainment television, television talk shows, local television news, general movie viewing, movies depicting military personnel, radio news, television magazines, television recruiting advertising, and newspaper recruiting advertising.

Hypothesis 1 predicted that respondents who rely on news for information about the military would have a negative attitude about the military and about serving in the military. Radio news is the only predictor of attitude about the military and about serving the military. Therefore, at first glance, Hypothesis 1 was partially supported because radio news use predicted attitudes about the military and about military service, but newspaper use and national television news use did not.

Hypothesis 2 predicted those who rely on entertainment for information about the military will have a positive attitude about the military and about serving in the military. At first glance, Hypothesis 2 was not supported when examining scaled measures of attitude about the military and about military service. However, a thermometer scale was also used to assess the likelihood of joining the Army or Marines. The single item scale did have significant predicators. Ethnicity ($b=-.31, p<.05$), newspaper use ($b=-.36, p<.05$), entertainment television use ($b=-.44, p<.05$), and use of movies depicting the military ($b=.48$, p<.10) were all significant predictors in determining young people's likelihood of serving. Caucasians were more inclined to serve than other ethnic groups. Newspaper use and entertainment talk show use were negatively related to and movies depicting the military were positively associated with likelihood of serving in the military. The results for the Thermometer measure often additional support to the Hypothesis 1 and partial support for Hypothesis 2.

People's media use and attention may impact their attitude about the war in Iraq. We were interested in determining what would predict attitudes about the war in Iraq. Income (b=.27, p<.05), use of newspapers (b=-.52, p<.01), use and attention to television entertainment shows (b=-.43, p<.05), and use and attention to movies depicting the military (b=.54, p<.05) were all significant predictors of attitude about the war in Iraq. Therefore, young adults and parents reading the newspaper or watching television entertainment shows had negative attitudes about the war in Iraq.

Hypothesis 4 predicted those who rely on recruiting advertisements about the military will have positive attitudes about the military. Hypothesis 4 was not supported. Hypothesis 5 predicted that those who rely on conversations to gain information about the military would have negative attitudes about the military. Hypothesis 5 was not supported. Hypothesis 6 predicted that those who have military experience within the immediate family would have positive attitude about the military and serving in the military. Hypothesis 6 was not supported.

Overall, the regression results were disappointing. The only significant predictors of attitudes towards the Marine Corps were income (b=.42, p<.05), talk radio use (b=.40, p<.05), and radio news (b=-.43, p<.05). Greater family income and greater use of talk radio were positively associated with attitudes toward the Marine Corps whereas greater use of radio news was related to less positive attitudes toward the Marine Corps. Income (b=.45, p<.05) and radio news (b=-.42, p<.10) were significant predictors of attitude toward the Army. Greater income was associated with more positive attitudes toward the

Army and greater radio use with less positive attitude toward the Army. Income (b=.28, p<.10) was also a significant predictor in determining the likelihood of joining the Marine Corps. Income (b=.33, p<.05) and radio news use (b=-.39, p<.10) were significant predictors in determining ones likelihood in joining the Army. Greater incomes was associated with more positive attitudes about joining both branches whereas greater radio use was related to less positive attitudes about joining the Army.

Multivariate Analysis

Hypothesis 3 compared parents and young adults' attitudes toward the military and serving in the military. Specifically, Hypothesis 3 predicted parents would have a negative attitude compared to young adults about the military and serving in it. To assess this question, a one-way MANCOVA was computed for group (young adult or parent) on the dependent variables of: attitude toward the Marine Corps, attitude toward the Army, attitude about joining the Marine Corps, attitude about joining the Army, and the one item indicator of enlisting in the military. Covariates included gender, age, and ethnicity. The omnibus results indicated nearly significant differences for the covariate of gender, Wilks' ë F(5, 109) = 1.94, p <.10, partial eta =.09. Subsequent univariate tests revealed significant differences for gender on the dependent variable of attitude about joining the Army F(1, 117) = 5.64, p <.05, partial eta^2 = .05. The pattern of means revealed parents were more supportive of youth joining the Army or Marines than young adults. Thus, Hypothesis 3 was partially supported. Parent and their children did not differ on their attitudes toward the Marine Corps or the Army. Parents had a more positive attitude about the Marines (M_p = 6.65, sd = 1.69; M_{ya} = 6.46, sd = 1.23) and the Army (M_p = 6.60, sd = 1.67; M_{ya} = 6.08, sd = 1.29) when compared to young adults. Also, they did not differ in terms and support for joining the Marine Corps or Army. However, males scored higher than females in the Army. Parents were more likely to encourage their young adults to form the Marines (M = 6.50, sd =1.81) and the Army (M = 6.38, sd = 1.84) than young adults.

Correlation Matrix

Hypothesis 7 and Hypothesis 8 predicted parents who have a positive attitude about the military would support their children's joining the military, and that young adults who have a positive attitude about the military would be more likely to join the military.

A correlation matrix was computed measuring attitude toward the Marine Corps, attitude toward the Army, attitude toward joining the Marine Corps, attitude toward joining the Army, and likelihood of enlisting. The results revealed that parents who manifested a more positive attitude about the military were the more likely to support their children's joining the military with all correlations significant ranging from r = .38 to .86. The same pattern was true for young adults, with all correlations significant ranging from r = .30 to .77.

Discussion

The use and attention of mass media sources as they affect the attitude of parents and young adults about the Marine Corps and Army. The study was conducted to determine if parents and youth differ in where they obtain information about the military and how it affects their attitudes of military and likelihood of joining the military. The goal of the study was to provide information to help recruiting efforts of the Army and the Marine Corps, the two services whose recruiting has been most affected by the Global War on Terror.

Our study was hampered by a small sample size. Consequently, this left many of our hypothesis unsupported. In a number of cases, we were approaching significance, but could not claim significance due to the small power. If at least 200 surveys could have been attained, the significance of the overall study would have been greater. However, we were able to find significance for several hypotheses even with a small sample.

The only significant predictors of attitudes towards the Marine Corps were income and talk radio use. Greater family income and uses of talk radio and radio news, were associated with positive attitudes about the Marine Corps. Use of radio news was related to less positive attitudes about the Marine Corps. For the Army, income and radio news use were significant predictors of attitudes about the Army. Respondents reporting greater family income manifest more positive attitudes about the Army.

Those relying on radio news information about the Army manifested less positive attitudes. We also found that income was a significant predictor in determining the likelihood of joining the Marine Corps. Greater family income was related to greater likelihood of joining. For the Army, income and radio news use were significant predictors in determining likelihood of joining their service. Greater family income was associated with greater likelihood of joining the Army. Use of radio news predicted less likelihood of joining the Army.

Our predictions also stated parents who have a positive attitude about the military would support their young adult joining the military and young adults who have a positive attitude about the military would be more likely to join the military.

As the Legree et al. (2000) study points out, the number of parents with direct knowledge about the military is dropping and suggests targeting parents in the services' recruitment strategies. Our results found parents who have a positive attitude about the military are more likely to support their young adults in joining the military. The same pattern was true for young adults. This supports Legree et al. (2000) study, where his research suggested that parental reports of positive attitudes are associated with adolescent enlistment behavior.

Our research posited parents would have a negative attitude about the military and about serving in the military when compared to young adults. However, attitudes regarding the Marine Corps and the Army did differ between groups. Also, the likelihood of joining either service did not differ across the group. Likelihood for joining the Army was higher for males than females.

Our hypothesis suggested those who rely on news for information about the military will have more negative attitudes about the military and about serving in the military. According to Kurtz (1999), more audiences are tuning in to get the news from different avenues, such as entertainment. For adolescents that are 15-18 years old, only 10% of their television time is spent watching news. For those 35 and older, they spend nearly double the time watching news. The results found radio news was the greatest predictor of attitude about the military and about serving in the military. However, our hypothesis was only partially supported because the other vehicles of news information, such as newspapers and television news, did not predict military attitudes.

We also predicted those who rely on entertainment for information about the military will have more positive attitudes about the military and will be more likely to serve in the military. Entertainment is just another form for audiences to gather information. Although it may seem as though what is watched, read or heard may be done so purely for entertainment, serious or real-life situations are being depicted to audiences. For our study we examined entertainment mediums such as movies, videogames, entertainment television, and primetime television shows about the military. Ethnicity, newspaper use, entertainment television, and movies depicting the military were all significant predictors in determining one's likelihood of serving.

The results offer only partial support for the positions that news might undermine, but entertainment might enhance, recruitment. However, two additional tests provide further support for these positions. First, the thermometer measure, which assessed the likelihood of joining the military, in contrast to the attitudinal scales, provide additional support. The results here indicated that greater use of newspapers and entertainment television reduced chances of joining the military, whereas use of movies depicting the military enhanced likelihood of joining. Second, media use predicted peoples attitudes about continued U.S. military presence in Iraq. The pattern was the same as reported above. Greater use of newspapers and television entertainment undermine support for the war in Iraq, whereas more use of movies depicting the military enhanced support for the war. Taken together, these results provide further support for our hypotheses: that news may undercut, and movies may bolster, recruitment efforts for both the Marines and Army.

There is limited research measuring the persuasiveness of military advertisements, but there is evidence showing how advertising in general can be a highly effective tool The television documentary *Merchants of Cool* illustrates the power of advertising and the rise of Sprite from relative anonymity in the beverage industry, to its relationship to hip-hop culture.

We predicted those relying on advertisements for information about the military would have positive attitudes about the military. However, this hypothesis was not supported in our study. Likewise, our prediction that those who had military experience in the immediate family would have a positive attitude about the military and serving in the military, was not supported. It is easy to conclude that the current war is having an impact on the attitudes people have about the military and serving in the military despite the fact that immediate family have served in the military.

Limitations

The limitations of our research are most directly related to the audience from which we used to draw our sample. Specifically, the limited location, age, time to draw the sample, and size of the sample, impacted our ability to provide greater significance to our results.

First, one of several limitations of our data are that our audience and sample only reflect those people in the Oklahoma, Kansas, and Arkansâs area. In order to obtain the most generalizeable results, future research should encompass a larger area. In addition, another limitation of our data was the age of the adolescent respondents, which was 16-18. Future research should expand the age of kids to 29, which corresponds to the armed forces recruiting standard of ages 18-29.

Other limitations include time restrictions and size of the sample. In the two week time frame in which data was collected, 1014 calls were made with 119 surveys completed. In future research, more time would be required to collect data from a larger sample. Future research should also seek other methods of conducting the survey, as our research was limited to phone surveys. Conducting the 20 minute survey through face-to-face, and/or mail-in surveys should be considered.

2

Changing Role of the Media in War

THE VIETNAM WAR: "THE FIRST TELEVISION WAR"

"Television was it"

Television is considered to be an influential social power. In the time of the Vietnam War almost all American households owned a television set and television became the most important source of information for the public. Thus, the media, in particular television, became a popular scapegoat to excuse American defeat in Vietnam.

After the end of the Vietnam War, television coverage of the conflict was highly criticized; according to critics, television influenced substantially the public and their faith in American administration. The media was transformed from a rather passive institution into an oppositional "player". Michael Robinson regarded the content of television news as the main variable: "Events are frequently conveyed by television news through an inferential structure that often injects a negativistic, contentious or anti-institutional bias...". In accordance with critics of the media, the Vietnam War was presented negatively by television, which influenced public opinion regarding support for the war. Therefore, it was television that affected not only the public, but also the officials in Washington. President Lyndon B. Johnson's withdrawal from reelection was often quoted as an example as well as his statement, "If I've lost Cronkite, I've lost Middle America" (said after Walter Cronkite, a CBS anchor, reported on the aftermath of the Tet Offensive).

Such oppositional reporting would be definitely labeled as abandonment of the principles of objective journalism. On the other hand, examples of the war coverage emphasizing patriotism and the positive presentation of American struggle corresponding to official policy in Vietnam were frequent in the early period of the Vietnam War. In such cases, no one was complaining.

Why to Fight in Vietnam?

Motives for American involvement in Vietnam were determined by political organization of the world after the Second World War. For the United States it was a question of national security to help any country which could be caught in a "trap of communism". The so-called Truman Doctrine became a basis for a new American foreign policy, "Containment Policy", which marked the political development of the world for decades. A key document, which codetermined American position in subsequent military conflicts, was a National Security Council report (NSC-68) from April 1950. This document called for taking initiative in a struggle against communism and the United States positioned itself into the role of defender of world freedom.

The first military conflict in the Cold War period and the first "limited war" of the United States was the Korean War. The notion "limited" means that the main aim of limited war is not a total destruction of an enemy, and the participants do not engage all available resources in a conflict (industrial, human, or military) ("Limited War"). Another aspect of limited war is a degree of involvement. The United States was not directly involved in Korea (the war was fought on the basis of the United Nations resolution), where the communist North attacked the "democratic" South. Thus, the Korean War represents the first demonstration of new American military policy in the Cold War period.

Though the Korean War had very similar political background as the Vietnam War regarding containment policy, it is often labeled the "Unknown War". The reason is clear: television broadcasting was still in its infancy. As the thesis deals with regular television coverage of military conflicts, the Korean War reporting will not be scrutinized. However, it should be pointed out that in the Korean War, as the first limited war the United States participated in, journalists were subject to censorship.

Why did journalists covering the Vietnam War gain free access to the battlefield and freedom to report on whatever they wanted? Daniel Hallin argues that official censorship would be impractical. First of all, the United States did not declare the war officially, some restrictions would have to be imposed not only on the journalists in Vietnam, but also in the United States, which was not possible. The question of legal jurisdiction constituted another problem. The United States held a position of assistant without the right to impose full censorship. As the conflict escalated, the number of accredited journalists increased (American as well as other nationality reporters). To prevent any leak of information it would have been necessary to include all journalists in Vietnam. However, correspondents accredited to American military troops had to agree on fifteen categories of information permitted to be published only after official authorization (troop movements, casualty figures). Except for these restrictions, journalists were free to go and report on what they wanted. Self-censorship and objectivity also played an important role. With a broad national consensus over the Vietnam War and objective journalism practices, an agreement with official policy was presumed. It was not only the reporting without formal censorship that made the Vietnam War unique. Covering the Vietnam War through regular everyday television broadcasting represents a turning point in war reporting.

TELEVISION COVERAGE OF THE VIETNAM WAR

Media-government relations during the Vietnam War could seem as oppositional at first sight. At the second, it is not so unambiguous. According to Hallin, "In situations where political consensus seems to prevail, journalists tend to act as 'responsible' members of the political establishment....In situations of political conflict, they become more detached or even adversarial, though they normally will stay well within the bounds of the debate going on within the political 'establishment'..." (*"Uncensored War"* 10). He argues that the same pattern could be seen in the Vietnam War and therefore more critical reporting of the war was just a result of normal routines of journalism. The only difference was that accredited journalists were not subject to censorship.

The Changing Image of the Vietnam War: 1968 as a Turning Point

What caused more critical tone of television broadcasting in the later years of the Vietnam War? Critics of the media argue that it was mainly "insensitivity" in relation to national policy, seeking for a dramatic story at any cost, or anti-establishment efforts that urged television reporters to present the negative image of the war. These critical reports had presumably substantial impact on the public regarding support for the war. According to journalists, more critical reporting was just a reaction to changes in American administration. First signs of disagreement over the military strategy in Vietnam appeared in 1967. Max Frankel, a prominent American reporter, formulated it in this way: "As protests moved from the left groups, the anti-war groups, into the pulpits, in the Senate...as it became a majority opinion, it naturally picked up coverage. And then naturally the tone of the coverage changed...". In addition, a decline in morale among American troops and the shift of antiwar movement into other parts of political establishment are stated among other factors that caused the change in the presentation of the war.

The Tet Offensive is claimed to be a turning point in the Vietnam War not only from the military and political, but also from journalistic points of view. In January 1968 Viet Cong forces attacked major South Vietnamese cities, which were under control of South Vietnamese government and American troops, in a large military operation. Though they were defeated, it was something nobody expected, either in South Vietnam or in the United States.

Tet Offensive coverage was criticized for being reported as American failure and that from that time on, reporters presented the war as an unavailing struggle impossible to win. This negativistic character of the Vietnam War reporting was allegedly regarded as a decisive factor in the decline of domestic support for the war. However, various studies dealing with television coverage of the Vietnam War did not confirm the premise that television and particularly Tet Offensive coverage caused decline in public support. The Tet Offensive was reported as a drama, but this could not be surprising when only a few months before the Tet the officials made an effort to convince the public that the "end of the war was in sight" (President Lyndon B. Johnson, General William Westmoreland). Moreover, the Tet Offensive represented a demonstration of North Vietnamese military tactics and power in a broader context; such organized military operations were not typical.

Tet Offensive reporting on television gave the sense that the war was not under control. An emphasis was laid on the destruction of cities; the frequency of broadcasting military casualties also rose. In general, journalists accepted the official line that the Tet was a military defeat for North Vietnam and Viet Cong, which was true: American and South Vietnamese troops managed to regain control over the cities. Most of the reporters were just not willing to accept official optimism about the victory in a short period of time. As a good example Walter Cronkite's famous report of the Tet Offensive could be given: "To say that we are closer to victory today is to believe, in the face of the evidence, the optimists who have been wrong in the past. To suggest we are on the edge of defeat is to yield to unreasonable pessimism. To say that we are mired in stalemate seems the only realistic, yet unsatisfactory conclusion" (Arnold 88). In this case, Cronkite was not just giving the facts but also editorializing. It is claimed that this report as a representative of critical coverage of the Tet Offensive brought the decline in public support of the war and also Johnson's decision not to run for reelection (Felman 10).

A new military strategy came with a new American president, Richard Nixon. The War was moved into the air. Escalation of bombing of North Vietnam meant also a shift in television coverage. Cameras could not be there, which meant no blood, no death on television screen, and a relatively "clean" image of war (*Enemy Image*). The process of Vietnamization, a gradual buildup of South Vietnamese Army in order to be able to fight without military assistance of the United States, was another step in an attempt to end American involvement in the "unpopular war". But the image of war changed considerably after the Tet Offensive.

Nevertheless, was the image of war really so negative? Journalists did not question the motives for the war, but only the course of action the United States took in Vietnam. The war became a stalemate and therefore the aim was to cease the war, in other words, to reach "peace with honor". Americans were still portrayed as "good guys" and journalists were using official sources of information as well as the soldiers in the battlefield to present news to the public. But as the consensus over the military strategy started to collapse, the media had to react. Thus the Vietnam War coverage suggests that the media only reflected political debate over Vietnam and the character of reporting, whether supportive or critical, depended predominantly on a degree of consensus within the establishment. To what extent the media and particularly television pursued its watchdog role during the Vietnam War is not so important. The fact that the media was regarded as an agent of defeat and the effects Vietnam War experience had on the media-government relations are crucial here.

Television as an Agent of Support

Before regular evening news broadcasting, which started in 1963, the news about the Vietnam War was presented on television in newsreels. Images the public could see were usually images of American military superiority and enormous power. Pictures of technical equipment and dedicated American soldiers were accompanied by patriotic texts and music. This "slightly" propagandistic tone reminded me of newsreels from communist Czechoslovakia and as much as the latter, this kind of propaganda was aimed at the public to support official governmental policy. The beginning of evening television news did not mean that newsreels were ceased to be broadcasted; the public gained an opportunity to see a completely different image of the war.

As television reporters covering the Vietnam War accompanied small troops, it was not surprising that reporters (especially of the younger generation) tended to identify with the soldiers. "American boys" became characters of drama called war. The war was presented from the soldier's point of view (*Enemy Image*). American foreign policy was reported from the "inside", right from those who were actually fulfilling it. The fact that soldiers became the main source of information for the reporters suggests that as long as the soldiers stayed supportive of the war, the reporters did as well. Findings about the Vietnam War reporting show that especially at the early period of the war, when the morale of the soldiers was good, the reporting from the soldier's point of view had very positive tone. Stories about American heroes and their humanity, competence, and morale could be seen on television screen very often in the early years of the Vietnam War. These images perfectly fitted into the official American policy line: American soldiers helping to free powerless peasants from communist tyranny.

And how was the enemy portrayed on television? Each drama has to have the "good guy" and the "bad guy" representing the forces of good and evil. It was obvious which position took American soldiers or, in other words, the United States. For drama on television screen, the conflict and clear contrast between good and evil are characteristic. While American soldiers were portrayed as national heroes, the other side, North Vietnamese and Viet Cong, were usually referred to as cruel, suicidal, and fanatical. Television created an image of a "terrorist", especially in relation to civilian casualties. In fact, majority of civilian victims shown on film in the pre-Tet period died in actions initiated by Americans and South Vietnamese. No reports focusing on political aims of North Vietnamese or history of the conflict appeared.

The public could see only images of the war going on in South Vietnam. American television reporters had no access to North Vietnam; however, some western correspondents were allowed access to cover the war from the other side. Pictures of ordinary people fighting for their country, their determination to win, and destructive consequences of American bombing campaign were presented to European public. Charles Colingwood, a CBS correspondent in Paris, brought first pictures from North Vietnam to American public in 1968 after bombing of the capital, Hanoi, where many civilians died and the city remained in ruins. Subsequently, he was accused of making communist propaganda (*Enemy Image*). No wonder that such images of destruction were not very agreeable to the officials in Washington who strived to maintain the positive image of the war and optimistic prospects for a military and political victory.

How the Media "Missing" the Vietnam War

One of the main criticized aspects of Vietnam War coverage was inexperience of war correspondents. Many of them were not familiar with the historical and political background of the conflict; most of the correspondents did not know the language and culture of Vietnam. It is also true that television reporters usually served only six-month tours. Some scholars criticized reporters for seeking only the story. In the case of television, reporting on events through simplistic images taken out of context was misleading according to him (Elegant). On the other hand, reporters were committed to present events realistically. For the first time in war coverage they had freedom to show what they regarded as exploitation on the American side.

According to a Vietnam War reporter Peter Arnett, the controversy over the Vietnam War coverage affected the relations between two generations of reporters. Older generation of journalists, who were part of the mainstream media, complained about inexperience of the younger reporters. Those were called "young crusaders", more critical in war coverage they were often labeled as not understanding the conflict in its full context and demanded to "get on the team". This meant presenting official statements, optimistic most of the time, and thus supporting the official military policy in Vietnam without questioning. And what if official version did not correspond to the facts? The public has the right to be informed; the question is to what extent the version we read or see on television agrees with the reality.

Reporters should present events objectively without personal judgments and without manipulating the images or the story. Therefore, when images are just fragments of the story, the media is responsible for presenting the story as much truthfully as it is possible. However, some cases of manipulation and "misuse" were claimed to happen in Vietnam. Cutting ears off a dead Viet Cong was often given as an example, as well as burning of village Cam Ne reported by a CBS reporter, Morley Safer. Nevertheless, the facts about the latter were rather controversial.

Safer was criticized for reporting an incident torn out of context. Search and destroy operations were under way in this area before the incident. Safer was then accused of concocting the whole story – he made the soldiers burn the houses and Cam Ne was a hamlet for training purposes (Safer). Two weeks after Cam Ne the public was presented with conflicting versions of the incident – houses were not destroyed deliberately but by ground fire (*Enemy Image*). Later, more facts about Cam Ne were revealed, the villagers were punished for not paying their taxes (Brush).

Images of American soldiers setting the houses on fire by lighters or flame throwers and pictures of desperate villagers were accompanied by Safer's report: "Today's operation is the frustration of Vietnam in miniature. There is little doubt that American firepower can win a military victory here. But to a Vietnamese peasant whose home is a – means a lifetime of backbreaking labor – it will take more than presidential promises to convince him that we are on his side" ("Village of Cam Ne"). It was the first time a reporter gave his personal judgment about the events. According to Safer, his main aim was to show "what the Vietnam War was really about", particularly for the civilians. It is clear that such a tenor of war reporting brought a shock not only to the public, but also to the officials concerned about maintaining more or less the positive image of military strategy in Vietnam. Images of American soldiers were considerably different from those American public was used to. Such events were not unusual, but this time a reporter with a camera was present, making critical evaluation of the event.

Personal judgments given by reporters do not correspond with the principles of objective journalism. Such abandoning of objectivity could be either supportive or critical. Cam Ne television reporting represents an example of questioning of American policy by a single man, which was not possible in previous war conflicts. This was the reason why Cam Ne meant a change in government's approach to television broadcasting. President Lyndon Johnson ordered the Department of Defense to monitor evening news since then (*Enemy Image*). His quote, "Your boys just shat on the American flag," tells its own tale.

The question of "picking a story" is also important. Here two events or rather Vietnam massacres are often contrasted. The first is a massacre in My Lai, where an American officer ordered to kill more than three hundred peasants allegedly collaborating with the Viet Cong. Though this happened in March 1968, the story was not revealed to the public until September 1969. The whole situation was even worsened by an attempt of the military to prevent its publication. In contrast, a massacre in the city of Hue during the Tet Offensive, where about three thousand residents were killed by Viet Cong, received minimal media coverage. Television reporters were criticized for not being interested in the Hue massacre: no report on television appeared. The My Lai massacre was definitely more embedded in the consciousness of the public, thus critics of the media regarded this fact as a fatal failure of professional journalism. According to William Hammond, the Vietnam War was first of all an "American war", as much as the American policymakers focused on efficacy of Vietnam policy, the public was interested primarily in what was happening to the American soldiers. Thus, the reporters focused on covering the Americans first (317). As Safer pointed out, "There was very little interest...in Vietnam, there was an interest in the Vietnam War" (*Enemy Image*).

Violence and "true horrors of war" presented on daily bases in television news were often criticized as well. The fact is that violent scenes or direct combat were not shown frequently. Only a small number of scenes that could be marked as violent (heavy fighting, killed and wounded within view) appeared on television screen. Television reporters usually showed military actions from the distance or the soldiers preparing for the action, moving into battle (Hammond 315). With images of combat violence, pictures of dead American soldiers are closely connected. Though dying was a part of the war and the depiction of it through television a part of a reporter's job, some limitations existed. Recognizable images of dead soldiers were not shown on television, for these controversial cases military rules as well as self-censorship worked (*Enemy Image*). Eventually, the American soldiers, alive or dead, were for the most part presented as heroes the Americans should be proud of. They were fighting for the "right thing" after all.

It is difficult to assess how exactly television coverage of the Vietnam War influenced the opinions of the audience. Television was the primary source of information. Walter Cronkite was even the "most trusted man in America" during the Vietnam War.

Pictures of the war represented another factor: people wanted to see what was happening in Vietnam. Nevertheless, experts on mass communication argue that rather than changing opinions of the audience, television could have had quite a contrary effect. It could rather reinforce the existing attitudes of a viewer. In a study of this hypothesis during the Vietnam War it was stated that 75% of respondents who considered themselves "hawks" (defined as those who advocate an aggressive foreign policy based on military power) thought Walter Cronkite was a "hawk". Similarly, a large number of "doves" (those who try to resolve an international conflict without the threat of force) regarded him as a "dove" (Hammond 315). Thus, television war coverage could be labeled as being rather contradictory, not taking unambiguously any side.

A NEW MEDIA-MILITARY STRATEGY

Television changed the presentation of war during the Vietnam War reporting considerably. New technology and the lack of censorship brought a different image of war to the audience. The former propagandistic tone of war coverage shifted into more critical approach. The clash between the media and the military, or in other words, the government, became more visible. According to critics, the media gained a substantial power over the public and thus over the formation of American foreign policy. And this must not have been allowed in the future, this power were to be restricted.

Panama: Operation Just Cause

Though the pool system was tested in several military operations, the invasion of Panama in December 1989 was considered to be one of the most important. In Panama the pool system proved to be a "failure". Not only the national pool was notified late and the reporters arrived to Panama after the combat had been almost over, but also regional reporters already present were restricted to cover the operation in order to "secure this right" for the national media pool. Moreover, technical equipment for the journalists in the media center was not sufficient. This failure of the pool system led to another reevaluation of media-military relations; the most important point concluded was the need to include public affairs beforehand; they were to participate in the operational phase of any military action. The military ought to hold regular briefings, reporters should be treated as members of units and coverage of military operation as wide as possible was to be provided. Five months later, the first Gulf War started and the pool system was tested again. More than 1,500 journalists reported on the war in military controlled pools.

Grenada: Operation Urgent Fury

Adversarial relations between the media and the military were fully manifested during the invasion of Grenada in October 1983. Though an action of lesser importance in relation to its extent, it was an essential step in media-military relations. The media was denied access to cover this military operation. First, they were not informed about the operation by the government and then the media was barred from the island. A pool of fifteen reporters was allowed access on the third day of the operation: in that time the action had been over (Pilnacek 22). The military justified the media exclusion by safety and security requirements. On the contrary, the media argued that the public had the right to be informed and the media ban was unconstitutional. As an NBC commentator John Chancellor put it, "Things get dangerous...when the government takes unto itself the function of informing the public...When your friendly government press agent, military or civilian, is your source of information, you ought to be worried" (Pilnacek 24). I believe this to be a clear proof of distrust between the media and the military.

This clash between the right to report war and the necessity to maintain operational security goes further in Grenada. This was the first military involvement of the United States after the Vietnam War and a new notion should be taken into consideration. The so-called Vietnam syndrome has been affecting American foreign policy for many years. In general, Vietnam syndrome refers to the reluctance of government and the public to get involved in a military conflict that could result in "another Vietnam". The course of the Vietnam War, media coverage, the decline in public support, and the "defeat" despite of military superiority were seen as the main causes of the crisis of authority after the war ("Vietnam Syndrome"). Thus, when the military considered the media to be responsible for the Vietnam War "loss", it was not surprising that the media was not allowed access to report the operation in Grenada.

After this intervention a debate over the presence of the media during any military action started. A panel of military and media experts, the Sidle Panel, was charged with the task to evaluate media-military relations on the basis of Grenada experience. Finally, the panel issued eight recommendations together with a statement of principle demanding cooperation between the military and the media. The media was to be integrated into a military operation, but only to the degree compatible with maintaining security and safety of American forces. The Sidle Panel recommended 1) early public affairs planning in the time of operational planning and 2) a creation of national media pool when there was no other option to secure transmission of information and security of American troops at the same time, the panel then suggested 3) voluntary compliance by the media with security guidelines established by the military and 4) the need of updated list of accredited correspondents for reporting potential military operations. The panel also recognized 5) the necessity of securing transportation and communication facilities. Reporters were to be accompanied by a military escort to assist them during an operation as well (Terry 12-13). These recommendations were criticized by the media; the military gained means of managing the media comfortably. The national pool should involve a limited number of reporters, the military decided where the pool would be present and what they could cover, and all the material had to be authorized before its publishing. These recommendations were perceived as a strict censorship but the media had no other option. It could gain at least some access to military operations; the media simply could not afford to be excluded.

TELEVISION COVERAGE OF MILITARY OPERATIONS IN GRENADA AND PANAMA

As the military restricted any access to Operation Urgent Fury, the media saw this as a serious violation of rights based on American democratic values and history (in all wars journalists accompanied American troops). The media was very critical about the restrictions and demanded to be incorporated into future military operations. Finally, the Pentagon introduced the pool system as a compromise. But was it really because of the right of the media to cover military operations? Some military representatives claimed that restrictions in Grenada led to stringent criticism of the operation in the media, and distrust in the military and government became deeper by the questioning of credibility of information the military provided (Combelles-Siegel 5). On the contrary, Operation Just Cause, where the journalists were at least partially allowed to report on the operation, received substantially less critical coverage.

Though the military blamed the media for critical reporting, a content analysis of media coverage of the operation in Grenada, conducted by Jonathan Mermin, showed that the mainstream media gave rather little criticism to the operation (only about 9% of paragraphs dealing with this subject matter). In comparison, reporting of the operation in Panama by the mainstream media was labeled as very positive (only 1.5% of references) (45-50). The question of independence from the official line given to the public comes into mind.

When reporters were barred from Grenada, justifications by the military to ensure safety of reporters and operational security were perceived as just some kind of cover; were the military and the government hiding anything? Questioning credibility of information during the operation by the media meant a serious problem, even when the media coverage was not so critical. This could represent another reason for the introduction of the pool system. As the proverb says, "Keep your friends close but your enemies closer."

The main difference in the coverage of Grenada and Panama operations appeared between questioning justifications for these conflicts. While both operations were open to relatively the same questions, they received considerably different coverage (Mermin 49). Primary reason for both American interventions, according to official sources, was the need to "protect" American lives in those countries. Fighting the Communism in Grenada and ceasing the drug trade in Panama were given as other justifications, and, of course, "liberation of the people", and promoting democracy could not have been omitted. But these justifications appeared to be rather questionable. Before the invasions, most of the American citizens in Grenada and Panama did not feel endangered at all. Neither did an assertion that a newly constructed airport in Grenada supported by the Cuban regime was serving for military purposes, prove to be well-founded. And though Manuel Noriega, the leader of Panama, was involved in the drug trade, he was not considered to be a "big fish", which highly contradicted the image he was given by American government. And how did the media deal with official justifications for the invasions? The mainstream media accepted them without scrutinizing their legitimacy; in the case of Panama, where the military was more "open" to journalists, hardly any critical coverage of this issue appeared.

Considering television coverage of both Grenada and Panama invasions, images the public could see were very much alike. In Grenada, as the journalists were denied access to the island, the only images reaching the public were shot by army cameramen. It meant that every image of the invasion was produced and authorized by the military, or in other words, the Pentagon. So what television received and the public saw in the newscasts was provided by the military itself (*Enemy Image*). Here the media served as the mediator of official information without any active role. Images of professionalism, smooth progress and military superiority presented the operation as a legitimate intervention and the United States as a protector of liberty and democracy. Though the media was outraged by the censorship, they accepted in large measure the official line of American government.

Similarly, official statements and information about the course of events in Panama dominated the mainstream media coverage. Although the pool of sixteen journalists was allowed access to cover the operation, the military successfully managed the message of the media. Again, the invasion was presented as an act of liberation: images of Panamanians holding the American flag, pictures of American soldiers bringing freedom to the country. But the reality seemed to be different. Reporters were interviewing only white middle class people who could speak English, they did not ask the people whose houses and property were destroyed by the bombing (the military hit twenty-seven targets in densely populated areas). The extent of damage was suppressed by showing the journalists only such places the military wanted them to see. Those journalists trying to get into the restricted zones (the attacked areas) were charged with breaking safety measures (*Panama Deception*).

However, it seemed that the media itself did not want to question the official policy either. On television the invasion was assessed from a tactical point of view regarding its efficacy. The question of casualties was also contentious. Only American casualties were reported on, as for the civilians in Panama, there was no coverage of this issue (it is estimated that about 3,500 to 4,000 civilians died during and after the invasion, American sources claimed about 250 to be an official number). In addition, what followed (or rather did not follow) the vote of the United Nations on the invasion of Panama was rather surprising. The United Nations condemned this military action as a violation of international law. Not only the media did not question justifications and legitimacy of this invasion during and after the operation, but also they ignored the opinion of the international community (*Panama Deception*).

Though the invasion was largely accepted by the public, critical voices coming from the academics and public-interest organizations appeared. However, the media did not reflect on them. An interesting thing is also the fact that the intervention in Panama received bipartisan support unlike the Grenada operation (criticized by the Democrats). The tenor of Panama coverage was much less critical (Mermin 59). Here Hallin's assumption about the connection between the disagreement among the officials and critical media coverage is confirmed. The media just reflected on the changing political debate over a particular issue in Washington.

Another reason for holding the official line could be simply commercial interests. The media is owned by large companies and when their interests are in accord with the official governmental policy, why to question it? The role of the media functioning as a watchdog is a good concept, but the media has to have some space to act according to it. And here again the independence of the media and its role in a war conflict comes into question.

After the Vietnam War, when the media was blamed for losing the war, it was clear that war reporting without censorship as in Vietnam had become the past. The military had to reconsider relations with the media and their future access to war coverage. First, they applied stringent censorship in Grenada but when they realized that this could backfire, they had to change their strategy. The "enemy" would have to be transformed into the "ally". The pool system was introduced with journalists controlled on their every move.

So what role did the media have in military operations in Grenada and Panama? Both operations were presented by the government to the public as the acts of liberation. The United States had "moral obligation" to intervene. Officially, they were defending American lives and democratic principles of the United States. Reporting official information about a military conflict should be definitely part of war coverage; however, this does not mean that other opinions should not be presented as well. During Grenada and Panama invasions, little criticism of these military interventions appeared and what is more important, the Panama invasion with at least some access of the media received almost no critical evaluation. With the restrictions applied it seemed that the military gained powerful means for managing the media message.

Independence of the media is one of the crucial principles of American journalism. While reporting on any military conflict, it is very difficult for journalists to avoid political and commercial pressures as a military involvement is usually the issue of great importance for a state. The media should also stay free from favor and present just facts. However, Grenada and Panama news coverage in the mainstream media did not maintain impartiality. Particularly television coverage could be labeled as disputable for its presentation or rather promotion of the official governmental policy during and after these operations. Images of American soldiers "liberating" the country, interviews with the people positively assessing the actions, and no pictures of damage and casualties helped to reinforce positive perception by the public. Thus, the media did not perform its checking function but served the government as a mediator for the message the public should have received. The pool system appeared to be effective (for the military) and went even further in the following American military involvement, the first Gulf War. And the image of war was changed again.

THE WATCHDOG ROLE OF THE MEDIA

Media has played a significant role in American society since its "birth". As access to information is essential to every democratic society, the media has a responsibility to provide objective information to the public. Freedom of the press in the United States is guaranteed by the First Amendment of the United States Constitution: "Congress shall make no law respecting an establishment of religion, or prohibiting the free exercise thereof; or abridging the freedom of speech, or of the press; or the right of the people peaceably to assemble, and to petition the Government for a redress of grievances" (*United States Constitution*). It is clear that authors of the Bill of Rights considered the free press to be a crucial part of democracy. These rights are basis for the media functioning as a "Fourth Estate" or a "Watchdog". By reporting on various issues the media should serve a checking function of elected officials and their execution of power.

From a historical point of view, Edmund Burke, a British statesman, philosopher, and political theorist, was the first one referring to the press in the eighteenth century as the Fourth Estate, and this term was later popularized by the Scottish author and historian, Thomas Carlyle. In his book Carlyle reported Burke's views, "...there were Three Estates in Parliament; but in the Reporters' Gallery yonder, there sat a Fourth Estate more important than they all...Literature is our Parliament too...Whoever can speak, speaking now to the whole nation, becomes a power, a branch of government, with inalienable weight in lawmaking, in all acts of authority...the requisite thing is that he have a tongue which others will listen to; this and nothing more is requisite. The nation is governed by all that has tongue in the nation. Democracy is virtually there" (Carlyle 147).

In connection with this function we come across another term – a "watchdog role" of the media. Lance W. Bennett and William Serrin define watchdog journalism as: "(1) independent scrutiny by the press of the activities of government, business, and other public institutions, with an aim toward (2) documenting, questioning, and investigating those activities, in order to (3) provide publics and officials with timely information on issues of public concern." According to Bennett and Serrin, the watchdog role of the media means documenting activities little-publicized to public scrutiny and clarifying these activities by asking probing questions of public authorities. Another level of watchdog journalism is then trying to find evidence of social ills, official deception, and institutional corruption. Whichever form of independent journalism, it is considered to be essential for keeping public authorities correspondent with values and norms of democratic society. Though this concept of independent journalism is highly idealized, it belongs to implicit aspects of every democratic country.

The role of the media to scrutinize decisions made by governmental officials is particularly crucial in connection with national involvement in a military conflict. The United States has been involved, directly or indirectly, in each major "war" since the Second World War. Thus, a discussion over American media coverage of these conflicts and the analysis of its role helps to clarify the fact that the media did fail to perform its checking function before and during the last military conflict, the War in Iraq.

As the media exercises immense social power and has a substantial impact on public opinion, it highly depends on relations between the government and the media. These three elements affect each other significantly. It is important to point out that the watchdog role of the media depends on a political background, which involves governmental strategy over particular issues and prevailing opinion of the public. Thus the checking function of the media is shaped by the "space" to operate left by the government and the public. This is particularly true in the time of a country's military intervention.

Danny Schechter discussing the media role during "war" argues that the historic concept of the "Fourth Estate" was transformed into a "fourth front" in the war plan (Schechter x). The media cannot afford to report freely on this issue. How can it be possible when the freedom of the press is constitutionally guaranteed? It depends on many variables such as political and commercial pressures.

The way in which the media presents war to the public involves not only reporting on particular issues, but also presenting the image of war. This again relates to the notion of watchdog role of the media. The image of war has been changing since the start of war photography. For today's coverage of military conflicts the period after the Second World War is particularly crucial. The reason is clear: the beginning of television broadcasting.

Before an analysis of the image of war during this period, it is important to outline the development of professional journalism and its function in American society concerning reporting on "war".

THE EMBEDDING PROCEDURE AND TELEVISION

American government gained a substantial power over the media by a process of "trial and error" through the decades, and war reporting is nowadays associated with the embedding system of reporters. Vietnam conflict is considered to be a turning point in media-military relations. The reason for this assumption is that the Vietnam War is regarded as the first war broadcasted live. Although the Korean War was considerably similar to the Vietnam conflict regarding political background of the Cold War, there was one big difference, television. The Korean War started when television broadcasting was a new phenomenon; therefore, this war could be seen only through photographs, which did not have such a direct effect on the public as war reporting on Vietnam (Cumings 1).

The Vietnam War was branded "the war lost in the living room". These conservative views were popularized in the early 1980s (a documentary *Vietnam War: The Impact of Media*; an article "How to Lose a War: The Press in Viet Nam" by Robert Elegant) (*Enemy Image*). Many scholars analyzed the hypothesis quite thoroughly and their findings do not confirm these assumptions. It was mainly due to the lack of strategy in Vietnam or rather disagreement about this strategy among the officials, and the fact that in later years of the Vietnam conflict the public, as well as the soldiers, did not see any point in staying in Vietnam (Bruce Cumings, Daniel C. Hallin, or William M. Hammond). The Cold War ideology was just not enough.

After the Vietnam War "fiasco" concerning the image of war and its presentation to the public, the government decided to apply substantial restrictions on war reporting. Following an example of the British government in the Falklands Conflict in 1982, during the invasion of Grenada in 1983 journalists were excluded from direct participation. The war was covered exclusively by army men; news about the conflict and its images were gained primarily from official sources (the Pentagon). After stringent criticism the Pentagon received, a new instrument for the war coverage was "invented". This so-called pool system was applied to a subsequent military conflict in Panama in 1989. This time, journalists were allowed access, but again they were highly dependent on the military (transportation and access to transmission facilities). These conflicts are seen as stages in media-military relations deriving from the Vietnam War experience, where the media role was associated with a significant power over the public.

The pool system went further in the first Gulf War. Journalists became subject to restrictions in the form of specific guidelines on reporting. They were not allowed to get into the war zone if not a part of the pool. Journalists could not choose what they wanted to report on and their reports were subject to censorship. As for the television broadcasting, material was provided by the military so the public could see just images of "hi-tech" and "clean" war. The public did not receive the real image of the war. Images to be broadcasted were censored and manipulated, especially those with Iraqi casualties; American public never saw the horror picture of the war. Instead of that, images of technological equipment and superiority, and clips of smart bombs were getting into American living rooms. The government created a new image of war: bloodless, surgical, clean war with technological heroes (*Enemy Image*).

The last American military conflict largely covered by the media was the War in Iraq. Journalists were fully embedded in the military, it could be said that the embedding system reached its "perfection". Many similar instruments used during the first Gulf War could be traced in Iraq (security review, military escorts, official briefings); some new instruments appeared as well (military training, permanent embedding, front line coverage). By embedding journalists into the military, the government ensured partly its position. Media-military relations are characterized by manipulation and propaganda, where the media serves as a communicator of the message needed to be sent to the public.

This system of information management is considered to be the product of post-Vietnam military strategy influencing the media, together with other factors (media elites willing to cooperate with the government, commercial interests, or the lack of funding of investigative reporting). It is clear that the Vietnam War coverage (particularly the period after the Tet Offensive) had an enormous impact on media-government relations and influenced the role of the media in war coverage for good.

American Journalism in the Twentieth Century

The modern concept of objective journalism is rooted in the period between two world wars. It was the time when facts were considered to be relative and subject to manipulation; values were seen as subjective. Journalists then took a position of unbiased and objective reporters of reality. At the same time,

American society was going through substantial changes in relation to the industrial revolution. Journalists became employees of news organizations gaining credibility and prestige.

Hallin mentions three principles central to American journalism: "independence", "objectivity", and "balance". Journalists should be free from external pressures (political, commercial); they should present facts, not to judge them; and finally, news coverage of controversial issues should be impartial, free from favor. However, it is not easy to stick to these principles. The Cold War period brought two different practices of news reporting where journalists turned away from the principles of objectivity. The first could be characterized by criticizing government and their foreign policy; the second celebrates patriotism, national values, and unity.

By introducing the principles of professional journalism and actually practicing them in reality, journalism became a part of the governing process. Journalists gained professional autonomy that involved access to governmental negotiations and inner information previously not available. In return, they were to accept certain standards of reporting (giving up presenting information with a political voice, partisan evaluation of political authority, but also giving access of administration to the media as a channel to inform the public). Journalists became more closely tied to the state. It is not surprising that they chose "the state" to be their primary source of information. On the other hand, they represented an important mediator for the officials to pass information to the public. One of the consequences would be the fact that sticking to the principles of objective journalism leaves space for manipulation by the officials. The truth is that the officials cannot control the media directly; however, their message is guaranteed to get to the public by their social status and political authority.

As an example of this professionalization the coverage of the period before the actual military involvement of American troops in Vietnam could be given. The Kennedy and then Johnson administrations successfully managed to keep this issue out of the media through the principles of objective journalism. Journalists usually focused on statements made by government officials, who were united as concerns the official strategy in Vietnam, and presented just the facts without analysing governmental decisions and policy. Moreover, one of the crucial roles in presenting an official military strategy had the president himself. John Kennedy's foreign policy rhetoric shows that he was able to justify American strategy in Vietnam in terms of idealism (the United States as a defender of world freedom and democracy) as well as pragmatism (emphasized historical and legal relations with the United States, complex strategy in economic and military assistance in relation to Vietnam's specifics) (Bostdorff, Goldzwig).

Therefore, considering objective journalism practiced in the early years of the Vietnam War, it corresponds with the official Washington policy after the Second World War. "Containment policy" requiring national consensus during the Cold War made it almost impossible to critically scrutinize foreign policy decisions. Critical voices were regarded as anti-American. Both the government and most of the journalists presented the Vietnam War as a part of counter-communist struggle of democratic society. This was just partially true. News about the Vietnam War as a struggle of nationalists against colonial rule, or a national revolution against feudal society did not appear. Later the presentation of the war changed as well as the public opinion. This change was not caused by journalists' coverage of the conflict (particularly television broadcasting), as many officials claimed, but the turn in the portrayal of the war was part of a larger change in American society (Dadge 110).

It is generally believed that 1960s and 1970s were the years of the free press. In 1966 the Freedom of Information Act (FOIA) was signed by President Lyndon Johnson, giving the limits to the government concerning previously unreleased documents and information. The public has a right of access to federal government agencies records (United States, *Freedom of Information*). The case *The New York Times Co. v. U.S.* is regarded as another influential legal decision. In 1971 the

Supreme Court of the United States decided against the effort of Nixon administration to prevent the publication of Pentagon Papers (a study of the United States decision-making process on Vietnam policy, 1945 - 1967) (Solomon, "Pentagon Papers"). Ironically, Nixon himself regarded this leak of information as politically advantageous to Republicans and harmful to Democrats. However, Pentagon Papers were dangerous to Nixon administration considering the importance and credibility of presidential office and government.

Thus the government had no direct means of influence over the media and their message. Successive administrations had to develop more vague instruments: calls for patriotism or an emphasis on commercial concerns of news organizations (Dadge 47). In the case of war reporting, this meant to tie the media more closely to the government and make them even more dependent on official sources.

When we turn on the television, we have a freedom to watch various presentations of one event and therefore which "version of a story" possibly to accept. The media has a responsibility to present information to the public objectively and their role of a watchdog is highly discussed especially in those cases in which they fail to perform it. This is also the case of the war in Iraq and attendant inconsistencies in justifications of American military action. But is the media the only one to blame? I believe that the media cannot perform its watchdog role fully with so many restrictions.

The term "Fourth Estate" suggests that the media represents a very influential social power. This power can be used in various ways depending on different conditions. The watchdog role of the media is one of them. This role requires a certain amount of independence to be performed considering the government and media elites, and also the acceptance from the public.

Professionalization of journalism in the thirties led to the tightening to the state. The principles of objective journalism became an everyday routine. Journalists had a guaranty of access to information from the officials; on the other hand, they were to present just facts and not judging. Professionalization also brought a new aspect into journalism. Journalists became part of larger companies privately owned and therefore financially dependent.

The importance of the media in a military conflict is unquestionable. The image of war includes oral comments as well as images of war. This is why the Vietnam War is considered to be crucial for the development of war reporting. Television broadcasting changed the image of war completely. Though television reporters covered the Vietnam War since the official American military involvement, television coverage was thought to be favorable as long as reporters stayed objective, if not supportive. When critical voices appeared, the freedom in reporting started to be inconvenient. Popular label of "loosing the Vietnam war" served as a justification for restrictions in war reporting of subsequent military conflicts. These restrictions have developed into the embedding system as we know it today. So what role does the media have in war reporting nowadays?

3

Military and News Media

NEW MEDIA AND MILITARY RELATIONSHIP

American journalism today has evolved such that several market-driven determinants strongly affect the outcome of printed news. With the internet's vast supply of free information comes a media dependency on advertisers looking to appeal to an audience determined by the stories and journalists chosen by the owners and investors. In the Pulitzer-Hearst era, journalists created sensational stories to gain greater circulation, as evidenced by the incitement of the Spanish-American War in 1898. This lavish misuse of hyperbolized events led to the coining of the term "yellow journalism" used to describe the intentionally misleading "news". With the current war in Iraq, "embedded reporting" can now be added to the list of terms coined and used to represent both the cooperation, and the mistrust between the American government and the American news media. In times of war, there is a delicate balance between government censorship of war correspondence and the right of the press to produce unregulated news stories. In essence, both rely on each other for propagation of war sentiment and both have the power to destroy each other's credibility with the American public. As Naval Reserve Commander Jose L. Rodriguez states, it is "a mix of cooperation and tension."

In Vietnam, the lack of an official declaration of war prevented the US military from making any formal regulations, thus it was forced to request that correspondents practice voluntary censorship. In 1971, the military created the Wartime Information Security Program to control the media, which quickly became obsolete as technology developed and there was no longer a need for field censorship. Without a formal contract between the military and the press, correspondents reported critically on the effectiveness of US intervention. Editors at home, however, reflected only military reports of success in Vietnam, and while some newspapers criticized military tactics, few, if any, questioned US policy. Then, in 1968, the Tet Offensive changed the media's perspective on war. As American troops began to lose significant battles for the first time, the public and press began to challenge America's decision to continue the fight in Vietnam. Ultimately, as journalists began reporting on the futility of sending more troops, the military began to blame the press for a lack of pro-war sentiment and the war's stalemate. Similarly, the press blamed the military for lying about the situation in Vietnam and trying to mislead the public. The mistrust between the military and the media that was established in Vietnam.is a sentiment that continues to be felt by both sides today.

In the war in Iraq, the media and military continue to look for a balance between censorship and free press. Whether to alleviate tension or to gain political and militaristic control, the Pentagon decided to be proactive about setting up safe media relations for the war in Iraq. Unlike previous attempts to keep the press away from the battlefield, the Pentagon established a system of "embedded" reporters, "a media representative remaining with a unit on an extended basis – perhaps a period of weeks or even months."3 In contrast, the term "unilateral" defines any un-embedded journalists who are not associated with a military unit, but instead are independent journalists, freelance journalists, or even journalists associated with a media organization. According to the ground rules established in an official unclassified government report from 2003, the purpose of embedding the media is "to facilitate maximum, in-depth coverage of US forces in combat and related operations." However, policy 2.A. reveals a military interest not only in in-depth coverage, but also in public perception:

Media coverage of any future operation will, to a large extent, shape public perception of the national security environment now and in the years ahead. This holds true for the US public, the public in allied countries whose opinion can affect the durability of our coalition, and publics in countries where we conduct operations, whose perceptions of us can affect the cost and duration of our involvement.

This declaration of strong US military interest in public perception of war reveals an obsession with the interaction between media and military and a dedication of both sides to cooperate in order to "tell the factual story – good or bad – before others seed the media with disinformation and distortions, as they most certainly will continue to do." Both the media and military claim to strive for truth: "[T]he public demands objectivity and journalists strive to achieve it, even though critics say they miss the mark. Even if the traditional notion of objectivity as an absolute standard is often unattainable, to abandon the concept altogether would open the door to undisciplined, irresponsible journalism." And in order to effectively and efficiently relay "the factual story," the Pentagon has chosen to embed media representatives. While appearing to be a perfect solution to the unsolved problem of unbiased and in-depth war correspondence, this new practice creates several unprecedented difficulties for both journalists and their readers.

The argument of this paper is twofold. First, it argues that embedded war correspondence in Iraq magnifies three specific types of biases inherent in all journalism: *reader-response bias, editorial bias,* and *sacrificial bias.* Then it expands this analysis of the limitations of objectivity to suggest more broadly that the effect of embedded reporting on the American public is a distraction from and desensitization to war, as well as a perpetuation of American overconfidence in military ability. Moreover, as the sexual tension inherent in the word "embed" implies, the intimate nature of the mediamilitary relationship is fundamentally incestuous, insofar as it is an illicit transgression of the principle of freedom of the press. Though it attempts to propagate pro-war sentiment and alleviate

American apathy, embedded reporting has actually given birth to an unprecedented hyper-dramatization of war.

READER-RESPONSE BIAS IN THE AMERICAN NEWS MEDIA

Journalism is not simply investigative reporting for the sake of finding truth; it is a capitalist enterprise with a market and consumers to which it must cater. In other words, a reporter will alter content and rhetoric based on a newspaper, magazine, or television station's audience, in order to best serve that audience's needs. In war correspondence then, considering the audience means that a journalist will inevitably censor the reality of war at his discretion. War correspondence is particularly conducive to censorship not only because it exposes the predominantly naïve American public to the brutality and ruthlessness of war, but also because the families of soldiers have a right to learn of their loved one's death in a respectful, tactful, and formal way. These pressures mean that embeds not only practice self-censorship, but also receive limited information and are denied intimate details for the sake of secrecy and military strategy. Because "unit commanders may impose temporary restrictions on electronic transmissions for operational security reasons," an additional layer of censorship evolves, which is essentially out of journalists' control. Similarly, the bias inherent in an embed's inability to see the larger picture of war contributes to a stratified filter of information that exemplifies the limitations inherent not only in the biases explored here, but in the restrictions placed on embeds as well. Despite necessary militaristic regulations, journalists wary of audience and public opinion practice self-censorship. This self-censorship is not only an inherent lack of objectivity, but also serves to create a fabricated version of reality.

Ultimately, self-censorship creates a relativization of information as it distorts reality through the eyes of the reporter. As embedded war correspondent Gordon Dillow writes, "The discomforts and dangers of the war were easily dealt with; accurately conveying the reality of it to the readers back home was not." He continues to justify his lack of objectivity by rationalizing, for example, that omitting the routine expletives of soldiers "was unavoidable" since "it wouldn't fly in a family newspaper, [and] neither would the constant jokes about sex and bodily functions." Dillow's article reveals not only his paternal over-protectiveness, but demonstrates a level of censorship that equates military personnel to singing schoolchildren. He even admits that the problem is obvious: "The result was that the marines sounded much more like choirboys in my stories than they really are." While he concedes the point that his stories do not accurately convey reality, he claims, "I didn't hide anything. For example, when some of my marines fired up a civilian vehicle that was bearing down on them, killing three unarmed Iraqi men, I reported it – but I didn't lead my story with it, and I was careful to put it in the context of scared young men trying to protect themselves… and sweet-faced, all-American boys hardened by a war that wasn't of their making." Dillow's strong connection with his soldiers, as well as his sense that "some things are simply too gruesome to describe in detail," caused him to take liberties with censorship, writing only what he deemed necessary and proper for a family audience. The problem thus becomes an inherent lack of objectivity that is paradoxically disguised by Dillow's openness and honesty with his reader: in admitting a lack of objectivity, Dillow gains credibility with his reader, who might then mistake his honesty for the truth value that his story actually lacks.

Dillow's argument is in itself a contradiction as he states that he both omits nothing and censors expletives and gruesome details for a family audience. This paradox emphasizes the fact that his reporting is in no way representative of objective truth. This is not to say, of course, that his article does not contain truth. In fact, he states that "the point wasn't that I wasn't reporting the truth; the point was that I was reporting the marine grunt truth – which had also become my truth." With respect to the reader-response bias, his "marine grunt truth" is in fact the "marine-grunt-truth-as-is-appropriate-for-an-Americanfamily- audience." Dillow's blanket justification for a lack of fact-based truth and his hasty relativization of truth opens the door to irresponsible journalism. If journalists abandon the pursuit of objective truth in favour of relativized truths grounded in personal experience and edited for audience consumption, then who will provide the audience with that necessary degree of objectivity? The question quickly becomes one of truth value in which truth is measured by an arbitrary and subjective gradient. It is unreasonable and illogical merely to generate truth labels in order to compensate for a lack of fact-based truth value in one's reporting.

Dillow's obligation to objectivity forces him to fabricate not necessarily a story, but a truth value, for the sake of catering to an audience that only wants to hear the censored "marine grunt truth." This choice suggests that the portrayal of war is affected by a desire to shape the opinions of the American public: journalists' self-censorship for the sake of catering to an audience skews the necessary reality of a story, making it subjective to and reliant on the people who, in reality, know nothing of the war itself. Embeds, however, are not the only ones attempting to cater to war sentiment at home. News media editors must also take into account the reaction of the American public, and as such, impose their own opinions on the stories received from embeds, altering both content and scope in the hope of providing what they feel to be a larger and more balanced perspective.

Bias in the American News Media

All journalists are employed by and accountable to their editors, and thus must be wary of editors' opinions. In political journalism, especially, reporters must be cautious of how their own political views measure up to those of their editors. War correspondence, however, has an entirely different effect on this reporter-editor dynamic. With the advent of technologies like satellite phones and lightning-speed digital imagery, war reporting in Iraq not only produces real-time correspondence, but a large volume of information which many media outlets send home to editors for rewrites before presenting the story to the American public. Both the relative speed of relayed information and the use of rewrites create an unprecedented problem of convoluted subjectivity.

In a panel discussion entitled "The LA Times Goes to War," Marjorie Miller, the editor of *The Los Angeles Times*, speaks to the success and value of embeds as well as to the responsibility of editors in organizing their information. "The embeds," she says, "were valuable as mosaic pieces. But they could only see as far as they could see and it was up to Tracy and Tyler [rewrites] to begin the process of putting some of those little pieces of the puzzle into perspective." While the initial purpose of embeds was to provide up-close firsthand war coverage, the media still seems to rely on two secondhand observers sitting in their comfortable LA office chairs to both rewrite stories and put them into perspective. Unlike past wars in which correspondence was telegraphed from military commanders, the American public now relies heavily on other American citizens who have not experienced war at all to relay valuable information. For embedded correspondence, information is relayed in real-time, and so the use of rewrites is equivalent to acquiring written notes from onsite reporters several thousand miles away only to be written into a story for the not-so-war-hungry American public. Clearly, liberties are taken with the information relayed through embedded reporters – liberties that are rather deceptively represented as an unavoidable balancing act: "What you were getting from the military, from Iraq, from allied countries, from other unallied countries was going into a main bar in LA....We were trying to balance the relative weight of all of that information." This approach may attempt to cover all ground as objectively as possible, but the mere use of a central editing hub narrows the scope of all incoming correspondence and filters it through the eyes of *LA Times* editors like Marjorie Miller, a process that introduces significant problems of subjectivity.

War correspondence politics are also quite complex in other news media outlets. After all, nationwide polls found that 86 percent of viewers received their news about war from television and more specifically, 70 percent from cable television. From the beginning of the war, television stations chose a particular stance on the conflict and continued to feed each report into an editing filter of patriotism, jingoism, or in rare cases, objectivism.

According to Julia Fox and Byungho Park's statistical analysis of objectivity in embedded war correspondence, of the three largest cable television networks –Fox, CNN, and MSNBC – CNN was "more objective in its coverage of the Iraq War...[and] attempted to bring different viewpoints to viewers with segments such as 'Voices of Dissent' and 'Arab Voices.'"

Fox and Park even quote a reporter with the *Chicago Tribune* who "criticized Fox [News] for its subjective reporting of the war [saying], 'We deride Fox News Channel for saying "us" and "our" in talking about the American war effort, a strategy that conjures images of gung-ho anchor Shepard Smith, like Slim Pickens in *Dr. Strangelove*, riding a Tomahawk straight into Baghdad.'" Columnist Clarence Page also disapproves of Fox "for embracing the language of the Bush administration in its newscasts.

It calls suicide bombers 'homicide bombers' and refers to the war to unseat Saddam Hussein as America's war to 'liberate Iraq.'" Statistics from viewer polls support these findings, as viewers say that Fox had a "great deal of media bias" 43 percent of the time compared to CNN, for which viewers saw a "great deal of media bias" only 27 percent of the time. These comparisons are only examples of the wide range of bias created by the media editing filter. Simply by watching Fox as opposed to CNN, one is more likely to gain a biased understanding of the war in Iraq. With respect to my argument, the stories fed by embeds are more likely to be altered or skewed by editing when editors preemptively choose a particular stance based on politics at home. An examination of editorial bias demonstrates the relative ease with which an already subjective embed's story can be made subjective not only to the opinion of the American public, as is the case with reader-response bias, but the opinion of news media editors in reaction to American politics and domestic war sentiment.

SACRIFICIAL BIAS IN THE AMERICAN NEWS MEDIA

In a capitalist society, reporters must sell any story at a good price, regardless of its level of objectivity, and are willing to get a good story at any price; a price that, in the case of embedded reporters, is often one's life. Reporters and even the American public at large must ask themselves whether it is necessary to use embeds to obtain the most in-depth and objective coverage, and if so, whether embedded war stories are worth the loss of more American lives. Jane Arraf, CNN's Senior Baghdad Correspondent and unilateral reporter, does not think so. In a panel interview with Michael Fumento and Paul Rieckoff on *The Al Franken Show*, Arraf replies to Fumento's criticism of unilaterals by saying, "there [have] been more than 60 reporters killed. Reporters don't have to go to Baghdad, take the risk of flying in, being hit by missiles as they're flying, go on that road to the green zone where they might be blown up. They can easily stay in Jordan..." Arraf continues to argue that it is often unilaterals who gain a better understanding of the war, as they have the ability to speak Arabic with the Iraqi people and understand both the experience of Iraqis and the plight of the American military.

But many reporters, like Michael Fumento, believe that risking one's life is necessary for getting the best story. In his article, "Covering Iraq: the Modern Way of War Correspondence," Fumento writes with great respect for embeds: "If you don't have the guts actually to cover the war, stand aside for those who do." His disgust for "hotelbound credit-claimers," resounds prominently throughout his article, making his position abundantly clear. A photograph along with the article shows his late editor Michael Kelly, who was killed while embedded in Iraq, and is accompanied by a caption that reads, "Embeds die in Iraq, not members of the Baghdad Brigade," referring to the "rear-echelon reporters" otherwise known as unilaterals. "[With] the sole exception of Steven Vincent, the only American journalists killed or even seriously injured by hostile action in Iraq have been embeds." Quoting Harry Truman, Fumento writes, "If you can't stand the heat, get out of the kitchen." While such impassioned rhetoric reinforces the skewed and opinionated nature of his article, Fumento also writes that when asked where he would want to be embedded, he replied, "'the redder, the better,'" claiming a willingness to sacrifice his own life for a story by embedding himself in the most dangerous war zone.

Unlike Fumento, photographer and journalist Stephanie Sinclair is unsure of her willingness to risk her life for the best pictures. In a recent PBS documentary on embedded journalism, "War Feels like War," Sinclair reflects on the danger of her current situation. "I'm a little wary. I really don't want to get hurt. It's just not worth it to me at this point. I don't really know enough about covering wars or any sort of real violent subject matter." Sinclair, who plans on continuing war correspondence for 15 more years, is still afraid of what she might lose: "I definitely don't want to go out on my first one. Not only would it be a bad way to die, but it would be a pretty bad way to be remembered." Photographer Marco Di Lauro of Getty Images, on the other hand, claims that war hardens reporters. In a conversation with Stephanie Sinclair, Di Lauro states that over time, experience in the field will change a reporter's willingness to sacrifice for a story: "You will be ready to kill another photographer for a better picture like everybody else is."

Regardless of whether or not the inherent risk of embedded reporting is justified by more objective and indepth coverage, an embed's ability to report objectively is affected by a personal willingness to sacrifice life. Like Di Lauro, NBC News Middle East Correspondent Richard Engel thought the war would harden him. And, in a way, it did. According to Engel, he went through four stages during the embedding process: Stage 1: I'm invincible. I'm ready. I'm excited. I'm living on adrenaline. Then as the war begins, Stage 2: You know what, this is dangerous, I could get hurt over here. And that starts to sink in. Then the war continues and friends start to get kidnapped or killed and you see bodies on the streets. Stage 3: I've been over here so long, I'm probably going to get hurt. And then at a certain stage, you hit rock bottom and you feel, I've used up my time. Stage 4: I'm going to die in this conflict. And that's a dark place to go into.

When Engel reflects upon his five years in Iraq, he wonders, "Has it been worth it? All the sacrifice? I think it has." But even if the sacrifice is "worth it," does greater sacrifice necessarily translate into more objective coverage? A reporter's willingness to risk his life for a story creates problems both on an individual level as well as for war correspondence as a whole. It is tempting to think that the more a reporter is willing to sacrifice, the better the story. However, a reporter can become desensitized to trauma and no longer relate to the American public on a humaninterest level. The reverse can also be true: a reporter willing to sacrifice his life for a story might be overly sensitive to the horrors of war and thus sensationalize suffering in stories. In either scenario, the amount of risk a reporter is willing to take with his life does affect the objectivity of the story and ultimately allows emotion to creep into a humaninterest piece as a desire for sympathy and pity – that is, sympathy and pity for the reporter, not for the soldiers. At this point, it is necessary to consider how sacrificial bias affects objectivity; whether the risk of death is ethical and, further, what risking civilian lives reveals about American capitalism with respect to the media. Why are Americans willing to risk more civilian lives in order to vicariously experience an intimacy with war? Does this willingness arise from national pride and a desire to justify overseas occupation? For that matter, a consideration of editorial bias suggests the following question: why doesn't the media save time, money, and lives by having Tracy and Tyler just write the stories from home?

It is possible that Americans are more than willing to overlook reader-response, editorial, and sacrificial bias due to a fascination with military strength, power, and domination – feelings that manifest themselves in embedded war correspondence. Rather than being concerned with the loss of objectivity, embeds fuel a fixation on technologically- advanced weaponry and the feelings of power that these weapons engender. In his article, "Grunts and Pogues: The Embedded Life," embedded reporter Gordon Dillow recalls the feelings of calm and strength he gained through being able to hold a grenade given to him by one of his marine grunts: "It had been more than 30 years since I'd held a grenade, and I knew that my having it violated written and unwritten rules. Still, it felt comforting in my hand." In the heat of the struggle, the marines, as well as Dillow, were willing to disregard military regulations for the sake of saving their own lives. If this is the case – that during times of war, when life is at risk, the rules do not apply – then a host of implications can be drawn from the controversy that embedded reporting causes. For example, where exactly is the line between embed and soldier? As colleagues "[who] operate as a part of their assigned unit," should embeds be expected to take fire for fellow soldiers? The ground rules would disagree. But when do the rules actually apply? When it comes down to life and death, objectivity is not merely impossible; it is the last thing on anyone's mind.

A MILITARY ESTIMATION OF EMBEDDED WAR COMMUNICATION

Both soldiers and veterans of the US military have their opinions of embeds, and the consensus seems to be a lack of breadth of scope. Dillow's article, while written about his own experience, provides a unique, secondhand account of the initial skepticism his marine grunts held for embedded reporters: They had been warned about us, I found out later. Be careful what you say to them, the Marines of Alpha Company were told before we joined them in early March...Don't [complain] about the slow mail delivery, don't criticize the anti-war protesters back home, don't discuss operational plans, and for God's sake, don't use ethnic slur words for Arabs. Better yet, don't talk to the reporters at all. They'll just stab you in the back.

To Dillow's surprise, the marine grunts not only saw embeds as an annoyance and an additional man to cover, but were initially suspicious of Dillow's loyalties. After getting to know the men of his unit, Dillow explains that "they realized that we weren't using our Iridium cell phones to alert the Iraqi army high command to the Marine's next move." Subsequently, Dillow was able to develop both trust and camaraderie with his soldiers. Eventually, the soldiers' initial mistrust grew into a desire to have their stories told accurately and affectionately to their loved ones at home. To the Marines of the Alpha Company, Dillow's "marine grunt truth" would suffice.

Paul Rieckhoff, an Iraqi war veteran devoted to the cause of bringing troops home from Iraq, does not agree that the embeds' reports are sufficient representations of truth. He argues that while embedded reporting sometimes produces useful media, the fact is that embeds are not getting the full story. He further suggests that it is impossible for embeds to report objectively when they, like the soldiers, must have a battlefield mentality. Rieckoff makes this view clear not only in his book *Chasing Ghosts: Failures and Facades in Iraq: A Soldier's Story*, but also in a panel discussion along with Michael Fumento and Jane Arraf on *The Al Franken Show*. Al Franken, the show's host, quotes Colonel Johnson as having once said, "Every man thinks meanly of himself for not having been a soldier." Rieckhoff addresses this quite frankly:

A lot of reporters really covet the [military] experience.... They like going over there. And they want to get their reporting chops. And we used to call them in the military "jock sniffers." They wanted to be part of the action. And I'm not saying this of all reporters, but there are some elements of that. And in my opinion, if you're embedded, you've compromised some of your journalistic integrity. You can't objectively cover both sides when I'm guarding your butt. And I've been there with embedded reporters and I think some of them do a great job. And I think honestly, Ms. Arraf, you're doing a wonderful job at CNN, but you're still only getting one side of it for the most part. You can't independently operate without US military protection now. So you're still only getting a very narrow understanding. And we think most of the people who have been there will admit that. Rieckhoff's statement sparked heated debate among the other two panelists, Arraf and Fumento.

Franken, playing the devil's advocate, immediately suggests that the best and bravest reporters are men and women like Jill Carroll and George Packer - "the people who have gone through that country without being embedded." Arraf strongly agrees and argues that embedding is not necessary to knowing the country and the people well. For instance, she states that "there are places you cannot go now without being embedded," yet, if you "know the country as I do, you go there, [and] can actually speak Arabic to the Iraqis," which, as she explains, is both necessary and sufficient in understanding the story in Iraq. Fumento, on the other hand, suggests that unilaterals are getting too comfortable sitting on the sidelines reporting secondhand information without actually experiencing what the soldiers experience. But perhaps it is actually the embedded journalists who exhibit a "false bravado," as Arraf claims, because they are attempting to credit themselves with a combat mission.

"Covering Iraq: The Modern Way of War Correspondence," Fumento addresses Rieckhoff's comment by saying, "Rieckhoff, an anti-war vet who was hawking his boring book...labeled those who actually go into battle with troops as 'jock sniffers.' To him, the Ernie Pyles and Joe Rosenthals of America's past were just a bunch of contemptible groupies." Fumento continues to mock Rieckhoff's statement by projecting his term "jock sniffers" onto journalist heroes of the past, where, under the photo of the famous flag raising at Iwo Jima, Fumento's caption reads: "The most iconic image of World War II, by 'crotch-sniffer' Joe Rosenthal." Fumento's response demonstrates the sharp contrast between the view of a soldier and that of an embed. While they might get along in the field, tension between the two still exists. Rieckhoff's proposed solution is more balanced, as he argues not for the factual storytelling of a soldier's plight, as one might expect from a veteran, but rather for the combination of correspondence gained by embeds, unilaterals, and non-American war correspondents. Ultimately, both Dillow's and Rieckhoff's accounts of soldiers' responses to embeds reveal the complexity surrounding an embed's inability to objectively view both sides while resisting the distractions of camaraderie, fear of the enemy, and pressure from soldiers to communicate their stories compassionately. Despite the military's skepticism of embeds and the tension created by mistrust in Vietnam, embedded reporting has changed the way the military views the media. As Commander Rodriguez points out, "The shift in the military's perspective of the media from that of an adversary to an ally was central to the mission" in Iraq and ultimately to the development of a symbiotic relationship between media and military.

THE CONSEQUENCE OF THE MEDIA-MILITARY CONSPIRACY

The media-military relationship does not simply cause a biased collection of war correspondence. In order to rally pro-war sentiment, justify America's desire to spread democracy, and glorify the American soldier, the media and military have teamed up to create a Hollywoodesque dramatization of the Iraq War, transforming reports on combat from a relay of unbiased facts to a red carpet media event. Together, they are manufacturing entertainment rather than offering information. In doing so, the media-military partnership has effectively distracted and desensitized the American public, strategically utilizing American overconfidence in war ability in order to justify the use of civilian embeds.

Preoccupying Americans with Journalism

Embedded reporters, whether they intend to or not, are keeping Americans occupied with stories of war correspondents rather than stories of war. By introducing embeds in the war in Iraq, the media-military machine is providing Americans with a convenient distraction: one in which embeds continue to glorify themselves and lead Americans to believe that they are winning a war, while the military continues to make poor decisions in Iraq that go completely unnoticed. Embed and foreign correspondent, Robert Kaplan, comments on this phenomenon in his article, "The Media and the Military," which attempts to justify the media-military intimacy created by the "embed phenomenon." He writes, "The Columbia Journalism

Review recently ran an article about the worrisome gap between a wealthy media establishment and ordinary working Americans. One solution is embedding, which offers the media perhaps their last, best chance to reconnect with much of the society they claim to be a part of." Embeds may be attempting to relate to the working American public, but in reality, their presence on a battlefield makes this "reconnection" impossible. Still, he continues, "the hundreds of embedded journalists aren't just reporting on this war; they're serving as surrogates for all civilians. And they've given the story a visceral immediacy, a that-could-be-me feeling." And it is precisely this feeling that keeps the public's attention drawn towards the media rather than the true heroes: the men and women of the American military who are dying in service of a country instead of the embeds who are "dying" to get a story. By creating this distraction which focuses attention on the death count of reporters rather than on the death count of soldiers and Iraqis, the media-military mechanism is operating a machine that symbiotically serves the interests of each. Should the Pentagon make a mistake with military strategy, it can simply force embeds to comply with the orders of the unit's commander. Similarly, the media gains inside access, is inherently biased, but the American public continues to believe that reporting from within troop operations leads to a closer representation of truth. Both at home and in Iraq, there seems to be an overwhelming notion that the true story is "embedded" in daily troop operations, and that with access comes an omniscient understanding of war. In reality, this complete understanding comes not from embeds whose scope is narrowed by limited information, but from a range of sources and stories able to contribute to a more objective truth.

The distraction caused by embedded reporting takes the form of a theatrical dramatization. "At first there is a build-up and expectancy of a Hollywood script about to unfold, but then reality hits and we are reminded that war feels like war." says journalist PJ O'Rourke. Instead of a Hollywood script, complete with the gut-wrenching thriller scenes of war movies like "Black Hawk Down," there is only bizarre uncut film of cameramen chasing soldiers through fields. War may feel like war, but it certainly does not look like it. Not only does this raise questions about the relationship between Hollywood and news media, fiction versus reality, but for those who have never experienced war, it begs the question: what does war actually look like? Ironically, the documentary, which is intended to expose the condition of necessary unilateral reporters, actually gives insight into what war might look like if there were no reporters in the field at all, and, instead, a video camera were simply left in the war zone to shoot uncut, unedited reels. Surprisingly, war does not have the rushed thrill of the Hollywood renditions. While at times soldiers are excited by the action and begin throwing around meaningless expletives, the reality of war appears to be a slow, daunting march towards an untimely and inevitable death. This march, however, does not end in Iraq. With increasing ubiquity, embedded reporting has become a phenomenon that cannot restrict itself to war coverage overseas. In transforming war correspondence into a cinematic narrative, journalists have followed wounded soldiers home, reporting directly from hospital beds. "The idea was simple," writes Anne Hull. "If the Pentagon was embedding journalists with military units in the invasions of Iraq, why couldn't it apply the same principle inside the nation's largest military hospital?" In her article, "Proposing a Variation on Embedded Reporting," Hull recounts her experience as a reporter embedded in the Walter Reed Army Medical Center in Washington, DC. Hull writes, "We'd locate ourselves inside a military hospital to explore the physical and psychological aftermath of war." The media- military machine thus does not stop in Iraq, but continues to impose itself upon soldiers at home. "We wanted a counterpoint to the ongoing stories and imagery of tanks rolling toward Baghdad, and Pentagon officials point at maps. It was time for a gut check. The casualties were starting to come home." Hull claims that once the terror and excitement of war is over for the wounded, they come home to an uncomfortable environment in which they become outcasts from mainstream society. However, as "War Feels like War" clearly demonstrates, the physical hardship of war is surprisingly similar to the hospital experience. This parallel demonstrates two realities: first, uncut war footage is not equivalent to the common Hollywood-esque perception, as demonstrated by uncut film. Second, the term "embed" is becoming a token of Operation Iraqi Freedom, showcasing a heroic embedded icon that displays the media-military intention of distracting the American public from combat and military operations in Iraq.

However, the media-military scheme does not stop with the embed icon. Rather, it forces a dramatization of the military experience similar to the one provided by war imagery used in film production, which inherently sensationalizes combat in order to sell movie tickets. This move raises the question: to what extent does the news media attempt to take its cues from or even compete with Hollywood in order to retain a captive audience? While that question is not within the scope of this paper, it is worth considering that, to some extent, the news media must obtain a universal audience in order to make money and, in so doing, must compete with other forms of media, both entertainment and "infotainment." It is easy to see how the news media might become susceptible to the habit of sensationalizing reality for the sake of selling stories. However, embedded reporting is the result of a combined effort, both media and military, to dramatize the war in Iraq.

American Apathy for War

This distraction then becomes part of an overall desensitization to the horrors of warfare, which is evidenced by the American public's indifference towards war. The surrogacy provided by embedded reporters is inherently contradictory in that it claims to offer a reconnection to and a link between war experience and the American audience. Yet, in reality, it merely serves as a filter through which Americans might read someone else's experiences and someone else's reaction to war. Short of having all civilians take military-assisted tours through Baghdad, it is quite impossible for the public to experience war; perhaps reporters are the closest substitute for personal experience. However, due to the inherent lack of objectivity, embedded reporters in particular may not be the best substitute, as they become a filter that actually puts one personal human experience between reality and the audience. In this sense, Americans are faced with the impossibility of personal experience and the dissatisfaction of being once removed from war itself. It serves only to create more apathy for and desensitization to war: after seeing the most gruesome pictures and reading the most glorified war stories, the American public is simply tired of trying to connect with war when, in actuality, it is not even possible.

American apathy for war is not only a problem for pro-war, Operation Iraqi Freedom supporters, but, as Paul Rieckhoff can attest, it is a problem for soldiers coming home from Iraq as well. "There's a war going on over there," says Al Franken, "and most Americans just don't relate to it at all." It is the one thing Franken, Arraf, Fumento and Rieckoff all agree on. "They [the American people] live life uninterrupted," says Paul Rieckhoff.

"It is patriotism light...and my biggest criticism of this administration is that they haven't asked the American people to do anything." To this, Fumento points out that every unit with which he was embedded complained, "Why don't the folks back home know what we're doing here?"- a question to which Fumento responds, "I'm afraid that a good part of the explanation is that reporters aren't getting out to them." This indifference to war becomes frustrating for reporters as well as for soldiers returning home.

MSNBC's embedded foreign correspondent Richard Engel speaks to this undeniable apathy from a journalist's perspective. In the onset of war, during the "Shock and Awe" Campaign "everyone wanted to know every sound and picture and image that we could get out of Iraq. Now five years later we have a huge infrastructure in the country, but the interest level has dropped dramatically. And that is one of the frustrating things, when you're in Baghdad and you want to tell a story and people don't want to listen." Even two years ago, claims Engel, Americans were more interested in stories of conflict in Iraq.

"Now nobody asks anymore. People don't want to hear it even on a personal level." Even Engel's family and friends grow tired of the constant reminder of their own lack of participation in the war effort. American apathy, then, seems to come from the guilt "every man [feels] for not having been a soldier," as well as from the media's contribution to the public's perception of war.

Out of necessity, the American public gets information from the news media. If the media cannot report objectively, then it is reasonable to expect very little interest from the American public in return. The sheer volume of information overwhelms Americans so that they either disregard the war altogether or naïvely accept the representation of war from whatever article or photo happens to slide across their desk on Monday morning. Part of this apathy and lack of concern stems from the comfortable lives most Americans live and the confidence and pride they seem to have in the nation's supreme military and weapons arsenal. So long as Americans feel that their presence in Iraq is morally justified by the spread of democracy, citizens will not be able to feel any of the effects of war – especially so long as there are no direct repercussions for the individual. American overconfidence leads paradoxically to an apathetic attitude towards war: what should breed patriotism actually generates both arrogance and indifference.

4

The Media's Role in Foreign Policymaking

THE MEDIA'S ROLE IN DOMESTIC POLICYMAKING

Media Selection of 'Legitimate' Policy Actors

The media acts as a powerful political actor, with its interests strongly tied to the status quo and that of other corporate policy actors, instead of the general public. Journalists and editors shape policy agendas by actively filtering issues, so that reporting conforms to their dominant news values - selecting what issues are covered and which sources are used. This tends to confine policy debate to the strict boundaries of current 'accepted wisdoms' set by the major political parties or institutional policymakers.

The conservative nature of these perceptual screens is strengthened by the media's 'need' for concision, which is especially dominant on television, with its appetite for sound bite politics. Creation of credible policy frameworks influence journalists in much the same way, leading them to rely on institutional actors (encountered on daily beats) who support their perceptions of a successful policy framework. Development of such close relationships with sources is very important to the policy process, and often results in what is described as "coalition journalism". Support for policies is also reinforced by, (1) credentialing supportive sources and disregarding opposing sources, (2) using labels to shorthand information about policies by placing them within frameworks (with their associated assumptions), and (3) by the way sources are then "in a sense forced, to reflect these perceptions" accepting the commonsense interpretation of these policy frameworks to protect their own reputations in the mass media.

Outsider groups find it difficult to voice opinions in the media and even when they do, official sources are contacted to 'balance' these stories to ensure 'objectivity'. These, often resource-poor groups, are compelled to use the media as a means of gaining recognition as trusted policy actors. However, due to the media's reliance on established sources they may need to resort to different methods to capture media attention - which may cause distractions to their legitimacy, as the news may focus on a group's event and not its politics. Media stereotypes of policies, individuals or groups can influence their respective abilities to determine policy outcomes. Furthermore, even if certain policies turn out to be successful, they may still be subjected to unnecessary reform, if their legitimacy has already been undermined in the media by the creation of negative stereotypes. Schiraldi and Macallair also illustrated the vulnerability of juvenile crime policymaking in San Francisco to media "manipulation…by election-minded politicians", showing how difficult it is for citizen campaigners to reframe official policy frames once they have been adopted by the media.

MEDIA RELATIONS WITH POLICYMAKERS

In the past it was believed that the media's influence on policy occurred in a straightforward fashion, with journalists clearly separated from the governing processes. Media investigations (initiated by popular public sentiment) prompt widespread changes in public opinion, citizens then organise and collectively pressure the government, which capitulates to popular pressure and makes the appropriate public policy reforms. This simple linear model has recently been described as the 'Mobilisation Model' - while in the past it has been referred to as a 'Popular Mobilisation' or 'Public Advocacy'.

This model assumes a strong democratic role for citizens in policymaking processes, a role which has been disputed by a number of political scientists, who suggest that special interest groups and other political elites dominate the policymaking processes, not the public. Protess *et al.* (1991, p. 19) support these contentions and suggest "that policymaking changes often occur *regardless* of the public's reaction" to active (investigative) reporting. By including ethnographic studies of journalists and policymakers in their study, they were able to show how prepublication collaboration between the two groups (journalists and policymakers) may be the real driver of policy agendas, not public opinion. These collaborations were seen to have a significant affect on policy outcomes. They illustrated how prior knowledge of upcoming media attention often enabled policymakers to exploit negative media attention as "policy opportunities". In this way, policymakers are able to manage their media coverage to maximise positive publicity for their policies. This is achieved by ensuring they were seen as part of the solution, even when they were responsible for the problem. This symbiotic relationship, entailing active collaboration between journalists and policymakers to determine policymaking agendas has been described as "coalition journalism" and would seem to stand in total opposition to the commonly perceived adversarial nature of investigative journalism. Guzzardi referred to the bond as *The secret love affair between the press and government,* asserting that the media had become a vital "force for legitimizing governmental institutions and free enterprise". Both parties gain by participating in "coalition journalism"; journalists obtain credentialed information and recognition by providing an 'important' legitimate story, while policymakers obtain publicity for their policy agendas. Perhaps the only loser is the public, who ends up losing challenging adversarial forms of journalism. In the light of this Protess *et al.* suggest that the "linear Mobilisation Model" be replaced with the more adaptive "Coalition Model" of investigative reporting.

Contrary to popular beliefs, Protess *et al.* (1991) also discovered that the amount of time being spent by muckraking journalists on investigative reporting is not declining. However, they reported a trend towards shorter investigations which, taken together with cuts in funding for longer term investigative reporting, is placing increasing pressure on journalists to replace adversarial journalism with coalition journalism. Investigative journalism is becoming less visible in the public sphere, as its work becomes more widely dispersed, conventional and less adversarial - staying closer to the borders of the dominant policy discourses. A further outcome of these changes is that as shorter investigative pieces are cheaper to produce, media outlets have less incentive to actively pursue policy stories for the duration of policy processes. Dominant news values, such as 'timeliness' further strengthen such practises by working to constantly change those issues on the public agenda, preventing any form of sustained media attention to most issues.

Media corporations may set policy agendas, but as the duration of policy attention cycles continues to decrease, influence of policy outcomes will be increasingly left out of reach of the public, and safely in the hands of established policymakers. So as coalition journalism becomes more institutionalised, the general public is being pushed further towards the margins of the policymaking processes, left ever more prone to manipulation from both the media and policymakers. Medler and Medler (1993) illustrated how easily the media (television in this case) can mislead viewers regarding the success or failure of environmental policies: creating unwarranted pressure for policymakers, who may feel the need to alter effective policies to safeguard their public standing, or preventing other policymakers from seeking solutions to ineffective policies. These media effects on politicians would be amplified if timed to occur just prior to elections, especially if the politician(s) in question did not have clear public support. Critically, to comprehend the complex media-policy nexus, it is necessary to understand which societal players are actively working to influence the media agenda. The importance of government's media management has already been mentioned in this respect, but not the other dominant actor in most policymaking decisions: corporations.

Affecting Policy Outcomes

Even if the media can set the actual policy agenda in some circumstances, this does not necessarily mean that they influence policy. Political rhetoric may appear to signal media impact, but if it does little more than pay lip service to media coverage, effecting only minor policy outcomes, then to what degree has the media really affected the policymaking process? Mortensen and Serritzlew examined local media influence on policy outcomes in Denmark, and demonstrated that media coverage actually has "limited consequences for actual policy decisions" even when "policy agenda and political discussions are affected by the media" (2004, p. 16). Reiterating this point they concluded that "the media are important for understanding the political agenda and the framing of decisions about special [or sensational] issues, but 'normal' politics and the broader policy priorities [or governmental issues] are largely unaffected". This partly confirmed the results of Soroka's (2002) study which suggested, that media influence is strongest with 'sensational issues', and weakest in 'governmental issues', which are predominantly policy-driven. Likewise, Protess *et al.* (1987) demonstrated that when a policy issue is 'nonrecurring' in terms of media coverage (a sensational issue), media power to influence public opinion (but not necessarily policy outcomes) is greater than with 'recurring' policy coverage (which are more synonymous with governmental issues). Taken together, these results present an interesting paradox for democratic governance, one in which media coverage of policy issues does not appear to affect most of society's actual decision-making.

THE MEDIA'S ROLE IN FOREIGN POLICYMAKING

Many studies have concluded that the media has a pivotal role in shaping government's foreign policymaking processes through a phenomena referred to as the CNN effect. This effect does not refer to the sole influence of CNN on policymaking, but rather on the power of global media networks to determine political processes through selective coverage of certain issues. This is particularly important, as most of the public rely on the media for access to foreign policy information. Gilboa notes that:

"The [CNN] concept was initially suggested by politicians and officials haunted by the Vietnam media myth, the confusion of the post–Cold War era, and the communications revolution. Despite evidence to the contrary, many leaders still believe that critical television coverage caused the American defeat in Vietnam. Since then, many have viewed the media as an adversary to government policies in areas such as humanitarian intervention and international negotiation."

To determine whether the media has the power to influence policymaking, Robinson (2000) devised the 'policy–media interaction model', utilising the theoretical framework of press–state relations outlined by Hallin (1986) and Bennett (1990). This model was applied to a number of US humanitarian interventions, which took place in the 1990s. The results showed, that critical reporting by the media with a strong pro-intervention frame had a 'strong' role in shaping the US government policies when policymakers were uncertain about their actions (resulting in the US intervention in Bosnia in 1995 to defend the Gorazde 'safe area') but a 'weak' role when government policies were already determined. Thus, the power of the CNN effect would seem to vary depending upon the existence of cohesive policies on foreign policy matters.

Where the media was commonly reported as driving foreign policymaking decisions such as the US humanitarian intervention in Somalia, critical research has shown the opposite to be the case. In fact, before the media really took up the case for intervention in Somalia, the government was persistently trying to raise awareness for it through press releases, which the media paid little attention too. The media only started to seriously call for intervention, after the leak of the president's decision to offer US troops to the UN for the intervention. Robinson notes that after this leak, the media tended to frame their reporting to support the president's decision by empathising with the Somali people and highlighting the positive aspects of the intervention. Alternative analyses of the

Somalia intervention using a 'realist' international relations approach support Robinson's case, concluding that the intervention was primarily due to American national strategic interests (Gibbs, 2000). Therefore, Robinson describes the medias role as being one of "manufacturing consent or indexing rather than the CNN effect". Governments directly benefit from this state of affairs by giving the impression of bowing to public opinion (which they equate with media coverage), despite the fact that their policy decisions may have been made long before media coverage of these issues began. Under such circumstances the media acts more as a tool of the policymakers themselves, rather than the public, by reflecting elite interests and opinions and manufacturing public consent.

COMPANY MANAGEMENT OF THE MEDIA AGENDA

Lawson Lucas Mendelsohn (LLM) is one of largest lobbying firms in the UK with many powerful clients including the *Royal Society for the Prevention of Cruelty to Animals* and *News International*: "Neil Lawson advised Tony Blair on campaign strategy, Ben Lucas conducted Blair's political briefings and Jon Mendelsohn handled the.. prime minister's contacts with business". Their massive financial resources and familiarity with key policymakers make them a perfect example of how asymmetric policy influence can be. Lawson and Lucas told undercover reporter Greg Palast how LLM recommends the indirect route of lobbying policymakers by "creating an environment" for clients by "placing things with columnists we know the chancellor [or relevant policymaker] reads". In addition, LLM runs a captive think tank, *Nexus*, to give their views (or their clients' views) legitimacy, and uses the *Socialist Environmental Research Foundation*, which acts as "a purchased front for retailers". Such services clearly provide a useful means, by which powerful businesses can influence the policymaking processes through the media. However, as public relations researcher Aeron Davis notes, corporate influence on business news is even more far reaching in its effects: "...the advantages of large corporate elites in business news...appear far greater than for political elites in mainstream news. As a result, journalists are left in the position of reporting outcomes or recording those conflicts that financial elites choose to play out in the media."

Powerful well funded corporate public relation campaigns work to forward pro-business policy outcomes by "excluding the media, the general public and rival elites from knowledge of elite policy-making processes". In fact, corporate and government public relations practitioners interviewed in the same study said that 50% or more of their activities involved preventing media attention. When conflict in the policymaking process is reported, it is mainly because discussions spill over into the public sphere, forcing those parties involved to release selected information to the media. However, the information that is released often limits the extent to which the policy issue can be placed in context and the degree to which it can be understood. Major reasons for this are (1) journalists tend to be limited in what they can reveal about negotiations due to their strong reliance "on small circles of public relation practitioners and elite sources", (2) information that is reported is targeted at specific decision-makers, so is often "exclusionary in its style and content", and (3) 'news values' do not favour the reporting of complicated policy issues, which has led to reduction in the reporting of such issues, and where they are covered, context is often lost making their relevance to longer patterns of change harder to determine. This all works to ensure that "macro-level trends are lost in coverage of the isolated micro-level event", so even when critical researchers emphasize the significance of such macro trends this "rarely result[s] in more significant media campaigns or public outcries".

This process is highly visible in the way that the mainstream media will occasionally attack lobbying, corruption, and certain taxes, but won't really criticize the underlying institutional problems associated with them. Undercover reporter Greg Palast found systemic evidence of corruption in New Labour (UK), and courting of lobby firms for favours. Yet despite the press taking up the story for a week after his exposé, the only person to be penalised was one lobbyist. There was no immediate parliamentary investigation and no calls from the media to demand the government to open its records. When the prime minister eventually called for an investigation, the Parliamentary Committee on Standards of Conduct concluded - after declining to use the evidence gathered by the Observer's investigations (which included tapes, faxes and witness statements) - that: "We may have serious problems but they are not of the gravest nature".

Davies concludes "that, for much of the time outside electoral campaigns, the role of the media in policymaking is more connected to the manufacturing of elite rather than mass forms of consent." Most corporate public relations resources aim to influence decision making through the business and economic press, which serves to "repeat the 'mobilisation of bias' identified in policymaking itself". This claim substantiates Hawthorne's (1993) finding, that the primary target of media coverage was an elite audience, who could directly influence policy, and the secondary target was public opinion. Manufacturing of elite consent also seems to be the main purpose of coalition journalism which primarily serves policymakers and media interests, before the public. Media corporations, acting as powerful corporate bodies, engage with credentialed policymakers to set both policy agendas and the legitimate terms of discussion. If there is sufficient disagreement, as to the terms of the debate among major political parties, then a fierce public debate can ensue under such limited conditions (confined that is within conventional truths). However, where 'official' opposition voices are united, it is unlikely that the media will challenge them, and policy issues will be strongly framed to support official policy positions. Powerful interests may still challenge official positions, but this will take place through more formal lobbying channels, well concealed from the prying eye of the media.

A Closer Look at Media Power when Policy Indecision Exists

Looking at the US intervention in Bosnia in 1995 as an example of strong media affects where policy uncertainty existed, even then, the media strongly supported the government's broader foreign policy agenda, and did little to question the dominant frames set by US policymakers. Prior to Bill Clinton's inauguration on 20 January 1993, the US 'elite' press (New York Times and Washington Post) "reacted only mildly" to the Balkan war. This served to legitimise the Bush (senior) administrations policies, whose "priorities were the Gulf states and Somalia" with strong opposition to "any further involvement with the developments in Yugoslavia". In stark contrast to the Bush administration, Clinton argued during his election campaign "for lifting the arms embargo against the Bosnian Muslims" and "had a much more positive attitude towards the Bosnian issue than... Bush", attacking "Bush's inaction" and charging "him with violating American liberal values in his foreign policy". As might be expected, if the media was to take their lead from policymakers (to manufacture public consent), the start of Clinton's presidency would have coincided with increased media coverage of the Balkans and indeed, already in his first year as president the elite press began to "intensely" address the issue of the Balkan war. During this time, Clinton's administration may have exhibited policy uncertainty, but their public commitment to the Balkans clearly raised the media ante, encouraging a stronger media focus on the ensuing developments in the Balkans. The media acted to exert pressure on the government, to take a firmer position in Bosnia, but they did so on the governments terms, showing strong (almost unquestioning) support to the Bosnian Muslims – who the US continued to illegally supply with arms from Iran and Turkey and with Mujahedin fighters which were "supported by Iranian special operations forces". The support the media provided to the Bosnian Muslims was strengthened by the Muslim leadership's utilisation of powerful PR techniques, which helped provide foreign journalists with pro Muslim stories. Early on in the conflict the:

"...Sarajevan Muslims realized the importance of both perception management and the need to disseminate their message to the world. This awareness, coupled with the expertise of their PR firms [including US firms Hill & Knowlton and Ruder Finn], resulted in a highly successful psychological operations campaign. Meanwhile, the more rustic Serbs proved no match for this competition."

In frustration with the unrelenting pro Muslim media coverage, Professor Jacobsen (Director of the Independent Committee in War Crimes in the Balkans) wrote to the editor of the New York Times, beginning his letter: "Your (deliberately?) myopic reporting on Yugoslavia mocks your masthead claim to objectively". The 'objectivity' of this type of journalism can be seen in the coverage of the three bombings in Sarajevo: in 1992 (the "Breadline Massacre"), 1994 (the Markale "Market Massacre") and a "Second Market Massacre" in 1995. All three massacres were reportedly carried out by the Serbs according to US media, despite the fact that UN officials and senior Western military officials claim that there was strong evidence suggesting that the massacres were undertaken by Bosnian Muslims. But why would US government and media show any favours towards the Bosnian Muslims? A Pentagon source frankly explained the reasoning behind US governments support for the Muslims in Bosnia:

"The simple facts are these: we are getting incredible pressure from the Saudis and others to help the Muslim cause in Bosnia. They remind us that the Islamic world provides us with all the oil we want at relatively low prices, that Islamic states have billions of petrodollars to invest in "friendly states" and offer a potential market of over one billion people for the goods and services of "friendly countries"; and finally, that the peace process between Israel and the Islamic world "should go better if Israel's main friend was also a friend to Islamic countries. When you weigh these facts against what 8 million Serbs can do for America's interests, its clear what direction our policy is going to take."

The media's siding against the Serbs naturally follows from their adoption of the US government's official foreign policy position. Therefore, if the media did strongly influence US foreign policy decisions regarding Bosnia (in 1995) as Robinson (2000) suggests, then it still did so on the government's terms. Instead of simply acting to manufacture public consent to align with US policy lines, as the US media did in Somalia, the media's role in Bosnia was more complicated (although the end result was still the same). Working within government led frames of reference, the media acted to highlight weaknesses in the US governments uncertain policy line toward the Balkans, and catalysed the development of firm policy objectives that drew from the conflicting policy preferences emanating from the Clinton administration. It served "mainly as a supportive arm of the state and dominant elites, focusing heavily on what is serviceable to them, and debating and exposing within accepted frames of reference". If the media was really being critical of government policy, there would have been a much wider debate surrounding the war; instead it was highly partisan and played up to the Clinton administration's geostrategic objectives (even if they were apparently poorly formed). This certainly calls into question the real ability of the media to effectively question or significantly influence foreign policy making, and fulfil its democratic function to the public.

Government Power of the Policy Agenda

Compared to domestic policymaking there is relatively less public interest in foreign affairs, which makes it relatively easy for government policymakers to dominate the media's agenda. From the wide array of 'potentially interesting' international stories going on at any one time, governments can actively distract media attention away from sensitive foreign policy initiatives (of which coverage might invoke more critical public reactions) by concentrating their PR machineries on less controversial policies. As noted before, in cases of policy certainty within any given government, the national media are extremely unlikely to challenge the government or focus any form of prolonged attention to the policies. Instead, as Chang concluded, the media is most likely to have an influential role in foreign policymaking when debates "spill from the closed circle over into the public domain" - which usually occurs when there is policy uncertainty within the political elites (1993, p. 24).

Despite the evident importance of foreign policymaking for democracies worldwide the media's apparent role in 'manufacturing consent' may be more easily understood, when it is considered that "the foreign policy establishment represents the most elite group within the government". Foreign policymaking also rates low on most citizens concerns, making it easier for corporate and government policymakers to control. The same is not true for domestic policymaking, where the level of interest and diversity of voices heard by the public is much larger. In practice though, the media's role is still much the same, with elite domination of critical policymaking agendas. Policies that will directly and adversely affect people's lives slip though unnoticed, with little media coverage, or never come up on the public (or media) agenda at all, due to the success of internal PR and lobbying activities.

Even when politically sensitive stories break into the media, revealing the true extent of politicians' conspiratorial dealings, they often seem to safely disappear (a bonus for politicians, but not democracy), barely registering on the public's consciousness. A current example is the leaked 'Downing Street Memo' which was first reported in the Sunday Times on 1st May 2005 (Smith, 2005). The minutes of this meeting revealed "that Straw and Blair had conspired to use inspections to lure Saddam into obstructing the UN, providing an excuse for war" (Medialens Alert, 2005 [27th and 30th June]) and then continued to lie about their true intentions: "war is not inevitable" (Straw, 2003) and "I hope, even now, Iraq can be disarmed peacefully" (Blair, 2003). The British (US and Australian) media had access to the memo, but this groundbreaking story was effectively killed to all intent and purposes. The Guardian's Jonathan Freedland described how "much of the coverage has sought to play down the documents' importance"; he even went on to suggest that the primary reason for this was that the media had decided that "voters were Iraq-ed out". How is this possible, how can such an important story literally drop off the public radar? Perhaps as Lee and Solomon surmise: "The world according to the mass media is not supposed to make sense; it is supposed to make money".

Davis warns about the risk of 'outsider' groups trivialising their policy goals through the process of reorientating their strategies (through "ideological shifts") to curry media favour. For example, these groups may focus on media friendly topics like personal corruption instead of more complicated policy issues like corporate crime or global warming.

Such practises can only serve to weaken our democracies, and therefore the underlying problems need to be addressed urgently – policymaking should not have to conform to media 'news values'. Corporate media cannot be relied upon to nourish our democracies while it simultaneously acts to erode our democratic institutions by excluding the bulk of citizens from elite policy discourses in the mass media or private elite communication spheres.

Herring and Robinison (2003) illustrate how effectively anti-elite ideas are kept out of the media according to Herman and Chomsky's (1988) 'propaganda model', by showing how the model itself has been ignored or dismissed within academia, especially by media scholars. However, with the rising concentration of corporate ownership of the media and the increasing dominance of what Davis (2002) referred to as *PR democracy* "if ever there was a time for the 'propaganda model' to be included in scholarly debates on media performance, it is now".

The internet may hold some hope for a more democratic media, but to ensure that the internet strengthens democratic processes it is vital, that its power is harnessed through appropriate legislation and regulation.

Unfortunately, the positive realisation of this technology for democracy seems unlikely, as so far the internet "has enjoyed virtually no public debate over how it should be organized and deployed" and the internet may just be seen as a "more effective way to commercialise the public discourse". Corporate colonisation of cyberspace is already undermining the democratic potential of this resource, marginalising many voices due to the domineering presence of large corporate portals and commercial media sites drawing most of the online traffic. Increasing market pressures on the internet mean that its democratising power is unlikely to be fulfilled unless there is sustained and coordinated pressure from all its users. This will require more critical approaches to the understanding of the implications of this new technology, as Mansell argues:

"Only a tiny fraction of research on new media makes explicit the researcher's own conception of the way in which power is articulated in society and its consequences. This unproblematic approach to new media must change in the future if we want to ask questions about how technological mediation is being fostered, about its structures, processes and consequences."

Founded on the principles of freedom of speech and private ownership, the media has been widely regarded as the 'Forth Estate' of government holding the Parliament, Judiciary and the Executive (or Crown) accountable within the democratic process. This stands at odds with the description provided by the analyses undertaken in this paper, which indicates that the media predominantly serves to *manufacture* consent rather than *deliberation* - a finding supporting by numerous recent studies. Bearing all this in mind, it is clear that the paternalistic description of the media acting as the Forth Estate urgently needs updating.

How should concerned citizens tackle these serious problems? The answer to this question depends on where one envisages the root causes of the problem to stem from. An analysis that firmly places the blame for democratic failures on the media's doorstep is in danger of ignoring the reform of deeper (often hidden) institutional structures which drive our current media systems - effectively letting politicians and corporate powerbrokers off the hook. This paper has tried to demonstrate, that this sort of limited approach to media reform would not provide any long-term solutions.

So although positive, it is unlikely that small media reforms (like public journalism) will be enough to reduce the commercial and corporate imperatives driving our existing media systems. Instead, a fundamental reform of the entire system is needed, together with a wider institutional reform of the very structures the media systems work within, our democracies. This will be a difficult task, due to powerful vested interests benefiting from the status quo, including media, political and economic elites. Reforms will need to be driven by vibrant grassroots campaigns mobilising public support across the political spectrum, to enable the citizens of the world to have a media system that works to strengthen democratic principles as opposed to undermining them. This task is challenging, but it will become easier once people begin to understand the media's role in policymaking within our democracies.

5

U.S. and China Media Diplomacy

THE U.S. MILITARY ROLE IN THE PACIFIC

Since the end of World War II the U.S. has been the dominant military power in the Asia-Pacific, and it deploys significant numbers of personnel in the region. A series of postwar bilateral treaties increased allies' dependence on the U.S. and created a structure for long-term U.S. hegemony in the region. The cornerstone of this policy was the Mutual Security Treaty, forced on Japan as the price for ending the formal U.S. military occupation. The U.S. presence has served several purposes over the years, most importantly the encirclement of the Soviet Union (and now Russia), China, and North Korea.

The U.S. acquired sites for training, refueling, and maintenance, and bases from which U.S. military interventions could originate. The most visible evidence of the U.S. role in the region has been the presence of the U.S. Navy. The 7th fleet, headquartered in Yokosuka, Japan, deploys 50 to 60 vessels, 350 aircraft, and approximately 50-60,000 personnel in the region. These forces can be quickly supplemented by Pacific Fleet forces operating from Hawaii. U.S. ships frequently make port calls around the neighborhood, and each visit constitutes an act of public diplomacy and is an overt expression of U.S. military might and interest in the region.

The U.S. security umbrella prevented Japan and South Korea from developing their own nuclear weapons systems. Advocates of the U.S. presence, both in the United States and in allied nations, would cite the past sixty-plus years of peace and stability in the region as evidence that these expenditures have borne fruit. U.S. hegemony in the region demands, however, a permanent and substantial presence of U.S. military assets now and into an unending future. This is at a time when the United States is facing huge budget deficits, is embroiled or is just recovering from costly land wars in Afghanistan and Iraq, and when the American people are being asked to reduce government expenditures by surrendering very popular entitlement programs at home. The commitments to Asia have been in place for so long that they have been taken for granted in Washington, and have not been seriously questioned or discussed in either presidential or congressional campaigns. Lind argued that: "because the hegemony strategy is so alien to American and international foreign policy traditions, and so potentially costly in its open-ended strategic and budgetary commitments, many of its supporters have suggested that it should be kept secret from the wider American public, since it is so at odds with what most Americans think." Lind further argues that the American people, if they really understood the nature of our hegemonic commitments in Asia, might balk at the notion that they should shoulder so much of the cost to provide global security while their allies get off so cheaply.

THE RISE OF CHINA

The Asia-Pacific is profoundly important to the rest of the world. The twenty-one nations that belong to the Asia-Pacific Economic Forum account for 40 percent of the world's population, 54 percent of its economic output, and 44 percent of its international trade. The rapid economic development of the region has stimulated global economic growth. The nation that has most accounted for this growth has been China, where, under Deng Xiaoping, the economy was changed from a centrally planned system largely closed to international trade to a market-oriented system emphasizing manufacturing for export. As a result, the Chinese economy has experienced unprecedented expansion. China now has the second largest economy in the world and the International Monetary Fund has projected that it will pass the United States and become the world's largest economy by 2016.

China has now decided to modernize its armed forces. In recent years, China has updated its land-based ballistic and cruise missile program (improving both their accuracy and range), enlarged its submarine fleet, and completed a new submarine base on Hainan Island. China now has approximately 66 submarines compared to the U.S. fleet of 71, and some experts claim that it could have 85 to 100 submarines by 2030. It has also significantly improved its communication, intelligence, and cyber-warfare capabilities. In addition, China has been working on anti-satellite weapons and lasers that could help shield the nation from incoming missiles. Finally, in an achievement that will be both symbolic and strategically important, China is developing its own aircraft carriers and a new generation of jet fighters.

The increasing military capability of China has been accompanied by a more assertive foreign policy. China has in recent years contested – or from a Chinese point of view has been challenged by– Vietnam (over the Paracel and Spratly Islands), the Philippines (over the Spratly Islands), South Korea (over Socotra Rock), and Japan (over the Okintori and Sankaku/Diaoyu Islands). China has asserted claims over large parts of the South China Sea. In defense of their claims of sovreignty, Chinese naval vessels have actively confronted and harassed American and Japanese ships operating in the area, including recent incidents with the *U.S.S. John S. McCain* and a survey ship called the *U.S.N.S. Impeccable*.

China has undeniable interests at stake. The reunification with Taiwan is a long-standing foreign policy objective of the Beijing government, and this alone is justification for the military expansion.

In addition, however, the Chinese remember the humiliation China suffered at the hands of the imperial powers in earlier decades, and there is a strong commitment that such indignities can never be permitted to occur again. Finally, China's economic vitality demands access to oil and other minerals and the ability to move finished manufactured goods by sea. Currently, almost 80 percent of China's oil imports transit the Indian Ocean, and thus could be subject to a blockade by a dominant U.S. naval force. Building up naval resources is a means to send a clear message to potential adversaries that China intends to protect its vital interests.

The new territorial claims, build-up of naval resources, and even the confrontational acts may be part of a long-term strategy not only for asserting its strategic foreign policy interests abroad, but also for intensifying feelings of nationalism at home. As Medcalf and Heinrichs observed: The growth of regional navies, and their more conspicuous use in asserting national interests, reflects the increased influence of nationalism in defence [sic] policy and posture. This seems especially so in China.

NATIONALISM REMAINS A KEY PILLAR OF LEGITIMACY FOR THE CHINESE COMMUNIST PARTY

This is beginning to manifest itself, among other ways, in the emerging forcestructure of the PLA-N: for instance, national pride would seem a major reason for China's-decision to acquire an aircraft carrier. China's naval nationalism might thus be seen as a 'prestige strategy': the Communist Party seeking to reinforce its domestic position through its external security posture.

The build-up of Chinese military assets, the continuing presence of U.S. forces in the region, the more assertive Chinese territorial claims, and the response by other nations (especially Japan, Vietnam, and South Korea) has led to a significant increase in what are known as "incidents at sea." As Medcalf and Heinrichs also noted: "The term 'incidents at sea' encompasses a wide range of maritime activities and situations. It can include maritime encounters that are either deliberate or inadvertent and involve any combination of ships, submarines and aircraft from military, auxiliary and civil organisations

[sic] of different countries – in this case, major powers of Indo-Pacific Asia." These incidents may include the challenging or "buzzing" of aircraft flying over open waters, the shadowing of surface vessels traversing the area, and even the collision between a Chinese fishing trawler and a Japanese Coast Guard vessel. One type of incident that represents a unique danger is known as "shouldering," or "dangerous or aggressive manoeuvring [sic] by one or more vessels in close proximity to those of another country. This kind of action is especially risky when opposing ships have no option but to take evasive action to avoid imminent collisions, as occurred during the Impeccable incident in March 2009." The Chinese vessels appear to have become more aggressive in their patrols and have been more willing to "shoulder" U.S. and Japanese ships. There is a danger that such confrontations could expand into other even more dangerous interactions between rival powers such as "accidental or reckless firing during military exercises; simulated attacks on ships or aircraft; electronic jamming of communication equipment; illuminating opposing ships, especially bridges, using powerful searchlights (known as 'dazzling'); and firing flares." Such activities significantly increase the risk that an adversary might miscalculate or misread the situation, and escalate the situation beyond control. The initial spark to provoke the confrontation might not even come in an interaction between U.S. and Chinese forces; an escalation resulting from an incident between China and Japan, for example, might immediately and severely test the seriousness of the U.S. commitment to protect Japan, and thus severely limit the choices available to U.S. military and civilian leaders.

Both nations have acknowledged that military-to-military engagements were necessary and could reduce tensions. For example, when Secretary of Defense Robert Gates met with his Chinese equivalent, he stated: "We are in strong agreement that in order to reduce the chance of miscommunication, misunderstanding or miscalculation, it is important that our military-to-military ties are solid, consistent and not subject to shifting political winds." The Chinese Defense Minister General Liang Guanglie responded by issuing his own statement acknowledging that their meeting was "positive, constructive and productive," while also declaring that the Chinese agreed on the importance of creating "sustained and reliable" military-to-military relations.

Chinese Media Diplomacy

A quick and superficial glance at Chinese media reports would suggest that there were similarities in the statements issued by the United States and Chinese governments or the media discussions of the need to enhance trust and develop military ties between the two countries. Yet a closer reading reveals noteworthy differences in how the issues were discussed and in the concerns in each nation.

The Chinese media cited statements by Chinese leaders as supportive of greater military-to-military collaborations, but these same reports indicated that the Chinese authorities were more modest in assessing the likely impact of such visits. These reports emphasized that creating trust was a worthwhile objective, but that trust would not occur without mutual respect. For example, the Xinhua news service reported that Vice President Xi Jinping told Admiral Mullen: "I hope the two countries' defense departments and armed forces will remove obstacles and promote their ties with mutual respect and mutually beneficial cooperation." This same theme was echoed by General Chen Bingde who told Xinhua "Only a country that respects others can gain respect from others."

General Chen also chided his guests with the statement: "I hope heartfeltly [sic] that our U.S. friends understand this and treat others in a modest manner and act cautiously." The importance of crafting a relationship based on respect also made it into the *China Daily*: "It is probably difficult for the superpower that is the U.S. to accept the rise of China as well as alter its attitude toward its emerging economy. However, once the U.S. realizes the consequences of the strategic confrontation and they respect and care for each other's core interests, there is no reason for the two sides to become opponents."

Chinese leaders communicated that they did not believe that the U.S. had been respectful of China's interests in the region or of its national resolve. They condemned U.S. joint military drills with the Philippines and Vietnam near the South China Sea, U.S. arms sales to Taiwan, and U.S. surveillance operations off China's coast. Xinhua declared these issues represented "China's core interests and therefore [they] need careful handling on the side of the United States if it expects to have a healthy relationship with China."

The *Global Times*' English-language publication that is read by many foreign visitors and residents of China, and which also has a substantial audience outside China, published many articles about these "core" issues during and after Mullen's visit. The arguments over China's legitimate interests in the "South China Sea" were described as a reason for the lingering tensions, and for the "small-scale war of words" between Admiral Mullen and General Chen. "The US has repeated that it does not intend to intervene in the South China Sea issue, but its behavior has given off opposite signals," *Global Times* quoted General Chen Bingde as saying after talks with his US counterpart. In the same issue, the *Global Times* warned "In the South China Sea, the US has spoken of participating in 'reconciling' the disputes among China, Vietnam, the Philippines and others. There could be armed clashes if they stepped over China's bottom line."

The *Global Times* reported: Since last June, there have been 20 joint military exercises held by the U.S. with other countries in the Asia-Pacific region. U.S. military power appears ubiquitous. This year, the U.S. has held joint exercises with Japan, South Korea, the Philippines and Vietnam, all of which envisaged China as the potential enemy. These military exercises have unsurprisingly created quite a stir around China."

The same article reported that in response to the U.S. actions China conducted joint exercises with Indonesia, Thailand, and Chile, and that there were advocates in China who wanted joint drills with many other nations. The article concluded: "in recent years, China has strengthened its military diplomacy. But compared to the U.S., China holds fewer joint exercises with other countries. This is related to China's diplomatic mindset that focuses on building a harmonious world." The slow pace of Chinese efforts to reach out to conduct joint exercises was thus not a reflection of a desire for secrecy, but resulted from the Chinese mindset that it was important to avoid war, for "we are strongly against the use of violence and direct conflict, and this points to the type of military strategy we have adopted at the moment. What we do in exercises is to largely focus on self-defense, military rescue or anti-terrorism."

China's "bottom line" was mentioned by Wei Guoan, who emphasized the U.S. decision to sell new arms to Taiwan was an obstacle to the creation of mutual trust. The article declared: "as regards the Taiwan question, [the] US is expected to keep the current status to curb any further moves on China's part. If the US clings obstinately to its own course and Taiwanese leaders resort to extreme measures, there might be an increasing possibility of collision." Wei Guoan, also warned that "If [the] US continued to take similar moves, [and] keeps [sic] on selling weapons to Taiwan... [improved] Sino-US military relations could only be a wish and fantasy as their insincerity might politically cripple the mutual trust." Shi Yinhong, director of the US Study Center at the Renmin University of China, told the *Global Times* that because the issue had divided the two nations over many decades it should be understood that "Contradictions over arms sales to Taiwan will neither disappear nor be solved overnight." He argued, however, that the nations should work to repair their relationship to avoid the potential escalation into conflict.

China also cast U.S. spy missions off its coast as insulting and as an assault on its sovereignty. At a joint press conference with Admiral Mullen on July 11, General Chen Bingde pointed out that recent missions by unmanned US surveillance spy planes had come as close as sixteen *nautical* miles off the Chinese coast, and that two Chinese Sukhoi-27 fighters attempted to intercept a US U-2 reconnaissance plane over the

Taiwan Straits on June 29. *The Global Times* cited the official statement offered by the Ministry of National Defense: "we demand that the US respects China's sovereignty and security interests, and take concrete measures to boost a healthy and stable development of military relations." The order to send out Chinese planes to intercept US spying activities was explained by Song Xiaojun, a Chinese military expert as "to show China's resolution to defend its sovereignty" since "it is impossible for China to deploy the electronic countermeasures needed to set up a so-called protective electronic screen in the air to deter reconnaissance." Another *Global Times* story mentioned the spy plane collision over the South China Sea in 2001 as an example of an incident that might have created a serious military clash to illustrate how direct military conflict would certainly disrupt the bilateral relationship. The article warned, however, that: "Ten years ago, China was much weaker than today. The incident was soon forgotten due to the 9/11 attacks. Had the collision happened today, the consequences would be far more difficult to predict."

The declaration that China's military expansion was for self-defense was not surprising, and certainly not new. Geng Yansheng, a spokesperson for China's Ministry of National Defense declared "China... firmly abides by a defensive national defense policy, does not take part in military confrontations and does not pose a military threat to any country. We ask the U.S.... to stop remarks and behavior that are not beneficial for mutual trust between the two militaries." The Chinese media explicitly contrasted China's foreign and military policy with that of the United States. While the

United States was a global hegemon eager to interfere in the interests of sovereign states around the globe, China was internally focused and had no such ambitions to dominate its neighbours. As the *Global Times* reported: The US quartered hundreds of thousands of military troops, set up dozens of military bases and continuously planned battles across the world. After the Cold War ended, it actively expanded its forces to the east and started the strategic envelopment of China.

In contrast, China did not dispatch a single soldier or establish an overseas military base in foreign countries, let alone to attack and capture other territories.

Chinese spokespersons also suggested that the U.S. should not be anxious about China's investments in its military since China remained far behind the U.S. in its military capabilities. For example, after Chen Bingde's visit to U.S. early in May in 2011, Xinhua (Chinese version) reported that Chen had observed that although China made rapid progress in building its military strength in recent years, this progress was a compensation for the deficiencies of the past. Chen summarized the military distance between the U.S. and China as huge; and that while "US defense spending stands at $700 billion a year and China spends 800 billion yuan ($123.6 billion), China's military equipment is about 20 to 30 years behind the U.S." Still another article argued: "the U.S. needs to adjust its attitude. It has to accept that China is growing into a militarily powerful country, and it should stop trying to frustrate this. Chinese military modernization is unstoppable, and any policy of blockade, sanction, or containment will only have a negative effect on Sino-American military relations. The only way forward is to welcome and accept the rise in China's military strength."

Admiral Mullen had declared before his visit to China that along with "greater military power must come greater responsibility, greater cooperation and greater transparency", the need for further transparency of China's military development was one of the most important positions that Mullen communicated to his Chinese counterparts during his visit. To answer this, a story in the *China Daily* reported that the decision to allow U.S. Admiral Mullen to visit a military base near Beijing was a significant step forward for China and an expression from the Chinese military that it was willing to be increasingly transparent. "The (U.S.) must have noticed it," said Zhao Weibin, a researcher at the Academy of Military Science run by the PLA. This optimistic view was challenged by a more sober assessment offered by the *Global Times* that warned:

A handshake cannot hide the truth of how these militaries have studied to guard against each other. Should even a sliver of the worst scenarios imagined actually happen, it would mean calamity for the Asia-Pacific region. However, how to prevent this from happening is more important for the two militaries, and a key step for major powers in moving from a zero-sum game to win-win politics."

The newspaper also spoke directly to Chinese military leaders coaching a more transparent style of interaction, declaring "military officials do not have to fake smiles when they meet. They can guide both the media and public opinion. The Chinese military can make things better by being more direct, in addition to showing U.S. counterparts around Chinese military facilities the PLA's low profile tradition unnecessarily compromises the intention it wants to display, and easily clashes with U.S. curiosity."

To answer Admiral Mullen's declaration that "the United States did not intend to abandon its commitments to the Asia-Pacific region", *China Daily* published an article written by Wen Zhao, a senior research scholar from the Center for US-China Relations at Tsinghua University. Wen commented that "In fact, the U.S.' increased military presence in the Asia-Pacific region is a very important part of its 'return to Asia' strategy, as indicated by Washington's strengthened military presence in Northeast Asia in 2010 following the rise in tensions on the Korean Peninsula and in Southeast Asia this year. Maintaining military superiority in Asia-Pacific, in Washington's eyes, is an important way of sustaining and prolonging its predominant status in the region." According to the author, however, it is Mullen's belief that China is developing military capabilities targeting the U.S. that challenges the long-established predominance of the U.S. in the Asia-Pacific region. "The establishment of a long-term and reliable military relationship between China and the US is in the interests of both countries, as Mullen has claimed. It is hoped that the US will do more concrete work in a bid to clear away obstacles and push bilateral military ties to develop in a stable and sustainable fashion." It is noteworthy that brazenly aggressive views were rare in the Chinese press. Most articles urged that "China should remain calm and continue its development to cope with any changes and work out a way for cooperation under the current framework of bilateral relations." Such moderate views were also offered in detailed interviews conducted by the *Global Times* with three Chinese academics who specialized in international relations. For example, Shen Dingli, the Dean of Fudan University's Institute of International Studies observed: After ten years of fighting against terrorism, U.S. national strength is exhausted. With factionalism in U.S., the slowdown of the financial industry and the steady progress of economic globalization, the U.S. can hardly find a way out. So it has become more anxious and lacking in confidence. Over the past decade, the Chinese economy grew by 450 percent in dollar terms, which was 10 times the U.S. economic growth rate over the same period. The U.S. hasn't adjusted to this new reality. But China's stand-off with the U.S. is still within the normal range of international relations. A stable situation in Asia is still the core U.S. goal.

This moderate view was echoed by Shen Jiru, a research fellow in the Chinese Academy of Social Sciences, who argued: Through dialogues at various levels, we should warn the U.S. that its greatest interest in Asia lies in making joint efforts with China to build a kind of cooperative relationship based on mutual respect and mutual benefits, in order to advance the two countries' common interests and meet the opportunities and challenges of the 21st century. We should actively commit to the guiding principle of friendship and partnership with neighboring countries and the policy of securing an amicable, tranquil and prosperous neighborhood. We should try to build a harmonious Asia together with various Asian countries and prove by actions that China's development is an opportunity for Asia and the world instead of a challenge.

Huang Ping, the director of the Institute of American Studies at the Chinese Academy of Social Sciences argued: "China will stick to the opening-up policy and the road of peaceful development, mutual benefits and harmonious relationships. Specific problems will be resolved specifically. Divergences are settled through negotiations. As long as what the U.S. does is beneficial to China's peace, prosperity and stability, China will always welcome it."

The Chinese press did give a voice to a few hawks who expressed very different views. For example, an unnamed author identified as a strategic analyst of the Energy Fund Committee wrote in the *Global Times:* The strategic goal of the U.S. in the South China Sea is maintaining a situation of no war and no peace. The U.S. has no direct concerns in Asian ocean disputes. So why does it take such a strong role in the dispute? This is part of the global strategy of the U.S. balancing power in different regions, as it has done in the past. It also interfered in the Taiwan Strait and causes tension on the Korean Peninsula. However, the U.S. feels that this is not enough to disturb China's development, and now it's trying to stir up Southeast Asia to make trouble for China.... China insists on peace. However, the U.S. and other countries make use of this insistence as a tool to press China now. We should stop insisting on peace when other countries are challenging our bottom line again and again. As long as China becomes strong and powerful in right way [sic], the countries that pay most attention to their own security interests will stop their defiance and get back to the friendship and partnership with neighboring countries.

Another *Global Times* article sharply criticized Japan for a strategy that seemed intended to contain China by "...joining hands with the U.S. and its allies, and prove[ing] its power through competition and friction with China."

U.S. MEDIA DIPLOMACY

U.S. media diplomacy toward China involves multiple ongoing meetings and press statements. The diplomacy began before the visits occurred, continued during each visit; and persisted when the visits were finished. The goal was to communicate that the United States was taking a moderate and even supportive position on Chinese military expansion, but also to express concern that a now powerful China was obliged to pursue more mature and nuanced foreign policy relations with its neighbours. Prior to departing for Beijing, Admiral Mullen directly expressed his commitment to improving communications between the two militaries. He declared in a public speech presented at the Center for American Progress that: "as many nations develop, they invest in their military but with greater military power must come greater responsibility, greater cooperation and just as important, greater transparency. When you talk transparency, particularly on security and defense matters, we inevitably come to the issue of military exchange. What the U.S., frankly, seeks, a sustained and reliable military-to-military relationship with China, is hardly unusual."

The U.S. also communicated to the Chinese government, to its allies in the region, and to Americans at home, that it would not abandon its commitments to the region despite the economic challenges it currently faced or the rise of China. During his visit to Beijing, Admiral Mullen toured a university and answered questions posed by Chinese students. In one such encounter he declared: "[The U.S. has] had a presence in this region for decades... and certainly the intent is to broaden and deepen our interests here and our relationships here."

Although the U.S. commander emphasized the positive commitments of his government, and the benefits that could be gained from cooperation, the U.S. media discussed the Chinese skepticism of U.S. motives and the fact that Mullen's Chinese hosts openly scolded him during his visit. For example, Chen Bingde, China's top army official, was described as having expressed "misgivings" about the U.S. decision to conduct naval exercises with the Philippines in the South China Sea at the height of recent tensions in June. The general was also said to have criticized U.S. plans to conduct "inappropriate" exercises with the Vietnamese Navy.

The *New York Times'* account of the Admiral Mullen's visit emphasized that winning "rapprochement between the world's leading military power and its fastest-rising one [was] a fiendishly difficult task," and asserted that China was engaging in a "breakneck modernization of its creaky military machine." The media frame was: while the United States was the steady, determined, and predictable power in the region, focused on the same set of commitments that had guided its policies, priorities, and partnerships in the Pacific since the end of World War II, China was upsetting the applecart, not only through its rapid economic development but also through its military investments and more assertive foreign policies. The newspaper article emphasized, for example, that China would soon have a new "still-secret class of advanced submarines," a "seagoing missile" that "could strike ships as far as 1,025 miles away," and "seven reconnaissance satellites." The article conceded that at some level, "China's military ambitions are understandable. The country's global trade footprint and its reliance on foreign fuel and raw materials justify building a sophisticated and far-flung military force to secure its interests, just as the United States has done." Nonetheless, the article warned that the Chinese intended to use new military resources "to rein in American military power in the western Pacific," and to serve "as a counterforce to the United States Navy's Seventh Fleet, which has dominated Pacific waters for a half-century or more."

American diplomats, foreign policy experts, and military leaders were cited in Wine's *New York Times* article as being concerned that China has not as of that time been willing "to sit down and tell us what they're doing and what missions these new platforms and weapons are intended to achieve." The newspaper reported that Americans were anxious that the Chinese have been "ambiguous about their motivations" and unwilling to engage in the types of military-to-military conversations that can serve to build trust and enhance understanding.

The willingness of Admiral Mullen to use the media as a forum for his public diplomacy was most evident in an unusual op-ed piece he published in the *New York Times* when he returned from China. The essay used America's most prominent newspaper and the newspaper most likely to reach elite audiences both in the United States and abroad, to argue the importance of enhancing U.S. – China military-to-military diplomacy. Mullen declared:

The military relationship between the United States and China is one of the worlds' most important. And yet, clouded by some misunderstanding and suspicion, it remains among the most challenging. There are issues on which we disagree and are tempted to confront each other. But there are crucial areas where our interests coincide, on which we must work together. So we need to make the relationship better, by seeking strategic trust. How do we do that? First, we've got to keep talking. Dialogue is critical. A good bit of misunderstanding between our militaries can be cleared up by reaching out to each other. We don't have to give away secrets to make our intentions clear, just open up a little.

Mullen discussed his visits with his counterpart PLA General Chen Bingde in the United States in May and in China in July. He explained that when General Chen was in the United States he showed him the capabilities of the Predator drone and invited him to observe a live-fire exercise. In return, he said that during his visit to China he toured the latest submarine, took a close look at a new fighter jet, and observed a counterterrorism exercise. What was most interesting about the article, however, was that Mullen emphasized that the conversations were candid and that there were disagreements. He acknowledged that the Chinese objected to continued U.S. arms sales to Taiwan and said they were told "the United States military will not shrink from our responsibilities to allies and partners." He declared that General Chen said that the Chinese "strategic intentions were purely defensive; I said that neither the skills they were perfecting nor their investments seemed to support that argument." Mullen, however, offered no apology for the frank disagreements. Indeed, he celebrated them because "at least we were talking."

The op-ed the Admiral identified the common interests that the United States and China shared: We're both maritime nations with long coastlines and economies dependent on unhindered trade. We both face threats of drug trafficking, piracy and the movements of weapons of mass destruction. We both want stability on the Korean Peninsula and in Pakistan. We both recognize the need for coordinated international humanitarian aid and disaster relief.

The Admiral then mentioned how the two nations agreed to conduct joint missions aimed at countering piracy in the Gulf of Aden. Still, he acknowledged, there were substantial differences dividing the two nations: "We still don't see eye-to-eye with China over military operating rights in the South China Sea. We still don't fully understand China's justification for the rapid growth in its defense spending or its long-term modernization goals. And we don't believe that China should be allowed to resolve disputes in contested waters by coercing smaller nations." Yet he also declared, in a bold and assertive American voice, that: "these sticking points aren't all bad. It's all right to disagree sometimes, to have substantial differences. In fact, sometimes bluntness and honesty are exactly what's needed to create strategic trust. And we need still more of it." Mullen even leveled criticism of the political leadership both in China and the U.S.:

Our military relations have only recently begun to thaw but China's government still uses them as a sort of thermostat to communicate displeasure. When they don't like something we do, they cut off ties. That can't be the model anymore. Nor can we, for our part, swing between engagement and over reaction. That's why the commitment by President Obama and President Hu Jintao to improve military-to-military relations is so important. Real trust has to start somewhere. And it shouldn't be subject to shifting political winds.

Although Admiral Mullen's arguments and those of other government spokespersons in the U.S. were communicated to public audiences through many of the most influential media outlets in the United States – such as the *New York Times* and the *Los Angeles Times* – it must also be recognized that such arguments did not appear in isolation. The American public was also exposed to arguments taking a far more skeptical view toward U.S.- China relations. For example, a blog published by the influential conservative think tank

The Heritage Foundation argued that "30 years of military-to-military interaction have not led to greater PLA transparency, increased safety in Sino-U.S. military interactions or greater cooperative approaches to challenge. Instead, efforts at engagement have led Beijing to believe that it has more leverage in military-to-military talks than Washington, because the U.S. appears almost desperate to have the talks, unlike China." The author further argued that:

Given the tight legal restrictions on what can be shared with the Chinese [imposed by the U.S. Congress], the one thing the talks do for the Chinese is to stave off the U.S. from pursuing its own national interest, for fear of jeopardizing U.S.-Chinese military-to-military links. This is consistent with Mao Zedong's tactic of 'fight fight, talk talk (da da, tan tan). Mao would negotiate, not in order to "get to yes" and reach a compromise solution, but to buy time, color his opponent's views, and influence third parties. The ultimate goal never changed, whatever the negotiating positions.

The suggestion presented was that the Chinese were scheming, pretending to negotiate in good faith, while clinging to the same rigid and ideologically focused political strategies that have defined the regime since it was founded. The argument characterized attempts to negotiate with the Chinese as dangerous and perhaps not always focused on "serving American interests."

These oppositional arguments shaped the domestic political debates in the United States, especially given the approach of the 2012 elections. China has long been cast as a hostile and authoritarian regime, especially in much conservative political discourse, and rhetoric that depicted the Obama administration as weak and vulnerable in dealing with a deceptive, steely, and ideologically committed enemy committed to an aggressive policy of domination over its neighbours resonated with many Americans accustomed to the narratives of the Cold War.

Countering such suspicions about China was an objective of Chinese media diplomacy.

One Step onward, One Step back

The visits by U.S. and Chinese political and military leaders in 2011 revealed that both nations wished to improve their military-to-military diplomacy and used the media to communicate their respective positions to multiple audiences. The combination of public statements by the officials and media coverage of the visits indicate that there were many substantial differences to be resolved along the way, however, including the persistent fly in the ointment: U.S. arms sales to Taiwan. Chinese leaders expressed opposition to these sales at every opportunity. As an example, General Chen Bingde said that China was prepared to cooperate with the U.S. in such areas as fighting sea pirates and providing disaster relief, but if the arms sales continued, Chen said that future relations would suffer. When asked how bad the impact of another sale would be, he replied that it would depend on the nature of the weapons sold. Despite the warnings, in September, 2011, the U.S. announced a new arms sales package worth $5.85 billion to upgrade 145 of Taiwan's fighter jets. Hong Lei, a spokesperson for the Chinese Foreign Ministry, warned that the move would damage U.S. military and security relations with Beijing. He declared: "The Chinese government and people strongly opposes [sic] it. The mistakes made by the U.S. inevitably hurt bilateral relations and cooperation in military and security of the two countries. The U.S. takes full responsibility for that." In the wake of the announced arms sales, China suspended several of its military exchange programs with the United States that were the fruit of the multiple visits and conversations that had occurred throughout the year.

A U.S. spokesperson downplayed the weapons sales and told the *Global Times* that the equipment sold to Taiwan was out-dated and should not be "seen as a challenge to China." Furthermore, he suggested that the arms sales reflected the "obligation that the U.S. has to the security of Taiwan." The spokesperson also explained the dynamics of U.S. domestic politics with regard to Taiwan: "Our political system is a very complicated one, and I'm sure there were many influences on what must have been a very difficult decision for our president. And of course, he made the decision which was less than what had been asked for, and less than what was pressured. For example, some 46 senators wrote to the president and wanted a higher level of arms sales and many friends of Taiwan encouraged it. So it is a balancing process." The Chinese were not persuaded, and frankly, given how U.S.-China relations have arisen as an issue in the U.S. Republican presidential campaigns, it is not surprising that this explanation was unpersuasive.

Perhaps motivated by domestic political pressures, in January of 2012 President Obama set aside the carrot and reached for the stick. The Pentagon released the 2012 Strategic Defense Strategy Document which emphasized the importance of military investments in Asia and doubled-down on its commitment to the region. As the Iraq and Afghan Wars wound down, the U.S. announced that it: *will of necessity rebalance toward the Asia-Pacific region*... The maintenance of peace, stability, the free flow of commerce, and of U.S. influence in this dynamic region will depend in part on an underlying balance of military capability and presence. Over the long term, China's emergence as a regional power will have the potential to affect the U.S. economy and our security in a variety of ways.

Our two countries have a strong stake in peace and stability in East Asia and an interest in building a cooperative bilateral relationship. However, the growth of China's military power must be accompanied by greater clarity of its strategic intentions in order to avoid causing friction in the region. The United States will continue to make the necessary investments to ensure that we maintain regional access and the ability to operate freely in keeping with our treaty obligations and with international law. Working closely with our network of allies and partners, we will continue to promote a rules-based international order that ensures underlying stability and encourages the peaceful rise of new powers, economic dynamism, and constructive defense cooperation.

The strongly worded document admitted that the U.S. actions were intended to counter China: "States such as China and Iran will continue to pursue asymmetric means to counter our power projection capabilities, while the proliferation of sophisticated weapons and technology will extend to non-state actors as well. *Accordingly, the U.S. military will invest as required to ensure its ability to operate effectively in anti-access and area denial (A2/AD) environments.*"

Despite all of the earlier rhetoric about cooperation, the U.S. signaled to the Chinese government, to its allies in the region, and to the American people that it would not reduce its military commitments even in the face of China's assertions of dominance in the region. The linkage of China, its most important trading partner, with Iran, an international pariah state, must have stung in Beijing; and, of course, it most likely reduced the likelihood that in the near future there would be significant military-to-military collaborations between the two nations.

CHANGES IN CHINA'S APPROACH TO MILITARY DIPLOMACY

While the PLA has employed many of these activities, programs, and venues for the past several decades, there has been some change in its approach to military diplomacy. The first, and most obvious change has been the PLA's willingness to conduct combined military exercises with its neighbours. There are likely many reasons as to why the PLA decided to conduct such exercises: Chinese officials pointed to the Sino-Russian combined exercise as a chance to practice a counter-terrorism scenario, while foreign observers speculated that the exercise was aimed at countering U.S. influence and showing off the new level of Russian-Chinese cooperation. The Russian press noted that the exercise was a chance to showcase Russian arms and boost arms sales to China. Still others speculate that these combined exercises allow the PLA to experiment with some of its new doctrinal concepts and test evolving command and control arrangements.

While this may all be true, one can also point to the PLA's foray into combined exercises as a natural outgrowth of China's increased regional presence in Central Asia, and its role as a regional power. As China plays more of a leading role in Central Asia—whether through institutions such as the Shanghai Cooperation Organization or economic investments in energy in Russia and Central Asia—it will likely continue to bolster regional cooperation, both politically and militarily, thus contributing to its national defense goal of shaping the international security environment.

A second change has been the PLA's increased participation in international efforts to counter non-traditional security threats such as terrorism, illegal drug trafficking, and maritime piracy issues. China's increased participation in countering these activities is indicative of two things. It recognizes that it needs, in many cases, international cooperation to solve these issues in and around its own borders. And Beijing sees that China's role as a global power requires it to be a participant in these issues.

IMPLICATIONS OF CHANGE IN CHINA'S MILITARY DIPLOMACY FOR THE UNITED STATES

Given these changes, there are at least three implications of China's military diplomacy for the United States.

- First, as China becomes an ever-stronger economic power, economic incentives will continue to clash with defense-related concerns, and this could have repercussions for US interests. The debate over lifting the EU arms embargo is likely just the beginning of many such discussions.
- Second, China's approach to military diplomacy is largely tied into its political agenda; therefore, when dealing with the PLA or when looking at China's military diplomacy activities as a whole, one must also consider Beijing's larger political agenda.

- Third, the PLA clearly conducts a comprehensive program of military diplomacy, and its overseas military activities are likely to become even more numerous as it continues on the path of military modernization. The more the United States can engage China in professional military exchanges, Track II dialogues, and other avenues to enhance mutual knowledge and transparency, the better off both countries will be in the future.

Activities Employed by China in its Military Diplomacy

The PLA employs a variety of activities, programs, and venues in conducting military diplomacy. These include such traditional activities as high-level strategic security dialogues, military functional exchanges, professional military education exchanges, the import and export of military weapons and equipment, and participation in peacekeeping operations. Other, more recent additions include increased participation in Track 1.5 and Track II dialogues, regional multilateral organizations such as the Shanghai Cooperation Organization (SCO), and, most significantly, the PLA's willingness to participate in combined military exercises with Kyrgyzstan and Russia.

Broadly, China's activities with regard to military diplomacy can be grouped into four categories:

Strategic-level Activities

This category includes Chinese efforts to shape the international security environment to support Beijing's national defense objectives at the strategic level through its use of military diplomacy. The PRC has three basic ways in which it does this: high-level defense consultations and dialogues with key global actors, exchanges between high-level military delegations, and arms transfers.

Defense consultations and strategic dialogues: China has engaged in frequent high-level consultations and strategic dialogues with countries with which it has strategic-level areas of cooperation or which are in areas of potential conflict. Recent highlights include:

- Strategic consultations between China and Russia, including meetings between the General Staff headquarters of the two countries' militaries in 2003-2004;
- Ongoing consultations with the United States on non-proliferation and bilateral security issues, including the Defense Consultative Talks, the eighth round of which took place earlier this month ; and
- Strategic dialogues with other actors that China perceives as important in shaping the international security situation, such as the United Kingdom, Australia, South Africa, and Japan.

Arms transfers: Arms sales and military technology transfers have a longstanding role in Beijing's conduct of military relations with other nations, and this remains the case today. China's arms sales have decreased markedly since the 1980s, when the emphasis was largely on the sale of arms and technology to help fund the PLA. Today, arms sales are apparently being used less as a money-making proposition, and more as a strategic end to accrue political influence with countries that the PRC perceives are important to its national interests. To wit, the bulk of China's arms sales are to African nations where it has energy interests, such as Sudan, Nigeria, Zimbabwe, and Libya, or to countries in the Middle East where it has longstanding political and economic interests, such as Iran, or to regional allies such as Pakistan and North Korea.

In terms of arms imports, the PLA has increasingly sought to acquire state of the art capabilities to support its military modernization program. Strikingly, whereas China's arms sales are largely done to support its political and economic agenda (i.e. the military supporting the political), when it comes to arms imports it is the political and economic agenda that is supporting the military.

For example, in the spring of 2004 China's civilian leadership used economic, diplomatic, and political elements of national power to pressure the European Union to lift its arms embargo.

China's relationship with Russia is another example. Closer political and economic relations between these two countries have manifested in increased sales of Russian arms and technologies to the PRC—which are also helping to keep Russia's cash-starved defense industries afloat.

Military exchanges: The PLA has an ambitious program of military exchanges. These include foreign visits by PLA Army, Air Force, and Navy personnel. According to the 2004 Defense White Paper, China has sent high-level military delegations to over 60 countries and hosted delegations from more than 70 countries. Recent highlights include Defense Minister Cao Gangchuan's visits to North Korea and Vietnam in 2006, and his 2005 visits to Russia and Central Asia, as well as to Egypt, Tanzania, the Netherlands, and Denmark. Other trips abroad by high-ranking Chinese officials include the President of National Defense University's visits to Israel, Jordan, and Ukraine in 2004.

Regional Activities

Many of the PRC's foreign military activities are aimed at bolstering relations with countries on its periphery, shaping its regional security environment, and ensuring that tensions do not erupt into armed conflict on China's borders. This is a tall order given that China has borders with fourteen countries, many of which encompass restive areas. Over the past decade, the PRC has made extensive efforts to settle border disputes and shore up relations with its neighbours. While this has led to *decreased* potential for state on state hostility, the PRC faces an *increasing* number of transnational threats such as drug and weapons smuggling, human trafficking, and international organized crime, to name only a few.

China's regional military diplomacy activities include:

- State to state military protocols with friendly border nations, such as the 1996 "agreement on Confidence-Building in the Military Field Along Border Areas," signed with Russia, Kazakhstan, Kyrgyzstan, and Tajikistan;

- Participation in military exercises with Russia and, to a far lesser extent, India; and
- Participation in (and leadership of) regional forums that deal with security issues such as the Shanghai Cooperation Organization.

China's relations with Russia deserve a special mention. Beyond the PRC's significant imports of Russian arms these two countries have over the past several years grown closer both politically and in the security realm. Since the turn of the century, border demarcation issues have been settled, friendship treaties have been signed, and joint statements espousing common viewpoints on the international order have been released. A recent example would be the pronouncement calling for a timetable for withdrawal of US forces from Central Asia, and in particular from bases in Kyrgyzstan and Uzbekistan.

This trend toward cooperation has become apparent in military relations between the two countries as well. "Peace Mission 2005," the Russian-Chinese combined military exercise, made headlines around the world. Conducted under the auspices of an anti-terror exercise, it was the largest combined military exercise the PLA had participated in. According to articles in the Russian press, a future exercise is in the works: shortly after the conclusion of "Peace Mission 2005" Russian media ran an announcement by the chief of Russia's General Staff that a second set of Russian-Chinese combined military exercises would be held in 2007, this time under the oversight of the SCO.

Professional Military Education Exchanges

A third type of activity the PRC engages in with regard to military diplomacy is professional military education exchanges through the PLA's professional military education system. This includes sending PLA officers abroad to attend foreign institutions, bringing in foreign instructors to teach as visiting professors and hosting foreign officers at Chinese military academies. Examples of these exchanges include the National Defense Science and Technology University, which has sent officers for graduate training at foreign scientific research institutes and higher educational institutions, as well as received foreign military delegations and visiting scholars. In addition, the PLA's Science and Engineering University has established an exchange program with the United States Military Academy at West Point. Finally, National Defense University has hosted foreign military exchange students through its Foreign Training Department.

In addition to education exchanges, the PLA also participates frequently in Track 1.5 and Track II dialogues with US think tanks, as well as government and academic institutions.

Cooperation in Non-Traditional Security Areas

China has stepped up cooperation with other nations to counter non-traditional security threats. In the post 9/11 era, Beijing has continued to cooperate with the US and others on countering terrorism, and has led several regional combined counter-terrorism exercises through the SCO. In addition, China has increased its participation (albeit somewhat contentiously) in peacekeeping operations, sending peacekeepers to Cambodia, the Congo, and Liberia.

Other non-traditional security threats loom on the horizon. It is possible that China, and the PLA, will have to deal with large-scale medical crises brought about by, for example, the spread of AIDS, another SARS outbreak, or a pandemic caused by Avian Flu or another such virus. It is conceivable, given this type of potential crisis, that the PLA will be forced into cooperating with other militaries on crisis response and containment.

Finally, it is worth noting what China does NOT do in its military diplomacy. The one element of military diplomacy that Beijing has not, and still does not, pursue today, is the path of forming traditional military alliances. By not entering into formal military alliances, Beijing allows itself the flexibility to pursue both its military and political agenda; and ensures that it has most freedom possible to shape its interests.

6

New Media and Today's Information of Military Operations

The Israeli-Hezbollah War of 2006 provides recent, glaring evidence of how the current information environment has impacted the way warfare is conducted today. Hezbollah masterfully manipulated and controlled that environment to its advantage, using (at times staged and altered) photographs and videos to garner regional and worldwide support. If this doesn't sound new, it shouldn't...especially if you are an Israeli. Hamas effectively used the same techniques to turn the Battle of Jenin in April, 2002 into not only a strategic informational victory, but a historical legend of resistance that lives on today in the hearts and minds of Palestinians.

The Israelis, having won total tactical victory in Jenin, literally snatched defeat from the jaws of victory by abrogating the information battlespace to Hamas. Certainly, United States military leaders can, at a minimum, empathize with the Israelis. Insurgent use of information as an asymmetric strategic means has been extremely effective in the current theaters of Iraq and Afghanistan leading Richard Holbrooke to famously muse: "How can a man in a cave out-communicate the world's leading communications society?" Had Holbrooke even superficially studied recent history he could have answered his own question. The monopoly enjoyed by nation-states over information as an element of power was rapidly lost as technology improved and as the means to transmit that information became smaller, faster, cheaper and, consequently, ubiquitous. And the outlook in that regard certainly does not seem to favour lumbering bureaucracies any time in the future.

These enabling technological capabilities have popularly been tagged "new media." Broadly, new media has been described as "that combustible mix of 24/7 cable news, call-in radio and television programs, Internet bloggers and online websites, cell phones and iPods." But, of course this menu limits the definition to present day capabilities and is quickly outdated given current and expected future technological advances. New media in this context quickly becomes "old" media, especially in light of projected asymptotic increases in speed and capacity. So, a more timeless definition should consider new media as any capability that empowers a broad range of actors (individuals through nation-states) to create and disseminate near-real time or real time information with the ability to affect a broad (regional or worldwide) audience.

If the United States military hopes to fight and win in a future information environment dominated by new media it must fully understand both the opportunities and challenges of that environment. This includes the ability to exploit new media to achieve military objectives and defeat an adversary's skilled use of it within real and perceived bureaucratic and legal constraints. A review of these capabilities and their use reveals a requirement for a significant cultural shift within the military, while recognizing that current planning processes remain valid. It also points to the importance of competing on the information battlespace, not only in counterinsurgency operations, but across the spectrum of conflict.

THE U.S. MILITARY: THE IMPACT OF NEW MEDIA

The impact of new media in today's information environment has significant implications for the U.S. military. The first, and perhaps most obvious, is that individuals and small groups (e.g. the terrorist franchised cell) wield information as a strategic, asymmetric weapon by very effectively leveraging new media capabilities. The lack of any bureaucratic structure further enables individual empowerment by also allowing a nimbleness of response that is the antithesis of nation-state governments. Additionally, the lack of governance of the World Wide Web allows any statements or positions to be presented without regard to truth, context or ethical foundation.

Current military doctrine espouses information superiority as the solution to the numerous dilemmas posed by new media:

To succeed, it is necessary for US forces to gain and maintain information superiority. In Department of Defense (DOD) policy, information superiority is described as the operational advantage gained by the ability to collect, process, and disseminate an uninterrupted flow of information while exploiting or denying an adversary's ability to do the same.

But this clearly is an unachievable definition of success given the challenges of the current and future information environment in which military operations take place. Individuals, empowered by new media capabilities, and unencumbered by bureaucratic processes and moral/ethical standards will continue to wield information as power asymmetrically. "Wildcards" will routinely gain resonance in the information environment and once the information is out it may be extremely difficult to refute or explain it (e.g. Abu Ghraib photos or Osama bin Laden's taped messages). Simply consider how corrections are made in mainstream print media. The correction is typically buried deep in the publication while referring to an article that likely appeared on page one above the fold. The chances of the original reader stumbling upon the correction are obviously slim. This reflects the "genie in a bottle" syndrome of today's information environment—once information is out of the bottle trying to stuff it back in is very difficult.

The Case of Jenin

The Battle of Jenin provides a relevant case study in both the impact of "wildcards" using new media means and the strategic impact resulting from a military that does not proactively and effectively manage the information environment.

Israel embarked on a military campaign in the spring of 2002 to root out entrenched Hamas terrorists in the West Bank of the Palestinian occupied territories. The Jenin operation specifically targeted approximately 200 militants operating within the city and was deemed a tactical success. The militant's infrastructure was destroyed, and a number of insurgents were killed and arrested. At the conclusion of the campaign terrorists attacks within Israel dropped off in the near term. However, the operation proved a significant strategic failure. Reaching the outskirts of Jenin, Israeli Defense Forces (IDF) restricted the media from entering the city. Thus, the information battlespace was abrogated to the militants. Framed digital photos of homes being demolished by Israeli bulldozers while frantic families looked on were transmitted quickly, and quite effectively, to the press and soon hit the international wires. Cell phones were the only means of communication to the city and so the press used uncollaborated cell phone interviews with Jenin residents to tell their stories. These interviews spoke of massacre within the city in emotive tone and content. While later disproved, those claims caused an international withdrawal of support for Israel. Further, Jenin remains, to this day, a mythical symbol of Palestinian resistance and Israeli ruthlessness among Palestinians.

The lesson of Jenin is that the military may be able to dominate the information environment in a localized geographical area for a limited period of time but these wildcards, using new media capabilities, become that limiting factor. So, if information superiority is effectively unachievable and information dominance can only be partially achieved how can the U.S. military succeed in the information battlespace? The answer is that the military can, and should be expected to *manage* the information environment on their terms. This requires playing a proactive role in shaping that environment as well as establishing processes to respond to those unforeseen stories that make dominance so difficult. Clearly, managing the "message" while controlling the necessary new media "means" represent critical challenges to that effort.

Nor should one be lulled into believing that the exploitation of new media as a military and strategic enabler is limited to insurgency operations. While insurgents use new media to affect perceptions, attitudes and beliefs (the cognitive dimension of the information environment) nation states most recently have acted to exploit dependence on new media (specifically the internet) in the physical dimension, revealing an important vulnerability. Russia was alleged to have taken down Estonian government, bank and newspaper websites in what may have been a cyber-attack test in May 2007[26] prior to their combined cyber and kinetic attack on Georgia in 2008. China's People's Liberation Army (PLA), the most obvious near peer military competitor to the United States, has gained notoriety recently by being implicated in taking down Pentagon internet capability in June 2007. The Chinese are transforming from a mechanized force to an "informationized" force and have stated intentions to use information warfare "as a tool of war (or) as a way to achieve victory without war...."

New media is now playing, and will continue to play an increasingly important role in how the United States conducts warfare. How the U.S. military effectively manages an environment dominated by new media, therefore, becomes increasingly important to success in warfare.

NEW MEDIA AND TODAY'S INFORMATION ENVIRONMENT

The current information environment has leveled the playing field for not only nation states, but non-state actors, multinational corporations and even individuals to affect strategic outcomes with minimal information infrastructure and little capital expenditure. Anyone with a camera cell phone and personal digital device with internet capability understands this. On the other hand, the United States military has increasingly leveraged advances in information infrastructure and technology to gain advantages on the modern battlefield.

One example from Operation Iraqi Freedom is the significant increase in situational awareness from network centric operations that enabled coalition forces to swiftly defeat Iraqi forces in major combat operations. Another includes the more prevalent use of visual information to record operations in order to proactively tell an accurate story or effectively refute enemy "dis-information."

Even a cursory look at advances in technology confirms what most people recognize as a result of their daily routine. The ability to access, collect, and transmit information is clearly decentralized to the lowest level (the individual). The technology is increasingly smaller, faster and cheaper. Consequently, the ability to control and verify information is much more limited than in the recent past. Nor will it get any easier.

In 1965, the physical chemist Gordon Moore, co-founder of Intel, predicted that the number of transistors on an integrated chip would double every eighteen months. Moore predicted that this trend would continue for the foreseeable future. Moore and most other experts expect Moore's Law to remain valid for at least another two decades.

So, if you're into control, as nation-states, bureaucracies and the military tend to be, the future may appear bleak since not only is the ability to access, collect and transmit information decentralized, the capacity to do the same continues to increase exponentially. With this in mind consider both the new media capabilities and methods currently used and where the future may be heading as the basis for understanding what this means for the warfighter.

The Internet

The internet is the obvious start point for any discussion of the impact of new media. It is important to note that the World Wide Web, as a subset of the internet, is essentially ungoverned, providing obvious freedoms and cautions. The web gives the individual a voice, often an anonymous voice...and a potentially vast audience. Websites are easily established, dismantled and reestablished, making them valuable to extremist movements. Islamic extremist websites grew from twenty to over 4,000 in only five years.

Web logs (blogs) are another example of the power that the internet provides to individuals along with the dilemma they pose for nation-states. There were 35.3 million blogs as of April 2006 reflecting a doubling of size every six months of the previous three years. Most of these, of course, have little effect on the conduct of nation-states or their militaries, but those that gain a following in the national security arena, can have a huge impact. President George W. Bush recently cited Iraqi bloggers to point to progress being made in Iraq, having apparently learned both the importance and value of blogs in 2004 when investigative bloggers cleared his name in the infamous CBS airing that questioned his military service. The U.S. Central Command actively engages dissident voices by participating in blogs that are critical of the war on terror noting "with the proliferation of information today, if you're not speaking to this forum, you're not being heard by it."

Video use and dissemination has skyrocketed as the capabilities of the internet have increased. The YouTube phenomenon's power and access is evidenced by its purchase for $1.6 Billion by Google only 20 months after its founding. Like blogs, YouTube serves a variety of purposes to include entertainment. But, also like blogs, YouTube can empower individuals to achieve strategic political and military effects where easy upload of their videos, without editorial oversight, allows access to a nearly unlimited audience. Thus, the use of the improvised explosive device (IED) by insurgents shifts from a military tactical weapon to a strategic information weapon when the IED detonator is accompanied by a videographer. And again, like blogs, the United States military has recognized the importance of competing in the video medium, using YouTube to show ongoing images of U.S. operations in Iraq.

While websites, bloggers and video proliferate in today's internet ("web 2.0") the "over the horizon" technology of "web 3.0" while in its infancy, is rapidly increasing in popularity. Web 3.0 is generally about being inside a 3D virtual world that is low-cost and emotive. This is the "metaverse" or virtual universe of applications like Second Life and others. Second Life is attractive as an opportunity to socialize where there is no need to compete and can be exploited as a tool for learning. Multinational corporations see a movement where they will plan and execute business plans in the 3D internet world. But, like the other internet based applications, web 3.0 provides opportunities for darker undertakings. The virtual universes show initial signs of providing training grounds for terrorist organizations and anonymous locations for criminal money-laundering.

Mobile Technologies

The internet clearly is part of the new media phenomenon, but the internet has not penetrated large areas of the world, especially in the poorest areas of underdeveloped countries. The cell phone, however, as a means of mobile technology, is increasingly available worldwide and deserves discussion as a potentially potent capability to affect national security and military issues; arguably even more so than the internet.

There are numerous examples of cell phone Short Message Service (SMS text) messaging shaping political campaigns by mobilizing and revolutionizing politics. It is used both to call people to popular protests as well as used by governments to provide misinformation in order to quell such protests. Text messaging is the medium of choice in overseas countries. It bypasses mass media and mobilizes an already persuaded populace as a means of lightweight engagement. Cell phones currently contain the technology to text, provide news, video, sound, voice, radio and internet. Mobile is pervasive in the third world. 97% of Tanzanians have access to mobile phones. Mobile coverage exists throughout Uganda. There are 100 million handsets in sub-Saharan Africa. Radio is the only media device more prevalent than mobile. Consider the economic implications of mobile technologies as well. 59% of mobile phones are in the developing world–over seven million mobile subscribers in Kenya alone. Efforts are under way to develop African specific mobile applications, e.g. distributing commodity prices (such as vegetable prices) to local village producers. Cell phones are used as credit cards in Kenya. You can pay for cab fare or for fish at the market with your cell phone. Cell towers are being raised in Lake Victoria to allow fisherman to call to shore with their catch numbers as they set out to market. Mobile phones are ubiquitous in Asia. There are over 400 million users in China. Farmers receive crop market prices from the Chinese government via text messaging in order to allow them to harvest at the best possible time.

Like any other new media capability cell phone technology provides opportunities and challenges. Many young Iranians are turning to cell phones as a means for political protest...an opportunity that can be exploited. On the other hand, criminals and terrorists can use cell phones to quickly organize an operation, execute it and disperse using phone cards to provide cover from being traced. On an international scale, the challenge is often in the same laws that provide individual protections in democratic societies. Witness recent court battles within the United States regarding eavesdropping on foreign conversations without a court order when those conversations may be routed through a U.S. cell phone service provider.

MAINSTREAM MEDIA IN THE AGE OF NEW MEDIA

Mainstream media certainly takes advantage of technological advances in order to remain competitive. Marvin Kalb, in the Harvard report on the Israeli-Hezbollah War notes that:

> *To do their jobs, journalists employed both the camera and the computer, and, with the help of portable satellite dishes and video phones "streamed" or broadcast their reports..., as they covered the movement of troops and the rocketing of villages—often, (unintentionally, one assumes) revealing sensitive information to the enemy. Once upon a time, such information was the stuff of military intelligence acquired with considerable effort and risk; now it has become the stuff of everyday journalism. The camera and the computer have become weapons of war.*

This real time reporting from the field has obvious impacts on the warfighter, but competition with new media for the first and fastest story also means that today's mainstream media is not your father's mainstream media. Because of the plethora of information available today, newspapers, which once competed for knowledge as a scarce resource, today compete for a new scarce resource: the readers' (or listeners' in the case of broadcast media) attention. Perhaps that is why increasing numbers of young adults turn to Jon Stewart's "The Daily Show" for their news. It should come as no great shock, then, that "good news" stories about military operations do not appear with regularity in mainstream print and broadcast journalism. Good news doesn't sell...because it doesn't grab the reader's (or viewer's) attention.

Of course in an environment where the speed of breaking news means viewership and thus advertising dollars, accuracy is sometimes sacrificed as well. In a strange twist, mainstream media now turns increasingly to bloggers for their stories and the most respected bloggers require multiple sources to verify accuracy. Consequently, the distinction between new and mainstream media sources becomes blurred, leaving it to the reader, already bombarded with information, to distinguish fact from fiction (or perhaps more accurately "spin" from context).

FIGHTING BACK: MANAGING THE NEW MEDIA ENVIRONMENT

The U.S. military has dealt with the new media phenomenon in fits and starts. Certainly one could argue that efforts to deal in this environment have largely been reactive rather than proactive. Soldiers using new media in the form of emails, blogs and digital photography revealed vulnerabilities of U.S. systems as well as operational tactics, techniques and procedures from current operations in Iraq and Afghanistan. This led to a top-down reemphasis on operations security, a program that has always existed, but never in the instantaneous world of information exchange, pointing again to both the power and danger of new media capabilities. The YouTube and blog response efforts outlined previously are encouraging, albeit reactive efforts to manage this environment. One area of new media the military proactively exploits is knowledge management in order to share lessons learned from recent operational experiences. Interestingly, this process was bottom-up driven in the form of a web site independently developed by junior officers known as CompanyCommand.com. While the power in this forum admittedly lies in the dynamics of people and conversations, its potential would not be realized without the global and instantaneous reach provided by the internet.

Reactive responses, however, will never allow the military to manage the information environment of today, nor the increasingly complex information environment of the future. Instead, a proactive approach to fighting in that environment is necessary. This requires a cultural shift in the military mindset but not a doctrinal change in the way military operations are planned. The military has muddied the waters somewhat in that regard. Recognizing the need to compete in the information battlespace they have grappled with the concept of "information operations" in doctrinal publications and applied the concept in current operations with mixed results. Most recently "strategic communication" has entered the military lexicon. Unfortunately these concepts are widely misunderstood by warfighters and often applied as afterthoughts by senior commanders in attempts to fix problems. Consequently, they become inherently reactive and often ineffective.

Senior military leaders have grown up in a culture that emphasizes kinetic warfighting skills, both in planning and execution. In order to ease the cultural transition from this world of bombs and bullets to one where information, driven by new media capabilities, is a significant weapon, it is best to work within both the language and planning methodologies inherent in that military cultural upbringing. Consequently, warfighters should consider and emphasize the "information effects" they wish to achieve in an operation. This focuses efforts on achieving a military objective, something commanders fully understand, and ensures the full range of capabilities available will be used to that end. The clear statement that will drive planners and subordinate units in that regard is the commander's intent.

The Commander's Intent, as part of the formal military planning process "articulate(s) the purpose of the campaign being conducted and the...commander's vision of the military end state when military operations are concluded." It serves as the impetus for operational planning. The key to proactively managing the information environment, then, lies in a clearly stated *information* endstate, that is, a description of what the information environment will look like at the end of the military operation. The information endstate should consider both the cognitive and physical dimensions of the information environment. The cognitive endstate includes the desired perceptions and attitudes of the target audience (e.g. the indigenous population or international community). The physical information endstate includes a description of the new media capabilities of the adversary at the conclusion of the operation.

A properly articulated information endstate will drive both planning and execution of the military operation with sensitivity toward the new media environment. Military courses of action will be analyzed against this vision and subordinate military units will carry out the operation in order to meet the endstate described within the intent. Sensitized to the commander' intent, planners "wargame" the courses of action with that endstate in mind. Consequently, the planners will consider an enemy's expected reaction to a friendly action in terms of the required information endstate. This will include recognition that a friendly kinetic action could result in an enemy asymmetric information reaction. Planners can then prepare for a counteraction to blunt the enemy information attack or choose an alternate course of action. Additionally, the information endstate will drive *how* subordinate units carry out their mission. Actions send loud and clear messages to a target audience. Where previously a kinetic solution may have been the preferred choice (driven by inherent organizational culture) the information endstate may instead drive the unit toward a different approach that achieves the stated cognitive effect on perceptions, attitudes and behaviors. The commander is now unburdened by unfamiliar concepts like information operations and strategic communication. To be sure, his planners and staff experts will apply those concepts to achieve the required information effect, but the key is that they will proactively do so. Nor will they limit themselves to information operations and strategic communication capabilities, but will use every available military capability available, in integrated fashion, to achieve the effect in support of accomplishing the military objective.

The information environment of today guarantees that "wildcards" will present themselves as unpredictable, disruptive forces to current operations. These incidents can significantly impact a military operation, whether the wildcard is the release of Abu Ghraib imagery...or terrorist internet video of gruesome beheadings. While the military response to such circumstances seems necessarily responsive in nature, current planning processes allow proactive consideration of such events as well. In military planning a "branch" is "a contingency option built into the basic plan.... It is used to aid success of the operation based on anticipated events, opportunities, or disruptions caused by enemy actions and reactions. It answers the question 'what if...?'" Like the commander's intent, however, it requires an organizational culture shift in focus to apply the existing process to the expected new media information environment...but the widely understood process does exist. While branch planning cannot account for every possible wildcard (thus the name) it should anticipate that wildcards will occur and, at a minimum, establish procedures to deal with them.

The Battle of Jenin serves as an example of what could have been if IDF organizational culture had prescribed that the information environment be addressed within the planning process. If the IDF Commander's Intent had articulated an endstate that addressed the cognitive dimension of the information environment would the battle have still resulted in strategic failure? Consider the effect of a stated military endstate where the people of Jenin would "remain neutral in their attitudes toward Israel" and "the international community would understand and support IDF efforts to defeat terrorism." Given that simple statement that drives planning and execution it is likely that the media would have been allowed to embed with the IDF during the battle in order to allow Israel to compete for international legitimacy. It's also likely that subordinate units would have carried out operations by using tactics other than bulldozing buildings to achieve their objectives in order to maintain Palestinian neutrality. Finally, branches to consider wildcards could have been developed that defined a process to address the now expected mis- and dis-information that the numerous cell phone interviews coming out of the refugee camps engendered. Those counter-wildcard procedures could have required IDF forces to carry helmet cameras to film operations to prove proportional response by the IDF and to immediately counter any framed or altered imagery distributed by the insurgents.

Given the importance of new media and the information environment, a statement of the information endstate must be required within commander's intent. This simple change in doctrinal requirement, supported by the military education system can drive organizational culture change and ensure the military proactively manages the information environment.

ASSOCIATION TO ADDITIONAL JOINT OPERATING CONCEPTS

Major Combat Operations

This *Military Support to SSTR Operations JOC* recognizes that SSTR operations can occur independently of MCO, or in combination with MCO in a theater conflict that includes the commitment to seize and hold former enemy territory, or, more ambitiously, to drive the existing political regime from power. When SSTR operations are conducted simultaneously with MCO, then the MCO and SSTR operations are inextricably linked from the very outset of the campaign and success in both operations is needed to achieve operational and strategic objectives. Planning, preparation and execution activities associated with SSTR operations crosses all lines of effort of the campaign and are not unique to the concluding stage of the conflict, previously called "phase 4." The planning and conduct of a military campaign that seeks regime change must integrate MCO and SSTR operations in a manner that is focused on both decisively defeating and expelling the adversary regime and "winning the peace" by helping a new host government create a new domestic order. The planning and conduct of more limited objective MCO, one that does not involve forcible expulsion from power of the enemy regime, requires the integration of SSTR activities into the campaign as well.

At any given time, the decisive combat and SSTR aspects of the overall campaign can, if not carefully planned and executed, create serious operational dilemmas for the Joint Force. While conducting major combat operations, the Joint Force Commander (JFC) must ensure that the campaign maintains focus on achieving the desired strategic end states, which is, setting the conditions for achieving stabilization, security, transition, and reconstruction objectives needed to create a new domestic order and a viable peace.

Therefore, within a joint campaign, the JFC, campaign planners, and even individual units, must continually balance their activities across the lines of effort throughout the campaign. For example, during MCO, the JFC should refrain from tasking friendly forces to destroy critical infrastructure needed to maintain security and provide essential services for the general populace, unless its destruction is absolutely necessary to achieve campaign objectives and desired effects. Similarly, care should be taken to actively protect key administrative facilities, ministries and the like from destructive attack and from looting, if feasible, because these key assets could be critical for successful SSTR operations by the new host nation government..

Mother country Defense and Civil Support

The main impact of the *Military Support to SSTR Operations JOC* on homeland defense will involve the fact that successful

SSTR operations can eliminate or prevent the emergence of a hostile government or ungoverned space that could serve as the breeding ground for hostile groups that hatch plots to threaten U.S. national security interests, including carrying out attacks on the U.S. homeland. Thus, effective SSTR operations can represent an important element of the forward region component of the layered defense concept set forth in the *Homeland Defense and Civil Support JOC.*

Additionally, the training, organization, and equipping of interagency partners for SSTR operations will have relevance for civil-military operations that address crises or disasters within the United States.

Deterrence Operations

Deterrence operations are relevant to certain aspects of the *Military Support to SSTR Operations JOC*. Deterrence achieved via the threat of cost imposition or the denial of the prospect of success certainly cannot impact the likelihood of a natural disaster. However, SSTR-related activities that strengthen the ability of a friendly government to create and maintain a safe, secure environment or reduce the grievances of the general populace can certainly impact the calculations of the antagonists wanting to unseat the friendly government through violent means. In addition, a nation's apparent will and capability to prevail in a regional conflict, including having the ability to defeat aggression by conducting effective major combat and SSTR operations could be an important factor in deterring such a conflict. Thus, through security cooperation programs, the USG and coalition partners can assist the militaries of friendly governments in developing significant MCO and SSTR capabilities, which can contribute to deterring regional conflicts.

Time Frame

This concept broadly describes how the future Joint Force will be expected to conduct military support to SSTR operations in the 2014-2026 time frame in support of national strategic objectives. In accordance with the *Capstone Concept for Joint Operations (CCJO)*, this JOC applies to operations around the globe conducted unilaterally or in conjunction with multinational military partners and other government and non-government agencies. It envisions military operations conducted within a national security strategy that effectively integrates all instruments of national power.

Assumptions

This *Military Support to Stabilization, Security, Transition, and Reconstruction Operations JOC* is premised on the following assumptions:

- The efforts throughout the Department of Defense (DOD) devoted to planning, organizing, training, equipping and otherwise preparing to conduct SSTR operations will be very substantial, roughly comparable to those devoted to preparing for major combat operations.
- U.S. Government departments and agencies beyond DOD will develop a core planning and rapidly deployable implementation capability with sufficient capacity for extended, sustained SSTR operations. There is significant risk that this assumption may prove false. Moreover, even if civilian capabilities to support SSTR operations double in the next 10-15 years, there will still be a capability gap that the military will be called upon to fill, even in a secure environment.
- DOD will support SSTR operations through the evolution and deployment of the net-centric operational environment (NCOE). The NCOE, whose cornerstone is the Global Information Grid, will provide information transport, information assurance, enterprise services, network management, applications, and knowledge management capabilities to facilitate SSTR operations. The NCOE will link DOD garrison and deployed organizations, and reach back elements to support the full range of military operations. DOD will also work with interagency, coalition, international, regional, non-government, and private sector partners who possess capabilities that can contribute to SSTR objectives to

ensure that they can effectively share information and collaborate in the assured DOD information environment.

THE PLANNED SETTING AND THE SSTR MILITARY DIFFICULTY

Failed and Failing States

The strategic importance of failed or failing states on the world scene has much greater salience in the aftermath of the tragic events of 9/11. Beyond purely humanitarian considerations, the nexus of state failure and transnational terrorism poses potentially catastrophic consequences to international security. Failed or failing states may arise as a result of the effects of globalization, economic collapse, resource competition, corrupt government, and/or failed social infrastructure. Failed or failing states frequently lead to the emergence of ungoverned spaces, which provide opportunities for warlords, crime bosses, tribal leaders, and religious authorities to gain control or compete for power. These groups will appeal to desperate citizens, and may offer sanctuary to criminals and insurgents. Additionally, terrorists, drug dealers, and criminal elements may use ungoverned areas as bases of operation to spread their influence among the indigenous and foreign populations.

Urbanization

With over 60 percent of the world population living in urban areas by the year 2030, the potential for urban combat significantly increases. In much of the developing world, insurgents and terrorists will exploit the density of major urban centers, finding money and sanctuary among the population and the complex terrain of a modern metropolis. Urban centers can also provide a steady stream of disaffected and unemployed youth, who can be recruited and turned into insurgents or terrorists. Additionally, complex urban terrain often provides insurgents or terrorists with asymmetric advantages, including more lucrative targets and broader support. Where political systems are weak and fragile and the economic base is overwhelmed, the combination of population growth and urbanization will foster instability and increase challenges to political control and public security.

In many of the major urban areas, the government's inability to provide the basic public services heightens the potential for chaos and civil unrest. Critical infrastructure most likely will be austere—water and sewer services in disrepair; limited or compromised electrical service; and inadequate educational opportunities and medical care.

Such cities may be ungovernable and increasingly run by an informal network of politicians, criminal undergrounds, and special-interest groups. The close proximity of various divergent ethnic or religious groups could ignite long-standing tensions, exacerbating already delicate balances. The diverse, fractured nature of the society and its internal instability means that external organizations with special interests or links to the society will likely influence SSTR operations.

The Strategic Setting

The United States will continue to face a complex array of security challenges, which are identified in the 2005 *National Defense Strategy* as the traditional, irregular, catastrophic, and disruptive challenges.

- Traditional challenges will be posed by states employing recognized military capabilities and forces in well-understood forms of military competition and conflict.
- Irregular challenges will be those posed by actors employing "unconventional" methods to counter the traditional advantages of stronger opponents.
- Catastrophic challenges will involve the efforts of U.S. adversaries to acquire, possess and possibly use WMD or other capabilities that produce WMD-like effects.
- Disruptive challenges will arise from the efforts of adversaries to develop and use breakthrough technologies to negate current U.S. advantages in key operational domains.

The United States will need to integrate the application of the diplomatic, informational, military and economic elements of its national power in order to meet these four challenges. In addition, the Joint Force must be prepared to meet all four of these challenges simultaneously and proportionally within any given area of operation.

If the U.S. military conducts a traditional military campaign during a theater war, it will almost certainly include a simultaneous SSTR operation. However, the SSTR operation within the traditional military campaign would most likely be characterized by non-traditional forms of military conflict. Hostile forces will likely opt to attack the Joint Force, U.S. allies, elements of the existing or new host government, and even the local population with various forms of irregular warfare, e.g., terrorism and insurgency. These "spoiler" groups may choose to employ weapons of mass destruction (WMD) or methods producing WMD-like effects to threaten or to attack critical U.S., allied, or host nation targets, should these groups come to possess such weapons. SSTR operations undertaken in the wake of the internal collapse of a failed state that possessed weapons of mass destruction would present "catastrophic" challenges for the intervening military forces conducting the operation. In such a case, highest priority attention will be focused on safely securing and ultimately eliminating the WMD capabilities.

Key Trends

There are certain trends in the current strategic environment that will likely figure even more prominently in the years ahead. It will be important to understand these trends, because it is very likely that they will directly impact both the frequency and character of future SSTR operations.

Ethnic and Spiritual Rivalries

Post-conflict stabilization, security transition and reconstruction operations during the past decade in the Balkans, Afghanistan, and Iraq have, in some cases, been triggered by and, in all cases, been strongly influenced by serious ethnic and religious differences. While not new, ethnic and religious conflicts pose a serious challenge to secular local authorities and external governments like the United States, which find themselves often conducting SSTR operations in highly charged environments. Moreover, long-standing ethnic, tribal, and religious-based conflicts are rarely resolved by external force alone but almost only resolved through political means.

Ethnic conflicts tend to arise when identities are challenged by the kinds of major social changes that accompany modernization and globalization. While current ethnic fault lines tend to be geographically centred, in the future, ethnic dynamics may have major impact on regional balances of power. Recognizing and understanding the ethnic dimension of an environment will remain critical.

Religious ideology is a powerful, driving social and political force. Those seeking national, regional, or global goals of dominance increasingly employ religion, particularly in its most extreme form, as a means to motivate oppressed, impoverished, or culturally adrift populations. Religious fundamentalism is attractive to those who feel victimized or threatened by the cultural and economic impacts of globalization and increased social interconnectivity. Additionally, there is a tendency for religious-based political movements to gain support when secular civic institutions of political authority appear unable to deal successfully with serious challenges, be they local or global in origin.

Network Global Media

Since SSTR operations are largely won or lost in the political and information domains, global communications and information dissemination are vital factors. Information will be at the heart of conflicts, permeating and influencing all operations by focusing on changing behavior and perceptions among target audiences. The velocity of information flows and the power of imagery can imbue a tactical act with strategic importance by relaying an out-of-context description or image of that act around the globe in a matter of minutes.

The media will provide a powerful means of influence because societies that have unprecedented access to information will be enormously susceptible to media impact. Media coverage of operations and the real-time dissemination of information will not only affect domestic politics, international relations and strategic interaction, but also have critical political and psychological impacts. Observers throughout the world will interpret actions on the battlefield and their consequences largely through the lens of omni-present media channels (e.g., television, internet, cell phones). Many world media outlets are not held to the legal constraints of "traditional journalism" (e.g., laws of libel, slander). Perversely, the very criminals or spoilers causing instability in fragile states may take advantage of the global media to carry out their operations or manipulate global perceptions of their "grievances."

Modern media information does not always penetrate "traditional cultures" that rely on information through the word of mouth. Moreover, traditional cultures usually defer to the opinions and views of authority figures (e.g., village leaders) rather than to outside media sources. In these cases, if the authority figures accept the legitimacy of the intervening force then it is likely that positive information will resound with the local populace. Conversely, if the legitimacy of the intervening force is criticized by the authority figures then negative, and often false, information can eclipse any positive media information.

Knowledge Diffusion

Advances in technology will spur technology diffusion that may enable minor states, non-state groups, and even individuals the ability to acquire and employ WMD and other weapons that produce mass effects. The large numbers of casualties caused by the employment of such weapons could rapidly undermine progress made in SSTR operations. In addition, access to advanced technologies can result in the development and use of highly sophisticated improvised explosive devices (IEDs) to disrupt troop movements and inflict heavy casualties.

Multiplicity of Actors

Another complicating factor is the proliferation of actors in the future security environment such as non-governmental organizations, private voluntary organizations, private companies, news organizations, and commercial security companies. The engagement of non-DOD actors dramatically increases the complexity of trying to characterize the battle space, determining who is supportive of U.S. efforts, who is neutral, and who is the enemy.

Globalization is producing intensified international interaction on a wide range of issues, often creating friction as the many cultures, religions, governments, people, organizations, and economic networks collide in highly competitive global settings. Increased economic globalization and the development of advanced information systems are generating enhanced worldwide awareness, as noted previously. This has influenced national and non-governmental policies and has resulted in increased roles for the United Nations, regional, non-governmental, and international organizations. When political circumstances allow the establishment of a U.N. Security Council mandate for SSTR operations, the United Nations should assume the responsibility of facilitating the unity of effort for all task execution and coordination.

MOST DEMANDING MILITARY PROBLEM CONNECTED WITH MILITARY CARRY TO SSTR OPERATIONS

The Joint Force of the 21st Century will face formidable challenges in the enormously complex and uncertain international security environment, some of whose most salient features. In the era of the "long war" against global terrorist networks, serious shocks—both natural and man-made—will have the potential to push a fragile nation-state or region into a deteriorating spiral of stresses on multiple elements of the government and society.

If a national government is weak, corrupt, incompetent, or non-existent then a triggering shock can seriously exacerbate an already difficult situation, producing widespread suffering, growing popular grievance, and often civil unrest, all of which can be intensified by several interrelated factors:

- The absence of adequate internal security, essential public services, and other key government functions due to ineffective, often corrupt governance; or the absence of any governing authority;
- Widespread lawlessness in an atmosphere of anarchy as well as sectarian conflict among ethnic, tribal or religious groups or between the incumbent government and its violent opposition;
- Very poor economic performance due to internal disorder, eroded infrastructure, and the destruction of key economic assets; and
- Extensive unemployment and pronounced economic disparities within the populace that breed pervasive dissatisfaction and help generate recruits for opposition groups.

Once such difficult conditions emerge, the drivers of instability and conflict tend to reinforce one another, creating a degenerating cycle in which conditions continue to deteriorate, and the feelings of insecurity and the grievances of the local population intensify. Without a countervailing force to break this cycle, these developments can eventually destabilize the interlinked political, economic and social systems that make up the fabric of a society.

Supporting Idea: Contingency Planning & Preparation

The objective of the planning and preparation stage of SSTR operations is to harmonize the many diverse civilian and military efforts within a comprehensive, integrated strategy for achieving the host nation's new domestic order. Coordinated civil-military planning has the potential to substantially strengthen unified action; however, it also has the potential to slow down the planning process. This may present an unacceptable level of risk in situations where time is of the essence and rapidity of response is a critical determinant of ultimate success. Certain situations may necessitate an abbreviated SSTR operation planning process. However, experience has shown that the absence of advance coordinated planning can undermine the ultimate success of SSTR operations; therefore, abbreviated SSTR operation planning should be used only rarely and where risk of delay is deemed to be extreme.

Situation Assessment. At the outset of planning, a crucial planning component is the development of a comprehensive situation assessment or diagnosis that places a premium on developing an in-depth knowledge of the underlying causes and dynamics of the conflict and the relevant aspects of a society's local culture as well as its political, military and economic systems. In particular, understanding the drivers of instability and/or conflict should be a central feature of this first phase of the planning process. The goal of this assessment is to fill knowledge gaps to enable the interagency planning team to develop a coordinated strategy and identify critical supporting tasks that are tailored to the unique conditions in the society at hand. The assessment process will include an independent Red Team review based on the premise of how to use the diplomatic, informational, military, and economic (DIME) elements of national power in order to affect the targeted political, military, economic, social, infrastructure, and information (PMESII) systems. This situation assessment must be continually refined and updated to reflect the latest intelligence and "on-the-ground" learning.

Desired End State, Goals and Objectives. The overall desired end state, major goals, and key objectives of SSTR operations should represent very significant achievements with regard to the creation of internal security, economic development and effective governance, and should be understood as laying the foundation for a more ambitious vision of the long term future.

When planning for the attainment of the SSTR operation goals and objectives, undertaken in conjunction and coordination with the Department of State's Office of the Coordinator for Reconstruction and Stabilization and, in many cases, multinational partners, civil-military planners should:

- Focus on event-driven stages and transitions rather than employing a purely time-phased approach. There are two major "lead change" transitions during SSTR operations: the first is the hand-off of the leadership role in the several MMEs between the foreign military forces, who took the lead in most areas initially, and the external civilian agencies. The second transition is between the external military and civilian agencies and the leadership of the existing or new host nation government. These transitions will very likely be neither simultaneous across the MMEs nor homogenous within all regions of the host nation at the same time for a given MME. These transitions are based upon clearly defined conditions established in the CONOPS and modified, if required, during the planning and execution phases. These conditions include, but are not limited to the expected security environment and the capability and capacity of the civilian organizations to carry out the activities needed to accomplish the mission.

- Set the right trajectory by ensuring that the initial activities undertaken within SSTR operations are consistent with and directly supportive of the longer term objectives and goals of the operation. This approach also emphasizes that actions taken in each mission element are not done in isolation, but rather as elements of a series of closely linked, concurrent civil-military efforts in a comprehensive and coherent rebuilding program. Setting the right trajectory also involves planning for the swift deployment of the essential military and civilian SSTR capabilities to the area of operations as soon as U.S./coalition forces begin to occupy and control host nation territory.

- Pay close attention to cultural traditions and sensitivities by focusing on the likely priorities and concerns of the existing or anticipated new host government. Additionally, civil-military plans must be informed in a manner described as "culturally and psychologically aware," that is, these plans are developed in a process that considers how any action will likely be perceived and responded to by the local populace and/or hostile elements.

- Allow for continuous learning and adaptation during execution by recognizing there are likely to be tensions between the operational plan and unanticipated exigencies on the ground. Critical to the support of such adaptive plans is the establishment of responsive feedback channels that allow planners and units to continually observe, assess, understand, adapt, and anticipate from the outset of the intervention. Additionally, these feedback channels should engender regular adaptations and adjustments to various aspects of the plan.

SSTR-Related Security Cooperation Activities. While integrated civil-military SSTR planning is crucial, certain pre-crisis military security cooperation activities can help create the conditions for the successful conduct of SSTR operations; or they can prevent the necessity for the conduct of SSTR operations in the future. Therefore, allocating adequate resources towards SSTR-related shaping activities prior to a crisis enables the U.S. Government to advance its interests using relatively modest amounts of targeted resources, rather than spending much more substantial, and often, massive amounts of resources to respond to a crisis. Finally, SSTR-related shaping activities enable the Joint Force, as well as U.S. civilian agencies and multinational partners to develop a better understanding of a specific region, which may prove critical for the successful planning and execution of SSTR operations.

SSTR-related security cooperation efforts are those activities that:

- Assist a fragile, stressed government or region thus preventing them from becoming seriously unstable, and/or

- Help build SSTR-related capabilities of partner countries in ways that directly support U.S. efforts with regard to the potential conduct of SSTR operations.

During pre-crisis and preventive security cooperation efforts, the Department of State has a central role. NSPD 44 charges the Coordinator for Reconstruction and Stabilization (S/CRS) with coordinating SSTR activities and preventive strategies with foreign countries, international and regional organizations, nongovernmental organizations and private sector entities. S/CRS will also develop strategies to build partnership capacity abroad and seek to maximize nongovernmental and international resources for reconstruction and stabilization activities. Additionally, The Secretary of the Treasury is responsible for coordinating with international financial institutions and multilateral financing bodies regarding the Secretary of State's SSTR work. Military security cooperation efforts must be closely coordinated and integrated, where applicable, with other U.S. Government Department and Agencies.

Establishing and Maintaining a Safe, Secure Environment

The objective of the efforts to establish a safe, secure environment is to create a situation where the security of the people, property, and livelihoods within the country is sufficient to allow the general populace to routinely go about its business. This includes freedom from external threats that could divert attention and limited resources from internal security efforts. A safe, secure environment will also facilitate the conduct of large scale, civilian-led external assistance efforts and host nation activities for reconstruction. Increased civilian participation enables the first key transition in SSTR operations as civilian-led external organizations providing assistance to the host nation assume lead responsibility across the various major mission elements.

Success across the several dimensions of SSTR operations is critically dependent on the ability of coalition military forces, working closely with reconstituted host nation security forces, to achieve a sustainable level of security in the face of determined, violent "spoiler" organizations. Ultimately, the ability of the existing or new host nation government to maintain a safe, secure environment—both internally and externally—will be a crucial factor in its gaining political legitimacy and widespread popular support. In order to permit the host nation government to focus on internal security in the early aftermath of a crisis, U.S. and coalition military forces will most likely assume direct responsibility for external security until the host nation can develop its own armed forces capable of protecting its territory from external threats. For example, one of the key activities undertaken by coalition military forces will be to secure borders and ammunition stores to preclude exploitation by hostile forces. This activity should be undertaken at the outset by coalition military forces while host-nation domestic military forces are carefully trained to take over the protection of the borders and ammunition stores as soon as is effectively possible. In order to establish a safe and secure environment, it will be essential that the Joint Force in combination with its coalition partners, if present, have sufficient numbers of forces with the capabilities needed to establish order and create positive pre-conditions for reconstruction. At times, the numbers of military personnel required to carry out effective military support to SSTR operations will exceed the number of forces needed to prevail during the sustained combat of MCO.

Measured, Discriminate Offensive Operations. When establishing a secure environment in the face of anarchy or armed opposition, U.S. and coalition military forces will conduct offensive and defensive air and land operations in a targeted, measured and highly discriminate manner. In some cases, the opposition may take the form of an armed insurgency, which employs terrorism as one of its primary means of attack. While the Joint Force must map, neutralize, and eliminate these terrorist networks, it must use measured and discriminate force in doing so.

Joint and coalition military forces conducting a COIN operation in the face of determined armed insurgents, will mount carefully targeted offensive operations to:

- Defeat, destroy or disrupt the coherence of hostile military forces;
- Kill or capture prominent insurgent leaders;
- Disrupt or preempt enemy operations; and
- Seize or destroy enemy support capabilities

Success in these efforts will greatly reduce enemy capabilities and discredit the enemy's reputation for effectiveness, while at the same time enhancing the reputation and effectiveness of the Joint and coalition forces and the host nation government.

Timely, measured and discriminate operations help to avoid furthering the insurgents' cause by mitigating potential negative effects, which might create more enemies during a given operation than those who are captured or killed. This approach should feature efforts to separate the hostile elements from the civilian populace. It will involve targeted raids on enemy force concentrations such as cordoning off specific areas and investigating specific locations to search for and apprehend individuals rather than resorting to destructive, fire-intensive "sweeps," which often produce substantial collateral damage. Finally, the success of measured and discriminate operations is heavily dependent on the availability of actionable intelligence, especially human intelligence, needed to precisely locate hostile forces and to carry out highly discriminate operations at the right time and in the right place, thus allowing the coalition forces to seize and maintain the initiative.

In order to establish a sufficiently secure environment for effective civilian-led reconstruction operations to take place, the Joint Force must do more than just defeat organized military resistance. It must also conduct operations to secure in stride: population centres, essential national and regional resources, and key infrastructure, including critical transportation and communications nodes, and key medical, water, sanitation, and power generation facilities. These efforts to defeat organized military resistance and secure critical assets must often be accomplished simultaneously, not sequentially. While overwhelming speed and precisely applied firepower are essential to those elements of the Joint Force locating and destroying organized armed resistance, those responsible for securing key objectives will be more deliberate in their operations, relying less on firepower and more on other capabilities, including those resident outside the military arm of the unified action SSTR efforts.

Force Protection. The coalition military units and multinational civilian organizations conducting SSTR operations must be protected from the efforts of insurgents or other hostile spoiler groups, who will seek to disrupt their rebuilding efforts and kill or maim their personnel. This protection will involve a mix of preventive offensive operations, combined with a variety of active and passive defense measures, including the establishment of protected areas (green zones), use of special security details, and specialized sniper and counter-sniper operations. Particular emphasis will be placed on protecting the military forces, their bases, their major movement routes, and critical supporting capabilities. Coalition defensive operations will also be mounted to protect the host nation leadership and critical infrastructure.

Recent experience has demonstrated that increasingly sophisticated IEDs, in particular, can pose a deadly threat to movements of materiel and personnel during SSTR operations. In the years ahead, additional threats will likely emerge, including possible terrorist use of chemical, biological or radiological weapons. Consequently, major efforts will be devoted to strategies and operations undertaken to counter high explosive IEDs and other advanced weapons. These will include attack operations to prevent or disrupt the manufacture and emplacement of IEDs and other weapons as well as active and passive defense measures to neutralize these devices prior to use and reduce the impacts of their successful detonation. Similarly, full dimensional protection measures must be undertaken to counter other critical threats such as those posed by suicide bombers, shoulder-fired, surface-to-air missiles, and unmanned aerial systems.

While effective force protection is an essential mission activity, it must not become the mission. During SSTR operations, direct personal interaction with the local populace is essential for developing supportive relationships and gaining the people's trust. Consequently, force protection measures must be consistent with patrolling methods and other activities designed to facilitate extensive, routine contacts with the local citizens. Persistent Presence with Small Tactical Units. Creating a secure environment will generally involve sustained tactical patrolling on a selective basis. This patrolling will be carried out in a way that produces close and culturally-sensitive interaction with local communities. These daily, grass roots, small unit operations should be marked by patience, persistence, and presence and a determination to grant no sanctuary to armed opposition elements. Small units, operating under mission orders, are particularly well suited for these persistent operations because they often act as their own intelligence "sensors" and can respond quickly to changing circumstances while developing and maintaining a rapport with the local people.

Dealing with WMD or Chemical, Biological, Radiological, and Nuclear Materials. If the U.S. military conducts SSTR operations in a country or region where stocks of WMD or chemical, biological, radiological, nuclear (CBRN) materials are present as a legacy from the previous regime, then timely elimination of these WMD and CBRN stocks, delivery systems, and possibly production facilities will be crucial for establishing a safe, secure environment. WMD/CBRN elimination refers to a process of systematically locating, characterizing, securing, disabling, and/or destroying a state or non-state actor's WMD/ CBRN programs and related capabilities (weapons production, key personnel, knowledge, and delivery means). Seeking out and eliminating WMD and CBRN materials in the SSTR theater serves the dual purpose of protecting the intervention force in theater and defending the U.S. Homeland by preventing potential adversaries from acquiring WMD or CBRN materials that could be used against the United States.

Growing Host Nation Role. Foreign military commanders can leverage and enhance indigenous security and intelligence assets by closely coordinating their multi-dimensional security building efforts with host nation security forces and political authorities. The goal of such coordination will be to get local leaders actively involved as soon as possible in these efforts so that they develop a stake in the process. Securing host nation participation may complicate operations and its outcome and, in some cases, result in lower levels of efficiency and effectiveness. Despite these difficulties, the security building results will take deeper root if host nation leaders assume ownership early on for the problems and their solutions.

Multi-Dimensional Nation-Building Operations Are Essential to Creating a Secure Environment. Recent experience has clearly demonstrated that even measured, carefully targeted security operations conducted by U.S. military and Iraqi security forces are not as effective in establishing a safe, secure environment as a more comprehensive approach that includes concurrent operations across the full range of major mission elements, e.g., humanitarian assistance, restoration of critical infrastructure, economic and political development.

Joint Force Commanders will likely conduct multiple civil-military operations to support these ambitious, multidimensional and concurrent undertakings across several challenging "lines of operation" that cannot be conducted solely by civil affairs (CA) units. CA personnel can help bridge the gap between the military and civilian-led efforts, but they are incapable of adequately organizing and managing the huge reconstruction efforts involved. Therefore, other units, including not only engineers but also large numbers of combat and support units, will need to be incorporated into these robust, "industrial strength" civil-military nation building efforts from the very outset of these operations until such a time as can be safely transitioned to civilian organizations.

Flexible, Adaptable Resources. In order for the U.S. military to undertake broader reconstruction efforts that directly affect security by enhancing the well being of the people and keeping large portions of the adult labor force gainfully employed, operational commanders should have access to adequate contingency funds that can be flexibly and adaptively spent ("Money is ammunition"). Recent operations demonstrated the high value of exercising this discriminate use of flexible funds through the extensive and wide-ranging use of the Commander's Emergency Reconstruction Program (CERP) funds. The availability of and flexibility in expending such funds will allow operational commanders to underwrite projects that provide humanitarian aid, restore essential public services, support the development of small and medium-sized businesses, and promote local political development in ways that produce tangible signs of progress within a relatively short time period. These visible accomplishments will help garner popular support and build momentum for longer term endeavors. Operational commanders should work with local community leaders to identify immediate, high-impact projects. Additionally, local efforts should be coordinated with larger reconstruction projects that are usually conducted by USAID and the Corps of Engineers.

The Central Idea

During SSTR operations, the primary focus of U.S. policy carried out by military forces, U.S. civilian agencies, and, in many cases, multinational partners, will be on helping a severely stressed government to avoid failure or to recover from a devastating natural disaster, or on assisting an emerging host nation government to build a "new domestic order" following internal collapse or defeat in war. The new domestic order refers to a series of new patterns of organization and process within the security, economic and political systems, which are significantly different than the previous character of these systems.

Whether responding to a devastating natural disaster or assisting in rebuilding a new domestic order, U.S. military efforts in SSTR operations will be focused on effectively combining the efforts of the U.S. and coalition militaries with those of USG agencies and multi-national partners to provide direct assistance and build self-sufficient host nation capability and capacity in several key areas. These efforts, which are called "major mission elements (MMEs)" or "lines of operation" are executed in a concurrent manner and are integrated and tailored to the specific situation.

Additionally, MMEs represent desired end states within the overall SSTR operation. The six MMEs are:

- Establish and maintain a safe, secure environment;
- Deliver humanitarian assistance;
- Reconstruct critical infrastructure and restoring essential services;
- Support economic development;
- Establish representative, effective governance and the rule of law; and
- Conduct strategic communication.

Within this setting, the Joint Force must be able to help establish a safe, secure environment and, simultaneously, work with interagency, coalition, multinational, and host nation partners to support the establishment of a new domestic order.

Throughout the conduct of military support to SSTR operations, the Joint Force will implement a continuous learning process that incorporates lessons learned into ongoing and future operations. This continuous learning process will be conducted through constant observation of tactics, techniques, and procedures (TTPs); assessment of best practices; understanding how to implement best practices; and adapting TTPs.

"High End" SSTR Operations

Each SSTR operation that the U.S. Government undertakes will differ in the mix and application of the MMEs. At the high end of the spectrum are SSTR operations associated with a U.S.-imposed regime change, assisting a faltering government, or responding to the collapse of a government caused by internal failure or military defeat. The worst case scenario, which would signify a "high end" SSTR operation. When conducting "high end" SSTR operations, the most critical determinant of success will be convincing the local populace to recognize the legitimacy of the existing or new government and to actively support the government's efforts to build a "new domestic order." If this situation includes the presence of armed insurgent forces, actively opposing the efforts of the existing or new host government, then this operation is a counterinsurgency (COIN) operation. During such "high end" SSTR operations, the Joint Force must not only provide force protection for military forces, but may also need to provide protection for USG civil agencies in order to allow these organizations to conduct their SSTR missions.

The design of the efforts to build a self-sufficient host nation capability and capacity in each of the MMEs should adhere to certain fundamental precepts.

- First, the lead responsibility for organizing and carrying out these concurrent nation-building efforts must be transitioned from the external military and civilian organizations to the existing or new host nation government as rapidly as possible. Transitions within the various MMEs are event-driven and will not occur simultaneously, but will proceed at their own pace; nor will transitions in a given MME occur at the same time in all regions of the host country.
- Second, the existing or new government must ultimately assume full responsibility for the range of challenges and activities designed to overcome the drivers of conflict and build the new political, economic, and security domestic order.
- Third, the provision of large scale assistance by the U.S. and other foreign militaries within SSTR operations will almost certainly prove acceptable to the local populace for only a limited period of time, after which external troops may increasingly be viewed as hostile imperial intruders rather than as a force for assistance and progressive change. Consequently, these militaries must make substantial contributions to SSTR efforts as

quickly as possible and then give way first to external civilian agencies and, ultimately, to host nation institutions to carry out medium to long-term reconstruction and development.

- Fourth, care must be taken, when providing direct assistance to a stricken nation, not to create extreme dependency on the coalition, or to provide services at U.S. standards that cannot be sustained over an extended period, thereby helping to undermine the legitimacy of the existing or new government.

Other Potential SSTR Operations

In major combat operations fought by the United States for objectives short of forcibly changing an adversary regime, some combination of the SSTR major mission elements may be carried out to achieve SSTR objectives in territories annexed from the defeated adversary.

These MMEs also may be drawn upon to help care for refugees displaced by the war and to directly assist the recovery of partner nations in the region, which suffered serious damage during the conflict.

Under a less challenging security environment associated with helping a stable government cope with the consequences of a devastating natural disaster, the U.S. military will directly coordinate its support of humanitarian assistance, and, in some cases, reconstruction efforts with the United States Agency for International Development (USAID) and other parts of the Department of State, including the Office of the Coordinator for Reconstruction and Stabilization, and the host nation. In addition, the U.S. military will often coordinate with multinational relief organizations. These efforts will generally focus on rapidly providing food, clean water, shelter, and emergency medical treatment to ease the suffering of disaster victims when their needs are most acute and will, if necessary, help to restore order in the disaster area. U.S. military personnel may also provide support to initial rebuilding efforts in the affected area.

Supporting Ideas

During the planning and conduct of military support to SSTR operations, it is imperative to achieve unity of effort through what the *Capstone Concept for Joint Operations* labels "unified action" in order to successfully integrate efforts across the "seams" of the wide range of U.S., nongovernmental organizations, and multinational military and civilian organizations involved in the many aspects of the operation. With respect to this *Military Support to SSTR Operations JOC*, unified action involves the successful integration and synchronization of the multidimensional efforts of the U.S. military, U.S. Government Agencies, and coalition partners as well as private sector actors and host nation agencies in pursuit of success in all of the MMEs. This unified action within and between the various mission elements is critical due to the strong interdependencies among the different rebuilding efforts, for example:

- Without the creation and maintenance of a safe, secure environment, there is little prospect that significant progress can be made in any of the other mission elements;
- Without progress in the other mission elements, it is unlikely that military forces will gain the trust and support of the population needed to gather timely and reliable intelligence that can enable them to find destabilizing forces and maintain a safe, secure environment;
- Progress in near and longer term reconstruction will rely heavily on the restoration of critical public infrastructure and essential services; and
- Successes in providing security and essential public services as well as visible progress in stimulating economic development are crucial to gaining the popular support and perception of legitimacy needed to create the new representative forms of governance that adhere to the rule of law and to carry out the many aspects of SSTR operations.

NATIONAL PLANNING GUIDANCE AND A NATIONAL CONCEPT OF OPERATIONS

Unified action must begin with common USG objectives and goals. Both NSPD-44 and DODD 3000.05 task the Departments of State and Defense, respectively, to identify states at risk of instability where potential SSTR operations are highly likely to be conducted. As the U.S. Government lead for SSTR activities, the Secretary of State should develop a *National Planning Guidance*, in coordination and consultation with the Secretary of Defense.

A *National Planning Guidance*, promulgated by the President, would provide USG-wide goals and objectives for each geographic region worldwide. Additionally, the *National Planning Guidance* would list those countries and sub-national regions with the potential for U.S. Government engagement in SSTR operations. This list would guide the development of standing interagency contingency plans, as well as serve as the unifying purpose for coordinated security cooperation activities in each region. When relevant and appropriate, SSTR contingency plans should be integrated with military contingency plans.

Unified action could also be further strengthened by the drafting and adoption of a *National Concept of Operations (CONOPS) for SSTR Operations.* This *SSTR CONOPS* would provide the basis for conducting SSTR operations, as well as for USG-wide exercises and rehearsals. This CONOPS would also create a useful framework for civil-military planning and for the rehearsal of key activities, including the processes of transitioning lead responsibility within the various major mission elements from external military to civilian-led organizations and ultimately to the existing or new host nation government.

In addition to having available national-level planning guidance and a *SSTR CONOPS*, the development of several important coordination mechanisms operating at the strategic, operational, and tactical levels would assist in developing the agreed-upon goals, shared situational understanding, plans, and execution oversight required to achieve unity of effort. While each of the mechanisms at the differing operational levels will have a distinct focus and objective, planners and operators must remain cognizant that these levels will inherently involve overlapping roles and require close, coordinated collaboration to assure successful SSTR operations. Many of the capabilities do not yet exist and will need to be developed by the Secretary of State in coordination with the Secretary of Defense.

Unified Action at the Strategic Level. Interagency (IA) coordination at the strategic level will continue to be governed by the National Security Council process. In the event of a crisis, the National Security Council may either establish a new high-level IA coordination group or expand an existing group. This group would develop the long term vision and goals for SSTR operations, based on the *National Planning Guidance*. Additionally, this group would promulgate guidance for coordination of IA activities during the operation and make decisions or recommendations on resource allocation issues. Membership in this group would include representatives from all of the federal departments and agencies involved in a particular SSTR operation.

Once USG strategic guidance is established, the coordination group should convene a series of interagency planning bodies, consisting of experienced planners from all the departments and agencies involved in the operation, would develop and rehearse the overall plan for the SSTR operation, as well as individual plans for each of the MMEs. The establishment of these planning bodies would require each of the relevant departments and agencies to create a cadre of civilian planners.

Unified Action at the Operational Level. In order to ensure unity of purpose, as well as unity of command, the development of a new interagency planning and execution oversight element, which could operate "split based" at both the headquarters of the geographic combatant command and forward in the field, would help ensure key perspectives, plans and capabilities from the various USG agencies involved in the SSTR operation are factored into the preparation of military plans and their execution. This IA planning element and execution coordination body, subordinated to the regional combatant commander, would work closely with, and may be embedded into, the Combatant Command's standing Joint Interagency Coordination Group.

The development of a new interagency coordination group, attached to either the senior U.S. civilian authority or the senior military commander on site, and able to be deployed to the area of operations to assist either of these senior leaders in integrating the multidimensional nation building activities, would also be useful. The group would maintain communications between the lower level interagency provincial teams and the senior U.S. representative in theater, thus helping channel information upward and guidance downward to the teams operating at the province level. Such a coordination group would require a cadre of deployable civilian personnel.

Unified Action at the Tactical Level. At the province level, interagency bodies embedded with the military or operating alone are valuable tools. The composition, organizational subordination, and modes of operation for these tactical interagency teams will be developed using the lessons learned from the Provincial Reconstruction Teams (PRT) in Iraq and Afghanistan, and from other SSTR operations undertaken in the past. PRTs would coordinate multi-agency activities on the ground. Therefore, these teams must be balanced with military and civilian personnel. As a result, relevant U.S. Departments and agencies will need to develop a cadre of deployable civilians to staff PRTs.

Multinational Involvement. All of these bodies, from the US-based strategic planning elements down to those operating at the province level in the field will, when appropriate, be expanded to include representatives from coalition partner militaries and civilian agencies as well as from the United Nations and other international and non-governmental organizations. Where possible and applicable, host nation planners should be integrated into the SSTR campaign design effort from the very outset.

Drivers of Instability and Conflict

While significant initial progress with regard to the other major mission elements associated with the conduct of a high end SSTR operation is critical to the establishment of a safe, secure environment, other essential components of SSTR operations include: the delivery of humanitarian assistance as long as it is needed; the sustained progress in the repair and enhancement of critical infrastructure and essential public services; the support of economic development; and the creation of more effective and representative governance. All of the efforts of the external civil agencies and foreign militaries must be focused on helping the host government develop and effectively employ, as rapidly as possible, the new capabilities and capacity needed in these critical areas.

The host government needs to develop its indigenous security, economic and political capabilities in order to successfully ameliorate the drivers of internal instability and conflict within the context of the "new domestic order" they seek to build. Building this new capacity is critical to enabling the host nation leaders at all levels to gain the popular support they will need to be able to carry out comprehensive nation building. The lion's share of the international assistance to these host nation efforts across the MMEs, including security sector reform, will be undertaken by civilian rather than military organizations.

Coalition Management. A first order responsibility of the JFC leading multi-national SSTR-operations is to establish and implement a plan for effectively managing the coalition military force and other multi-national partners. This multi-national effort will generally consist of three separate entities: foreign military forces, foreign civilian government organizations, and non-governmental organizations (NGOs).

The commander of the lead nation must be cognizant of all the capabilities, limitations, and varying rules of engagement within the military coalition and must appropriately manage and coordinate the efforts of the partner militaries throughout the duration of the mission. Additionally, the commander should leverage cultural and historical ties between coalition forces and the host nation that could positively impact the mission.

Non-military members of the coalition will not fall under the direct chain of command of the JFC; however, the JFC must continually coordinate activities with these entities in order to ensure unity of effort. Coordination with foreign, non-military government organizations and NGOs can be particularly challenging because these organizations typically have their own objectives and missions and will not necessarily want the coalition military forces to impinge on their independence and jeopardize their neutrality. Nevertheless, NGOs will often operate in the area of operation of the coalition forces and the responsibility for coordinating with and, in many cases, protecting their operations will fall on the commander of the lead force. In many instances, a JFC leading a multi-national operation will be operating under an U.N. mandate and may function under a variety of U.N. structures in the host nation depending on the manner in which the U.N. Security Council Resolution is written and the extent of the U.N. structure established in the host nation. In light of this operational structure, the JFC and preferably all forces supporting the JFC, must be well trained regarding operations in a U.N.-mandated environment and must clearly understand their roles and responsibilities under these conditions and how they differ from conventional missions.

Broader Security Sector Reform. In order to expand and solidify the safer, more secure environment, U.S. and coalition forces will focus on training and equipping host nation security forces (both military and police forces), integrating them into the conduct of internal security operations and enabling them to take the lead in the conduct of internal security operations as rapidly as is feasible. Critical elements of this activity include:

- Embedding U.S. and coalition advisory teams into host nation units. These advisory teams enable continuous, "round-the-clock" training as well as facilitate the development of positive relationships with the local populace that build trust and rapport.

- Establishing a joint, military-police intelligence sharing and planning framework. The joint participation of military and civilian police units from intelligence assessment to planning and ultimately to the execution of operations will generally produce more effective operations. Intelligence sharing between military and police organizations enables coordinated actions against threats to public security (e.g., organized crime, civil disturbances).
- Avoiding "mirror imaging" the organization and capabilities of U.S. forces. Security training of host nation militaries must be specifically tailored for the types of forces that the host nation needs to develop and local military traditions.
- Building the institutional infrastructure. A critical component of this reform effort will be the development of the public sector institutional infrastructure (e.g., Ministry of Defense, Ministry of Interior, National Security Council, Human Rights Ombudsman, etc.) needed to support the new military and police forces. In virtually all cases, this must be designed to reflect civilian control consistent with the legal norms of the host country; it must also focus on the creation of a judicial system, including correctional institutions, to enforce the rule of law.

Deliver Humanitarian Assistance. The objective of the effort to deliver humanitarian assistance (HA) is to rapidly relieve or reduce human suffering, as well as to improve the capacity of the host nation to provide essential services to its population, and better prepare for future disasters. It is also important to closely coordinate all HA efforts with civilian agencies (public and private) to expedite the transition from U.S. military to U.S. and host nation delivery of HA and subsequent stabilization activities.

Humanitarian assistance is generally limited to providing victims of the disaster immediate access to the basic human necessities, e.g., clean water, food, shelter, sanitation, public health, and medical care. In this situation, immediate medical coordination and integration with other relief organizations will be essential, as well as the ability to rapidly augment the host nation's medical infrastructure.

HA can be delivered either following governmental failure due to internal collapse or defeat in war, or following a devastating natural disaster, such as a flood, tsunami, or earthquake. In the wake of major theater war, especially in a contested environment, the Joint Force will most likely play a leading role in delivering HA during the initial stages of the operation. Under these circumstances, joint medical units must be prepared to provide specialized care to non-U.S. military personnel such as the local populace, detainees, and contractor support personnel.

Reconstitute Critical Infrastructure and Essential Services. At the outset of SSTR operations, especially within a contested, hostile environment, efforts to reconstitute critical infrastructure and restore essential services will primarily be a military-led activity. The objectives of this effort will be to:

- Protect and secure critical national and regional infrastructure, natural resources, and strategically important institutions, e.g., government buildings, religious sites, courthouses, communications needed to support SSTR efforts. The Joint Force Commander must consider limiting and/or avoiding damage to this infrastructure during the planning and execution of combat operations and ensure that proper force is applied to secure this important infrastructure; and
- Establish or create procedures and processes for the provision of essential services, e.g., providing clean water, telecommunications services, electrical power, sewage and garbage disposal, medical care, and education that are deemed essential by the Joint Force Commander to promote stabilization and to preserve freedom of action for the Joint/coalition force. Services deemed "essential" will vary according to the assigned mission and will be based on numerous factors such as national objectives,

expected duration of the mission and international legal obligations. Commanders at all levels will conduct civil-military operations to meet legal obligations and preserve their own freedom of action.

The rapid reconstruction of critical infrastructure, including key transportation systems and telecommunications networks, and the restoration of essential public services must be accomplished with an eye toward the creation of a durable foundation that supports a wide range of longer term efforts to develop a diversified, modern economy in the host nation that is effectively integrated into the global economy. Therefore, it will be essential for the military to work with U.S. and international civilian organizations and host nation government officials to identify, fund, and directly support strategic projects in those areas critical to demonstrating visible signs of progress. Rebuilding efforts should also use local labor where possible, which fosters employment and gives the populace positive options through clear improvement in quality of life.

As the security environment becomes increasingly safe and secure, the planning and implementation of longer term infrastructure reconstruction efforts will be transitioned to civilian-led external assistance organizations and the existing or new host government.

Support Economic Development. In the short-term, the objectives of the effort to support economic development are to assist in the early recovery of local and national economic activity and to lay the foundation for sustained economic growth. In the long-term, the objective is to launch economic development activities that establish a legal, financial, and regulatory environment where economic activity is derived from legitimate, formal transactions in accordance with the rule of law and to foster successful economic development in a variety of key economic sectors.

While civilian entities will lead the bulk of this mission element, U.S. and coalition military forces will play a supporting role within the short-term objective of stimulating economic recovery, especially during SSTR operations mounted in connection with a theater war. Military activities will tend to focus on generating small projects that employ members of the local population and help generate income, e.g., municipal clean-up, restoration of basic infrastructure. It is crucial that the efforts of U.S. and coalition forces in the economic arena set the conditions (i.e. set the trajectory) for the longer-term economic development objectives. As noted earlier, operational commanders will often use their CERP funds in innovative and entrepreneurial ways to assist near- and mid- term, local business development efforts.

However, it is possible for CERP-funded activities to actually retard longer-term economic recovery if they do not contribute to the longer-term, sustainable growth objectives. Close coordination with U.S. and international development agencies at the earliest feasible point in SSTR operations will help ensure these development activities complement one another.

Long-term economic development efforts will be led by these U.S. and international development agencies (such as USAID and the World Bank) NGOs, and private sector actors—all working closely with the emerging host country leadership, both national and local. Achieving the longer-term objective of creating stable economic institutions and processes and supporting significant development within key economic sectors requires initiatives that address the specific economic root causes of instability and conflict in the host country, which may include:

- Reducing widespread poverty, deprivation, and socio-economic inequalities by developing and implementing a comprehensive and inclusive economic growth strategy.
- Enhancing workforce skills and employment opportunities through targeted education and training programs, developed with local community involvement and market-sensitive private sector engagement.
- Reducing illicit, informal black market activities through legal reforms, strengthened enforcement activities, and aggressive efforts to provide alternative income sources to the traffickers.

- Putting in place the necessary incentives (laws, policies and practices) that enable domestic and international investors to create jobs, social benefits and hope for the future.

Establish a Representative, Effective Government and the Rule of Law. In the wake of a MCO in which U.S. and coalition forces have forcibly expelled the adversary regime and occupied its territory, the United States and its coalition partners, as occupying powers, will need to create a temporary "military government." Despite being labeled military, the occupation government may be military, civilian, or mixed in composition. In most cases, this temporary government will likely be a civilian led civil administration that exercises executive, legislative, and judicial authority throughout the occupied territory in accordance with international law. Guidance regarding the precise form of governance and the performance of these key governing functions will be determined by the President, in consultation with his senior advisors, and may also involve an international policy making group. The highest priority tasks for this civil administration will be the maintenance of law and order, which will be carried out in a manner that seeks to preserve the pre-existing legal order (where applicable), and the care of the civilian population to ensure it receives adequate food, water, shelter, and medical treatment. Other key functions of this administration will include reconstituting essential public services and fostering the recovery of the national economy.

During military support to SSTR operations, efforts will get underway to rebuild or help create host nation government structures that will ultimately assume the responsibility to govern. These new structures should be representative and inclusive, responsive to constituents, and accountable for their actions. Political reform efforts must take into account deep-seated rivalries and distrust among ethnic and religious communities, should they exist. The new political arrangements must provide all groups/communities with the opportunity to participate meaningfully in the governance process, including mechanisms to protect minority groups from discriminatory actions by the majority.

Activities within this mission element will be led primarily by civilian organizations. However, in the opening weeks of military support to SSTR operations, especially when the environment is hostile and contested, the Joint Force may need to engage in early restoration of local governance activities such as restoring city/regional councils, developing transparent reconciliation processes, and resolving property claims and disputes.

Military efforts in the area of governance must take into account existing local and cultural laws. Additionally, early governance reform activities must help set the trajectory toward the political end states established as both the mid-term goals and long term vision associated with the SSTR operation.

Conduct Strategic Communication

Strategic communication is the focused United States Government processes and efforts to understand and engage key audiences to create, strengthen or preserve conditions favourable to advance national interests and objectives through the use of coordinated information, themes, plans, programs, and actions synchronized with other elements of national power. The objective of strategic communication efforts and supporting communication strategies is to understand and engage key local and foreign audiences in order to create, strengthen, or preserve conditions favourable to achievement of overall stabilization goals and objectives. Reaching the local population quickly through the media is critical to defeating extremist and criminal challenges to local stability. Therefore, strategic communication efforts must be pro-active, anticipating opposition strategic communication capabilities and preempting or rapidly responding to adversary communication methods.

The development of strategic communication messages must take cultural sensitivities and perceptions into account. In order to facilitate this effort, DOD personnel expertise and capabilities should be enhanced with the appropriate linguistic, historical, and cultural training. Sustaining credibility at all levels is an essential goal for strategic communication. Therefore, strategic communication messages cannot be empty rhetoric: in order to maintain credibility and trust with friends and foes alike, including the American domestic audiences and coalition partners, all messages must be consistent and transparent. Additionally, overall strategic communication plans must be coordinated with the Staff Judge Advocate, public affairs officer, as well as information operations and operational planners to ensure messages are in compliance with DOD and other national guidance.

Throughout the operation, the primary supporting capabilities for strategic communication within the DOD—public affairs, information operations, and defense support to public diplomacy, must be continually coordinated and synchronized, both horizontally and vertically:

- Information Operations. The focus of the IO planning will be on influencing, disrupting, corrupting, or usurping *foreign* adversary human and automated decision-making processes, while protecting human and automated decision-making processes of the Joint Force engaged in SSTR operations. To conduct IO, the Joint Force will employ offensive and defensive information means to degrade, destroy, exploit, and influence an adversary's information-based process while protecting its own.
- Public Affairs. The focus of public affairs planning will be on conducting public information, command information, and community relations activities that provide truthful, timely, and factual unclassified information about SSTR activities to host nation, and U.S. domestic and foreign audiences. These information activities will be critical to efforts to manage expectations, as well as to gaining and sustaining support within each of the target audiences.
- Defense Support to Public Diplomacy (DSPD). The focus of DSPD is to understand, engage, influence and inform

key foreign audiences through words and actions to foster understanding of U.S. policy and advance U.S. interests regarding SSTR operations. DSPD incorporates DOD's support to USG strategic communication, and can collaboratively shape the operational environment in support of USG information activities through security cooperation efforts. DSPD may also involve multi-media programs to assist selected host nations and the DOS in reaching foreign target audiences, but may also involve specific actions by DOD forces.

Generally, visual information provides the ability to advise, plan, synchronize, and rapidly acquire and distribute visual products (still and video) to external audiences in support of commanders' strategic and operational objectives operations. All VI information activities are essential to information sharing between DOD elements, U.S. Government agencies, and multinational partners prior to, during, and after the completion of SSTR operations.

Vignette

The following is an illustrative vignette that describes how the future JFC might conduct a successful high-end SSTR operation within a hostile, contested environment. Additionally, the vignette highlights the linkages among the military problem, military support to SSTR operations, the central idea, supporting ideas, and anticipated functional and operational capabilities. This vignette also illustrates how the JFC can collaborate with multinational partners, as well as the pre-SSTR operation planning activities that contribute to the successful execution of SSTR operations.

Beginning in 2015, an international coalition, led by the U.S. military, becomes engaged in a major combat operation aimed at decisively defeating a foreign government that had provided protracted materiel support to a global terrorist organization responsible for detonating a WMD in the largest city of an important U.S. ally. Joint major combat operations, waged concurrently on the land, and from the air, sea and space, are conducted with precision and achieve decisive effects, resulting in the swift defeat of the perpetrating government. In the wake of major sustained combat and the defeat of the perpetrating government, the Joint Force swiftly adjusts itself accordingly to carry out a successful stabilization, security, transition, and reconstruction operation. The SSTR operation objective in the near term is to establish a safe secure environment throughout the host nation, recognizing that this is the necessary precondition for success in all other parts of the SSTR effort. This security effort is part of a multidimensional campaign conducted concurrently to effectively reduce the drivers of societal conflict and, as a result, build a new domestic order in the host nation and, more broadly, viable peace internationally in which the host nation's populace can prosper long into the future.

The seeds for success in this high-end SSTR operation were sown prior to the intervention during relevant preparatory, planning and theater security cooperation activities that included the following salient components:

- A high-level, joint interagency planning team, through effective coordination mechanisms, developed an in-depth situational understanding of the complex dynamics of the society at hand, including the wider environment. The body of information openly shared across both civilian and military agencies included an expert assessment of the causes, ideologies, aims, organizations, capabilities, methods/approaches, and external support for irregular threats that already existed in the host nation and those that would likely coalesce in the wake of the deposed government. Other areas probed included identifying the sources of societal conflict that required a mitigation plan, as well as the key power brokers whose influence and legitimacy should be (and was) significantly leveraged throughout the SSTR operation;
- This joint planning team, comprised of senior military and civilian representatives, developed the long-term vision for the host nation, the goals for the operation based on situation-specific intelligence, guidance for

integration of interagency activities during the operation, and decisions or recommendations on resources. Policy conflicts and disconnects were effectively identified and reconciled as part of this planning process, thus increasing the scope of unified action in the field once the operation commenced;

- This planning body also ensured that the individual plans for each of the MMEs within the SSTR operation were synchronized and aligned with the long-term vision for the host nation's new domestic order;
- The MCO and SSTR operation phases of the campaign were planned coextensively in Washington, at the headquarters of the geographic combatant command as well as forward in the field to ensure interagency perspectives, plans and capabilities were sufficiently factored into the preparation of military plans and their execution. For instance, SSTR operation-related considerations affected the targeting of ordnance during major combat operations to avoid inflicting unnecessary destruction to the host nation's critical civilian infrastructure;
- A Joint Force estimator modeling program defined the force requirements for this situation-specific operation. The real-time database identified available units and potential sources to fill capability gaps and supported adaptive planning throughout the campaign. This enabled rapid identification and generation of appropriate interagency deployment packages for such tasks as governance, judicial, law enforcement, economic, humanitarian, and reconstruction support. In the initial weeks and months after major combat operations ceased, these interagency packages enabled the Joint Force to immediately respond to urgent humanitarian needs as well as administer public services with an appropriate mix of military and civilian assets, while minimizing delays to providing sustained relief;

- An international initiative that was launched ten years before this crisis had achieved its primary goal of training and equipping a standing military force, a majority hailing from neighboring nations. These states chose to enter the coalition thereby greatly increasing the capacity of the combined force available to help conduct the SSTR operation, while also strengthening its perceived legitimacy in the eyes of the indigenous populace; and
- Other military shaping activities in the region that bore fruit during this SSTR operation in the form of the granting of critical transit and access arrangements to support coalition military operation to defeat the perpetrating state included the establishment of combined training, exercises and other military-to-military interactions; creating programs to cover such issues as defense security cooperation, international military education and training, and international arms cooperation.

Consistent with the well coordinated MCO and SSTR operation plans, major combat operations left minimal damage to the host nation's critical infrastructure, including its major natural resource sites and governmental buildings; this, respectively, proved critical to spearheading efforts at reviving the economy and creating a new host nation government. Despite this advantage, the war severely disrupted virtually all aspects of normal life in most parts of the country.

In the wake of our victory in the sustained combat phase of the war, the Joint Force quickly shifted its dynamic mix of conventional and unconventional forces to counter irregular threats that sought to take advantage of the subsequent turmoil and chaos to undermine our SSTR operation efforts, in particular our operations to create a safe, secure environment. Tactical defensive operations occurred seamlessly following Joint Force control of populated territory, preventing the incidence of property crimes from surpassing anticipated levels during the brief, albeit critical period, of anarchy following MCO. The

Joint Force, recognizing that security of the populace is the indispensable cornerstone of SSTR operation success, executed the plan to integrate and synchronize all the major mission elements—establishing a safe, secure environment, meeting obligations to the civilian population under international humanitarian law, restoring critical infrastructure, assisting economic development, helping create effective representative governance, and supporting strategic communication, with varying emphasis at different times and in different parts of the nation, depending on the situation on the ground. Each major mission element was, on the whole, conducted in consonance with the other MMEs, thus minimizing the size and number of "gaps" that adversarial forces were able to exploit.

Joint Force Commanders entered the SSTR operation recognizing that there was no "success template" that could be laid down across the various intervention activities, and therefore allowed for the different MMEs to be flexibly tailored to unique situations that invariably arose over time. In particular, significant educational and training resources related to SSTR operation activities across the DOD enterprise equipped unit leaders with the adaptive mindset and operational art necessary to succeed in this particular operation. Troop leaders, from the JFC all the way down to company commanders, were prepared physically, emotionally and intellectually to work in and through the post-war chaos, turning the inherent complexity of the situation to their collective advantage. U.S. troops were similarly well trained and otherwise prepared to conduct this challenging SSTR operation.

Adaptability was also supported by superior tactical intelligence resulting from sufficient manpower focused on its timely collection and rapid analysis. In fact, the high fidelity and accuracy of the tactical intelligence created for many units a benevolent, self-reinforcing cycle that underpinned success across the other MMEs: it enabled timely, discriminative, precise operations to counter insurgent activities, thus enhancing the perceived legitimacy of ongoing coalition operations, leading to more sources of actionable intelligence, which in turn furthered counterinsurgent efforts, and so on.

In terms of force sizing, the extensive use of small units further enabled tactical operations to be conducted in a timely, measured and discriminate fashion. Large unit operations were occasionally necessary to conduct a full-scale offensive operation against concentrated bands of adversaries in well identified locations. However, the Joint Force achieved greater success in countering various insurgent elements with smaller units that fostered closer contact with the populace and avoided over-reliance on "kill or capture" operations that, while decisive, risked creating more animosity as a function of collateral damage.

Progress within the other MMEs, conducted concurrently, allowed the overall coalition SSTR effort to reduce the underlying drivers of conflict in this host nation. These drivers included widespread official corruption, degraded essential services, longstanding and intermittent bouts of sectarian conflict, and the lack of an independent judiciary and/or trusted penal system. The initial phase of activities across the MMEs set the right trajectory towards the primary SSTR operation objective: each major activity thrust was aligned with ultimately producing a self-sustaining host nation capability and capacity to govern its own affairs without substantial external support.

Execution of the capability and capacity building efforts within the MMEs was greatly facilitated by the augmented use and availability of adequate amounts of CERP funds, which had become a highly flexible funding mechanism following appropriation reforms by the U.S. Congress. Enhanced CERP funds coupled with flexible contracting arrangements, many prepared prior to the onset of combat operations, ensured that no time-sensitive opportunities to jumpstart SSTR activities were squandered.

Commanders used these CERP funds for a variety of projects, all of which resulted in measurable progress towards improving the provision of essential services (such as food, power, clean water, the disposal of waste, and rudimentary medical care), developing the economy, strengthening the infrastructure (including building and restoring schools and hospitals) in a sustainable manner, and developing key institutions (e.g., police forces, an independent judiciary and media, etc.) that are essential ingredients for a prosperous civil society.

One critical way that unit leaders used resources for the greatest effect was by exercising best efforts to get the general population actively involved in confronting challenges and implementing culturally acceptable solutions. Assisted by economic development specialists from USAID, the Joint Force played a key role in both short-term and long-term economic development efforts. A paramount consideration of the short-term effort was to find productive ways to employ a large percentage of the young and middle-aged men of the host nation, which meant in effect that almost every household had a legal means for income. The focus on local employment as a key consideration in contracting initial reconstruction activities also prevented insurgent elements from capitalizing on concrete elements of civil discontent.

Security was further strengthened over time with a full-scale, comprehensive effort to train, equip and advise host nation security forces, both police and armed forces. The Joint Force in this endeavour benefited greatly from global security cooperation programs that created a number of discrete, deployable teams from multinational coalition nations, which were specifically designed to fulfill this mission. A general precept that guided enormous progress in this dimension was avoiding the temptation to train the new host nation security forces "in our own U.S. image." Instead, the Joint Force trained and developed the indigenous military in a manner that befitted their purpose and situation. This allowed many indigenous forces to combine with the Joint Force in conducting internal security operations earlier than would have been possible if full-scale combat capabilities were first required.

The Joint Force also achieved significant benchmarks early on in the SSTR operation in promoting lasting institutions of responsible, representative governance. In particular, the Joint Force was able to accurately assess the state of the existing society's legal system and helped the indigenous people develop and implement a new legal system that struck a balance between local cultural norms and universal notions of how the rule of law is supposed to operate (e.g., proportionate punishment, the right to a fair trial, humane treatment of prisoners, etc.).

Beyond the rule of law, the SSTR operation made significant progress in forming, and in many cases reforming, the governmental bureaucracy. These political reform efforts were designed to provide effective, inclusive, and responsive governance at all levels, while also accommodating deep-seated rivalries and distrust that existed among certain ethnic and religious communities. The new political arrangements were always crafted with an eye towards ensuring that all indigenous groups/communities had the opportunity to participate meaningfully in their political governance.

Civilian experts from U.S. Government agencies and multinational organizations were often supported by military units in this political endeavour. However, in some cases, where resources were limited, the military engaged directly and principally in these wide-ranging tasks. As a result, the public administration of the host nation was noticeably strengthened over time, especially once ministries were established along functional lines that were able to manage the host nation's governmental programs in a reasonably effective manner. Ministries were formed at the national, provincial and local levels, and were comprised in rough proportion to the society's overall ethnic demographics to prevent potential sectarian strife over the control and use of these institutions.

The Joint Force strived to transition governance responsibilities to these indigenous ministries as soon as was practicable to, among other things, demonstrate to the populace the limited duration of the Joint Force intervention and to provide avenues for the indigenous government to win the allegiance of its population, further isolating the insurgency and other sources of instability. The combination of restoring capability and building self-sufficient capacity facilitated the transition to legitimate local governance and the ultimate reduction of coalition efforts leading eventually to full withdrawal.

Certainly, the Joint Force's collective effort to build the capacity and capability of the host nation was not without significant, albeit isolated, setbacks. The use of widespread, indiscriminate violence by insurgent elements at key junctures challenged the credibility of the Joint Force to provide for the lasting security of the host nation populace. Longstanding and deep-seated ethnic and religious rivalries within the society also proved a vexing challenge to surmount. Nonetheless, the Joint Force helped institute a number of national and sub-national reconciliation mechanisms to diffuse tensions and provided a number of productive, peaceful venues aimed at fostering inter-ethnic trust and transparency.

During the final stage of the SSTR operation, the Joint Force successfully culminated its efforts to have the host nation be able and willing to accept responsibility for the conduct of activities across all the major mission elements. This transition was based on the new host nation government's capacity to sustain the rule of law, meet humanitarian needs, provide essential services, foster economic development, and govern responsibly without substantial external assistance. In the final months of this last transition stage to host nation self-reliance, the Joint Force withdrew in substantial numbers until only a modest routine military assistance team remained in the host nation.

Capabilities

Stabilization, security, transition, and reconstruction operations are manpower and resource-intensive operations and mandate the development of an agile Joint Force, as well as a robust civilian force, that can work cooperatively with each other, allowing the collective effort to carry out effective full-spectrum operations. The effective conduct of SSTR operations requires a range of functional and operational capabilities across the Joint Force, U.S. Government departments and agencies, and multinational organizations. Functional capabilities are those capabilities that allow the Joint Force to perform tasks that occur across all aspects of SSTR operations; thus, functional capabilities are required to successfully carry out each of the major mission elements throughout the campaign, e.g. creating shared situational awareness among diverse stakeholders. Operational capabilities focus on capabilities associated with accomplishing a desired end state (i.e. major mission element) within a SSTR operation, e.g., delivering supplies of food and medicine, rebuilding a power generation and distribution system.

Functional and operational capabilities are made up of a series of critical and enabling capabilities. Critical capabilities focus on the primary abilities that allow the force to accomplish a desired effect. Enabling capabilities support critical capabilities and allow a force to accomplish an important task that underpins the accomplishment of a desired effect. Due to the multiple foci of the various SSTR mission elements, many required capabilities may reside outside of DOD. This section outlines ten SSTR operational capabilities and their corresponding critical and enabling capabilities.

Functional Capabilities

U.S. Government Institutional Agility. U.S. government institutions must be able to distribute funds, goods, and services rapidly and efficiently to successfully conduct SSTR operations. Critical and enabling capabilities include:

- Critical capability. The ability for DOD to systemically plan, program, budget, and allocate funds for SSTR operations.
    - o Enabling capability. The ability for U.S. commanders to have access to contingency funds that can be spent in a flexible and adaptive manner.
    - o Enabling capability. The ability for U.S. commanders to rapidly bring to bear reliable, expert foreign and domestic contractor support a wide variety of SSTR undertakings.

- Critical capability. The ability of all U.S. government agencies to systematically plan and execute humanitarian, development, and reconstruction projects within an integrated strategic and operational framework.
    - o Enabling capability. The ability for non-DOD U.S. Government Agencies to plan for, rapidly deploy, and sustain civilian specialist assets in the area of SSTR operations for longer tours to maintain the needed capacity and expertise.

Command, Control and Coordination. In military terms, command, control, and coordination is the ability to exercise authority and direction by a properly designated commander over assigned and attached forces in the accomplishment of SSTR missions. Additionally, command, control, and coordination is the ability to conduct a coherent operation with the interagency, coalition, and multinational partners. Therefore, DOD must be able to effectively coordinate and integrate efforts between elements of the Department of Defense, engaged U.S. Government agencies, intergovernmental organizations, and nongovernmental organizations in order to accomplish SSTR objectives.

This capability requires the ability to manage and make available relevant, accurate information to appropriate stakeholders. Inherent in this capability must be the ability to protect and defend information systems by ensuring their integrity, authentication, confidentiality, and non-repudiation. Critical and enabling capabilities include:

- Critical capability. The ability to conduct integrated, parallel, and distributed planning within DOD, across the U.S. interagency community, with coalition partners, and with other multinational organizations.
- Critical capability. The ability to conduct seamless knowledge sharing among DOD elements, U.S. Government agencies, and multinational partners prior to, during, and after the completion of SSTR operations.

Battlespace Awareness/Understanding. Battlespace Awareness/Understanding is the ability to develop situational awareness and understanding and to produce intelligence through persistent and pervasive observation of all domains. Critical capabilities and enabling capabilities include:

- Critical capability. The ability to develop intelligence requirements, coordinate and position the appropriate collection assets, from the national to the tactical level.
    - Enabling capability. The ability to conduct persistent surveillance of critical enemy activities in difficult and denied areas by using sensors to capture timely, relevant, and interoperable source data.
    - Enabling capability. The ability to locate, tag, and track hostile elements in all domains.
    - Enabling capability. The ability to produce information from exploited all-source information and provide intelligence in an assured environment.
    - Enabling capability. The ability to make information and intelligence available to support the User-Defined Operational Picture.
    - Enabling capability. The ability of DOD to disseminate information to the appropriate members of the interagency community to ensure consistent communication.
- Critical capability. The ability to understand the cultural context in which operations take place, including the culture of coalition partners, civilian organizations and agencies.

Joint Force Generation and Management. In order to successfully execute SSTR operations, Services must be able to man, equip, and organize resources to ensure the JFC has the capabilities to support USG objectives for the SSTR campaign. Additionally, Services must be able to develop the Joint Force with the necessary skills to conduct SSTR operations. Critical and enabling capabilities include:

- Critical capability. The ability to craft rotation policies among the major components of the U.S. Joint Force.
- Critical capability. The ability to package personnel and equipment into optimal units to meet the demands of a JFC for SSTR operations.
    - o Enabling capability. The ability to provide DOD surge or niche capabilities from a steady state environment to a crisis, in ways that do not degrade combat readiness.
- Critical capability. The ability to instruct personnel to enhance their cognitive thought and leadership skills for SSTR missions.
    - o Enabling capability. The ability for Professional Military Education to develop curricula that includes: foreign language capabilities, regional area knowledge, and understanding of foreign governments and international organizations.
- Critical capability. The ability to train DOD and non-DOD personnel to enhance their ability to perform specific SSTR-functions and tasks.
    - o Enabling capability. The ability to develop and conduct individual training for DOD and IA personnel on the planning, conduct, and support of SSTR operations.
    - o Enabling capability. The ability to develop and deliver extensive, specialized, pre-deployment SSTR training across several operational areas.
    - o Enabling capability. The ability to collect, assess, and rapidly integrate SSTR lessons learned into DOD SSTR training curricula at all venues and levels.

Operational Capabilities

Create a Safe, Secure Environment. Creating a safe, secure environment requires the elimination or neutralization of hostile actions or influences of adversaries, criminal elements, or other illicit actors. Additionally, creating a safe, secure environment requires the Joint force to enable sufficient security to allow the conduct of large-scale, civilian and host nation-led activities. Critical and enabling capabilities include:

- Critical capability. The ability of Joint Force to conduct focused yet measured offensive and defensive operations against the leaders and military forces of hostile groups.
    - o Enabling capability. The ability to plan and execute security operations with coalition partners and the military and police forces of the existing or new host government.
    - o Enabling capability. The ability to use both kinetic and non-kinetic means to capture and defeat terrorists/insurgents, often in dense urban environments, while minimizing collateral damage.
    - o Enabling capability. The ability to carry out a mix of targeted offensive attacks to disrupt IED manufacture and emplacement, active defense efforts to neutralize implanted devices, and passive defense measures to reduce the impact of detonated IEDs.
    - o Enabling capability. The ability to interdict, seize and eliminate WMD and CBRN materials, as well as the ability to operate in an environment in which WMD/CBRN has either been used or is threatened to be used by adversary forces.
- Critical capability. The ability for the U.S. Armed Forces to train, equip, and advise large number of foreign forces in the full range of SSTR-related skills.

Deliver Humanitarian Assistance/Disaster Relief. Delivering humanitarian assistance/disaster relief requires capabilities that enable the immediate provision of basic necessities (e.g., water, food, sanitation, public health, medical care) in order to relieve or reduce human suffering. Additionally, providing humanitarian assistance involves helping improve the capacity of the host nation to provide essential services to its population, and better preparing the nation for future disasters. Critical and enabling capabilities include:

- Critical capability. The ability to coordinate and integrate with USG agencies and multinational organizations in order to support humanitarian assistance and disaster response efforts.
- Critical capability. The ability to obtain and redistribute essential supplies, food and medicine from within an affected nation, or deliver essential items that are not available locally or regionally, to disaster sites.
    - o Enabling capability. The ability to promptly deliver and operate water purification and electrical power generation equipment in devastated regions.
    - o Enabling capability. The ability to provide flexible and agile joint medical forces, capable of conducting sustained operations in multiple locations.
    - o Enabling capability. The ability to provide timely emergency medical treatment and prophylaxis to people impacted by natural or man-made disaster;
    - o Enabling capability. The ability to construct and operate camps and facilities for migrant and/or internal displaced person

Reconstitute Critical Infrastructure and Essential Services. Rebuilding/improving critical infrastructure requires capabilities that enable the protection of critical and strategically important institutions. Critical and enabling capabilities include:

- Critical capability. The ability to conduct immediate reconstruction of critical infrastructure and essential services.
    - o Enabling capability. The ability to protect key infrastructure that provides essential services to the population.
    - o Enabling capability. The ability to repair or construct roads, bridges, tunnels, and airfields for road, rail, and air transport.

- o Enabling capability. The ability to repair or build primary health care clinics, administrative buildings and hospitals.
- o Enabling capability. The ability to build or restore schools and provide text books and supplies.
- o Enabling capability. The ability to build or restore water purification plants, electrical power generation grids and telecommunication networks.
- o Enabling capability. The ability to repair or construct sewage disposal systems and collect and dispose of garbage.

Support Economic Development. Supporting economic development requires capabilities that enable the establishment of economic processes and institutions where the bulk of economic activities are derived from legitimate transactions.

These capabilities include those that will be largely provided by civilian economic development specialists from the interagency community, who are supporting SSTR operations. Critical and enabling capabilities include:

- Critical capability. The ability to assist the host nation in developing near-term reconstruction and longer-term economic development plans, e.g., reestablishing the central bank and government payment mechanisms, rationalizing revenues and expenditures.
  - o Enabling capability. The ability to design, fund and implement public works initiatives to rapidly provide employment for the local populace.
  - o Enabling capability. The ability to help plan and financially support a variety of small-, medium-, and large-sized business development programs to stimulate the economy.

Establish Representative, Effective Government and the Rule of Law. Promoting representative, effective local and national governance requires capabilities that enable the establishment of political institutions and processes that will be accepted as legitimate by the host nation population. Critical and enabling capabilities include:

- Critical capability. The ability of the USG to deploy and sustain civilian specialists over an extended period to assist the host nation in developing the new governance system.
  - o Enabling capability. The ability to assist in the drafting of local and national laws, designed to establish the rule of law, accommodate communal differences, and provide legislative oversight of military and security forces.
  - o Enabling capability. The ability to assist in the organization and training of personnel to work in the various government ministries and agencies.
  - o Enabling capability. The ability to assist in the creation of civic groups, political parties and representative governance at the national, province and local levels.
  - o Enabling capability. The ability to assist in the training elected officials at all levels about constituency building, accountability, transparency, participatory decision-making and conflict management.

Conduct Strategic Communication. Conducting effective strategic communication requires capabilities that enable the Joint Force to engage key local and foreign audiences in order to create, strengthen, or preserve conditions favourable to achievement of overall SSTR goals and objectives. Critical and enabling capabilities include;

- Critical capability. The ability to design and disseminate information in various forms to influence the views of adversary, neutral, and supportive audiences.
  - o Enabling capability. The ability to broadcast U.S. and coalition intentions and to help the local population find quick survival relief.

o Enabling capability. The ability to plan and synchronize joint public information and joint psychological operations activities and resources in order to communicate truthful, timely, and factual unclassified information about SSTR activities to the appropriate audiences within the area of operation.

7

Military-media Relations of Conflict

CURRENT APPROACHES TO MEDIA SELECTION

How are Media Really Selected? Little valid information exists on media usage for training or the process by which media are selected in corporate America. Surveys such as Training magazine's "Annual Industry Report" draw superficial conclusions about media usage. These conclusions give no information about how different media are used in the training process, or why particular media are used more than others. For example, the 1994 report concluded that the most commonly used medium to deliver training in American industry in 1994 was videotape, followed by lecture, and one-on-one instruction. This conclusion is based on the percentage of respondents who indicated whether each of a list of media was used for any training in the organization. In addition to providing no information on the quantity or type of training delivered with each medium, Training magazine's survey illustrates the fuzzy thinking that permeates the conceptualization of what constitute media in the training field. Media (such as videotape) are confused with media-independent instructional events or methods (such as lecture and one-on-one instruction).

Surveys such as Training magazine's do bear out informal observations of an increasingly complex array of media being employed to deliver training. In particular, computer-based multimedia/interactive videodisc systems are growing in popularity in corporate and military training (Fletcher, 1990; Nowakowski, 1994; Froiland, 1993; Industry Report, 1994). However, there is great variation among programs that bear the label "multimedia". While some principles for designing interactive multimedia instruction are appearing, there are currently no models to guide the micro-level media choices that must be made in order to produce a multimedia program. For example, how should designers decide which parts of a program should employ video, which information should be displayed in text, what material should come from audio narration, and which parts of a trainee's performance should be recorded?

No one has conducted a cognitive analysis of how expert training managers and designers make decisions about media; therefore, we do not know how training managers and designers really arrive at decisions regarding which media will be used to deliver particular training programs or components of programs. Neither do we know of any data on when decisions about media are made in the training design process. Most linear instructional design models include media selection as a post-design, pre-development activity. In our experience, the primary medium is often selected before the start of design, either because an organization has committed to one delivery system for all training, or because a company wants to be seen to be employing the latest technology. What might appear to be premature acts of media selection fit a new general theory of decision making proposed by Langer (1994). She suggests that calculated decision making (in any domain) may be a myth. Langer argues that the processes that are most generally understood as leading to decisions, such as integrating and weighing information in a cost-benefit analysis, most often are postdecision phenomena, if they occur at all. Instead,... information gathering is undertaken to make options that appear the same, look different. The information search ends when one reaches a cognitive commitment. Cognitive commitments are frozen or rigidly held beliefs that unwittingly are unmodulated by context. Once a cognitive commitment is reached, choice follows mechanically, without calculation.

"OBJECTIVE" APPROACHES TO MEDIA SELECTION

Kemp, Morrison, and Ross (1994) suggest that there are three different approaches to media selection: (a) selection based on what is readily available; (b) selection on the basis of what a trainer is most familiar with or most comfortable using (this assumes that a human trainer is the principal medium); and (c) selection on a more objective basis whereby some guidelines can be followed so that selection can be justified in a nonsubjective manner. The problem is that most existing objective guidelines are questionable. Even the authors of popular media selection models emphasize the lack of theory and research to support their recommendations. For example, Anderson (1983) prefaces the second edition of his book on media selection with the statement that "Media selection is NOT (and may never be) a precise science...charts are simply intended to organize that activity in a more systematic and thorough manner". Romiszowski (1981) states that there is no reason why the reader should agree with the selections he makes for particular examples in his book, "as some of the questions [to be answered during the decision-making process] call for value judgments". Kemp, Morrison and Ross (1994) state that "although each of us might answer a question differently and end at a different place in a diagram, the decision would be acceptable as long as you can justify the answer to each question as you proceed". Gagne (1965) suggested that "most instructional functions can be performed by most media". Schramm (1977) also argued that most media have "a wider spectrum of usefulness than is sometimes appreciated".

Media selection rules based on anything other than practical considerations are difficult to justify because there is no evidence that any medium either (a) makes a unique contribution to learning or motivation or (b) cultivates unique or transferable cognitive skills. Any measured achievement gains found in media studies can be attributed to uncontrolled differences in the novelty of the media, the content of the programs being delivered, and the instructional methods embedded in the programs. Taking the most extreme position on media, one might be tempted to suggest that if media do not matter in terms of instructional effectiveness, then perhaps how media are selected may not matter either, as long as the organization can bear the cost of the media selected.

One would like to think that organizations applying systematic or objective approaches would make "better" decisions than organizations making decisions based largely on intuition or experience. Unfortunately, there is little research evidence to support the superiority of systematic selection. The only two published studies we find that have attempted to examine the relative merits of media selection models and intuitive approaches produced conflicting results. Romiszowski found that novices using media selection models made "better" decisions about training media (as judged by educational technology experts) than advanced experts who used their past experience. Braby found that an intuitive approach was judged to be as "useful" as the most useful of the ten systematic models compared.

Existing Media Selection Models

There have been no studies of the relative value or utility of different media selection models. However, it is generally agreed that there are more similarities than differences among existing models. We refer the reader to Reiser and Gagne (1982), Romiszowski (1988), Main and Paulson (1988), and Heidt (1989) for comprehensive reviews of existing models. Heidt (1989) concluded his review of existing approaches as follows:

None of the models developed to date can be regarded as an easy-to-handle satisfactory instrument. Some only identify factors, which should enter the decision-taking process, while others suggest procedures, in which usually a sequence of difficult operations ends in some commonsense decision. Research so far has not been successful in discovering how the factors commonly agreed upon as relevant should enter the selection process nor what the consequences of alternative media decisions really are. Because of the complexity of educational situations, the selection remains a matter or subjective good judgment based on the consideration of a large list of potentially relevant factors.

Companies such as AT&T (American Telelphone and Telegraph Company, 1987) and the military have documented their approaches to media selection. Some organizations have created menu-driven computerized tools based on existing paper-based flowcharts, matrices, worksheets and checklists. However, whether paper-based or computer-based, there is often a dissociation among the media selection inputs, outputs, and the process of matching the inputs to the outputs. Often factors recommended as inputs are not included in the decision-making tools. For example, Reiser and Gagne (1983) recommended matching media to different events of instruction, but they did not include events as decision points in the flowchart and worksheet they provide for implementing the process. AT&T's (1987) approach to media selection includes factors such as objectives, tests, and instructional strategies as inputs, but how media might be matched to these is not discussed. With such gaps in the documented procedures, one wonders how users fill in the gaps as they move through the stages of the selection process.

Two-stage process of media selection. Existing media selection models generally conceive of media selection as a two-stage process. The first stage involves the selection of a set of candidate media to match task, trainee, and instructional event characteristics. The second stage involves selecting among the candidates based on practical considerations such as relative cost and convenience. Before describing in more detail the selection criteria and rules embodied in existing media selection models, we will first consider how these models portray the outputs of the selection process, (i.e., how they depict what is being selected). We will argue that there has been a tendency to blur the distinctions among media, media attributes, and methods, and that the first step toward a more rational approach to media selection involves clarifying those distinctions.

What is being selected? Most media selection models conceive of their outputs as subsets of a laundry list of alternatives that mix individual delivery devices such as radio, chalkboard, human trainer, or computer; gross categories of media such as broadcast media, print media or multimedia; and media capabilities or attributes such as audio, motion, or two-way communication. Many lists of media options also include items that refer to either what is being delivered (e.g., demonstrations, simulations, diagrams, or concrete models), or the kind of activity in which the trainee is engaged. Some authors divide the list into categories. For example, Cantor (1988) used a three-level categorization which consisted of twelve generic categories (such as television, audio, and computer-assisted instruction), some major variants within each category (for example, variants within the television category were video cassette with linear playback, video disc, and interactive television with logic), and finally, specifically identifiable devices or processes within each variation. Seels and Richey (1994) classified media into four types: print media (which present text and graphics), audiovisual media (which present auditory and visual messages), computer-based media, and integrated media (which encompass several forms of media under the control of a computer).

Twenty years ago, Heidt (1975) highlighted many of the problems inherent in attempts to list or classify media that might constitute options for delivering training. He noted cases where categories were too broad; for example, he thought that still pictures neglected instructionally important differences between an illustration in a book, a slide, or an overhead projector transparency. Heidt also noted superfluous distinctions such as the distinction between film-strip and slide. He pointed out cases where some of the media listed could not exist independent of other media, for example programmed instruction. Heidt suggested that some approaches allowed for hardly any specific discrimination between media and non-media.

Recently, variables such as interactivity, learner-control, linearity, and learner-centeredness have been associated with particular media or categories of media. Interactivity is often associated with computers, but not other media. Computers certainly permit immediate two-way communication between trainees and the system; however, two-way communication can be accomplished by a combination of what might traditionally be regarded as one-way (i.e., non-interactive) media. For example, a trainee could complete a hands-on assignment and be videotaped while doing it; the videotape could be mailed to a human who views the videotape and generates an oral, written, or videotaped critique, which gets delivered to the trainee at a later date. While this use of media may seem cumbersome and an inefficient way to provide coaching, there is evidence that such delayed feedback may in fact be more effective than immediate feedback, if retention and transfer (as opposed to speed and accuracy of performance during training) are the goals.

Linearity of presentation and use is often associated with print and audiovisual media, while non-linearity is portrayed as a feature of computer-based and integrated media. Linearity is really a two-dimensional attribute, one dimension pertaining to the linearity of the format in which the material is stored, the other dimension pertaining to the extent to which the material can be accessed randomly. Instructional material may be stored in a fixed sequence, for example in a book or an audiotape, but the information can be accessed in a non-linear manner. Learner control is also a multidimensional construct, encompassing dimensions such as control over sequence and pacing, control over information access, and control over number and type of contexts for practice.

One media classification system which avoids the association of variables such as interactivity and learner control with particular media is that of AT&T (1987). AT&T divides media into six categories: visual media, audio media, printed media, physical objects, human and situational resources, and computers. The only problem with this scheme is that computers can deliver audio and visual material and so encompass audio and visual media. Humans can also deliver audio material, or at least verbal material orally. What distinguishes humans and computers from other media is their ability to monitor a students' behavior, and generate or prescribe a response to that behavior.

Media, media attributes, or methods. In our view, there are two main sources of confusion in lists of media options and attempts to categorize them. The first source of confusion is a lack of distinction between media and methods; the second is a lack of distinction between media and media attributes. It is important to separate instructional methods, media attributes, and media because one cannot make direct links between media or media attributes and the psychological processes involved in learning. However, one can link instructional methods to cognitive activity. What aspects of training can be directly linked to media and methods. Media influence access to training, cost of training (development and delivery costs), and efficiency of training in terms of time to learn; methods primarily influence learning and motivation, although they may also influence efficiency of learning. For example, providing immediate feedback (an instructional method) may increase the speed with which learning occurs. Clark (1994) has argued that all methods can be formatted for delivery in a wide variety of media, with different consequences in terms of access, cost, or time to learn, but with similar learning consequences.

Instructional methods. An instructional method is an external representation or activity that supports an internal cognitive process necessary for learning. Different levels of support are possible depending on the extent to which one wants to reduce the cognitive processing burden on the learner. A method can only be defined in terms of the cognitive process or processes it targets. For example, a key cognitive process in learning is the compilation of procedures by analogy to examples. The presentation of worked examples or demonstrations during training are methods that facilitate this process. Another key cognitive process in learning is the ongoing monitoring of the state of one's knowledge in relation to a goal. The provision of practice activities and the detection and reflection of errors in performance are methods that support this process.

A cognitive process that optimizes the investment of effort during learning is the maintenance of a perception of the task as a moderate challenge. Methods can monitor and modulate both objective and subjective perceptions of difficulty. Objective difficulty can be adjusted by adapting the complexity of the task a trainee works on, or the amount of scaffolding provided during task performance as a function of performance on the current task, so that the current task is most likely to be just at the edge of the trainee's zone of proximal development. Subjective perceptions of difficulty can be monitored by asking students direct questions or watching for verbal and physical cues from the learner. Verbal strategies, such as commenting on the difficulty of an upcoming task can be used to manipulate the trainee's subjective perception of challenge. None of the methods previously described are media-specific, but they do require media that can permit the ongoing monitoring and adaptation of what is presented to trainees, that is, media that possess the "attribute" of adaptability to individual trainee performance.

Media attributes. According to Levie (1989), a media attribute is a functional feature of a medium that allows the medium to transmit particular kinds of information, and to process particular kinds of trainee responses. For example, ability to transmit audio, to display motion, to display text, to give non-linear access to information, to monitor performance, and ability to deliver individualized feedback are all media attributes. Levie suggested five categories of media attributes: sensory modality (e.g., visual, auditory, tactile), symbolic modality or symbol systems (e.g,, verbal, nonverbal), design cues and codes (e.g., color, motion, shading, music), locus of control (i.e., extent to which trainees can control pace and sequence), and interactivity (i.e., extent of coordination between student responses and feedback). Kozma (1991, 1994) suggested three categories of media attributes or capabilities: technology capabilities (physical, mechanical, or electronic), symbol system capabilities (e.g., spoken language, printed text, pictures, numerals, musical scores, maps, graphs) and processing capabilities (e.g., display, reception, storage, retrieval, organizational, translation, transformation, and evaluation). A media selection process based on media attributes would match attributes to instructional requirements and then search for a set of media that possessed the necessary attributes.

Media. A medium is an instructional resource that incorporates a cluster of media attributes or capabilities (Kozma, 1991). Different media combine different sets of attributes. Some media have a broader range of attributes or capabilities than other media. For example, "multimedia" consists of a computer-based integration of a large number of information presentation attributes, such as video, audio, graphics, and text; a narrower range of response processing attributes, such as acceptance of selections from presented options on the screen, or acceptance of verbal responses; and all of the capabilities of the computer to analyze trainees' actions and generate responses to those actions. Interactive video combines the information presentation attribute of video with the monitoring, analysis and adaptive capabilities of the computer.

Links to cognition. A medium does not have any influence on cognition; neither do its attributes (Clark, 1983). A medium's attributes merely permit the delivery of some method that has cognitive consequences. Some authors have suggested that media or media attributes can have cognitive consequences. However, Clark (1994) argues that any learning benefits that have been attributed to media or media attributes can be traced to media-independent methods. Each new wave of media spawns a group of proponents who attempt to attach cognitive consequences to the newer media or newer media attributes rather than to methods which are the real source of the hypothesized cognitive effects. Interactive video and hypermedia are two of the latest media types that have been associated with learning benefits. Hypermedia are media that share the attributes of non-linear structuring of and/or access to information. This information can take many forms including text, pictures, video and audio, depending on the other attributes of the particular medium. Books are a form of hypermedia since they provide non-linear access to information, but recent interpretations of hypermedia have associated this type of media almost exclusively with computerized banks of information.

If we categorize non-linear structuring of and access to information as media attributes, then we should be able to identify an instructional method or methods those attributes can deliver. Two different instructional methods have been linked to the non-linear structure and access attributes of hypermedia. Spiro et al. (1992) suggested that having learners explore the same units of information from multiple perspectives induces the acquisition of a denser, more flexible network of knowledge about that particular domain. Thus, the instructional method facilitated by hypermedia might be support for acquisition of dense, flexible knowledge. The media attribute that facilitates delivery of this method is non-linear access. Another instructional method facilitated by hypermedia, according to Jonassen and Wang (1993), is support for acquisition of expert-like knowledge structures. By structuring information in a set of hyperlinks that reflect the semantic network of experts, learners are likely to internalize a similar semantic network.

The Cognition and Technology Group (1990, 1993) have used interactive video as a means to deliver anchored instruction, facilitating learners' acquisition of knowledge that is situated in contexts similar to those in which they will be expected to use that knowledge. The interactive video portions of their programs, for example, the Jasper Woodbury mathematics series, could be delivered in other media. The critical media attribute in this case is the ability to present scenarios or problems in a realistic situation. The goal-based scenarios employed extensively in Andersen Consulting's training programs were adopted as a non-media-specific approach ; however, Andersen Consulting is increasingly using multimedia environments as an efficient way to combine the attributes necessary to present realistic scenarios, provide on-line informational resources, and to monitor and coach trainees when necessary.

Before outlining a media selection model where media attributes are linked to separate components of training, we will first consider how existing media selection models advocate matching their lists of media options to tasks, trainees, and instructional events. The main characteristics of existing media selection models and the limitations of the models.

Matching media to task types. Many media selection models, for example, Reynolds and Anderson (1991), and AT&T (1987), advocate matching media to Bloom's (1956) three-way categorization of learning tasks: cognitive, psychomotor, and affective. However, the distinction is not sustained in the flowcharts and diagrams to guide the decision-making process, giving the impression that task differences make no difference to the kinds of media that could be used to train them. Flowcharts, diagrams and checklists, which accompany the models, focus on matching media to instructional requirements of tasks in general, requirements such as the need for interaction or motion visuals. No guidance is given on what might lead one to decide that a particular task requires the use of motion or still visuals. This is not surprising given the inconsistency of research on the effects of different types of presentation on learning, and the fact that most studies do not examine the differential effects of different media or presentation modes on different types of learning outcome.

Recent research indicates that it is the manner in which types or modes of presentation are combined (and not the mere presence or absence of a particular mode) that influences cognitive load and processing during the encoding of information. For example, presenting the commentary on a diagram in auditory mode rather than in text beside the diagram seems to reduce the load on working memory. Mayer and Sims suggest that concurrent presentation of two representations facilitates the making of more referential connections between the visual and the verbal representation, which in turn facilitates transfer. This dual-coding theory is not dependent on task type.

In general, there is little empirical evidence that any particular type of information is absolutely necessary for the learning of any task. For example, it is not clear if is it necessary to see a real demonstration of a procedure; a stylized sequence of still images might be enough to convey the nature and sequence of the steps to a trainee. A trainee may be able to fill in the gaps and attempt to do the procedure after seeing only the still images, or possibly having seen only a verbal description of the steps. In fact, less complete representations may induce deeper cognitive processing.

Theories of situated cognition would suggest that the greater the authenticity of the context in which a trainee practices the skills being learned, the greater the potential for transfer. However, the extent to which a practice activity should have physical and functional fidelity to the real situation is unclear. In the first stage of learning a skill, that is, the stage of controlled processing, less fidelity may facilitate the construction of appropriate procedures for task performance. During the second stage of skill learning, where sequences of actions and decisions become associated with task stimulus conditions, greater fidelity may aid transfer of the procedures. Thus, it may be that media attributes need to be selected to match different stages of learning (regardless of task type) rather than to different types of task.

Reiser and Gagne (1983) suggested matching media to Gagne's five categories of learning task: verbal information, intellectual skills, psychomotor skills, cognitive strategies, and attitudes. However, Reiser and Gagne's specific recommendations for media were related not to five task types but to a two-way distinction between tasks that require a trainee to learn to do something (intellectual, psychomotor and cognitive strategy objectives), and tasks whose objectives are that the trainee should be able to state or believe something (verbal information or attitude objectives). This two-way categorization of tasks is similar to the distinction between declarative and procedural knowledge. Declarative knowledge can be thought of as knowledge "about" things or knowledge "that" something is the case. Declarative knowledge helps one answer "what" and "why" questions. Procedural knowledge is knowledge that links goals to conditions and actions for achieving the goals. Procedural knowledge helps one take actions and make decisions in particular situations.

According to Reiser and Gagne, tasks with "do something" objectives require media that permit precise corrective feedback. Reiser and Gagne listed portable equipment, simulations, computers, programmed texts, and interactive TV as media appropriate for training intellectual and motor skills. They recommended motion picture, slide/tape, TV, filmstrip, printed text, surface layouts, models, mockups, and audio as media suitable for training attitudes and verbal information. Reiser and Gagne assumed that the learning of verbal information (or declarative knowledge) did not require monitoring and precise feedback; thus, a medium that could deliver information only would be sufficient.

In contrast, we would suggest that all tasks require information presentation and practice, and that media selection decisions should be based on the type of information and practice a particular task requires. For example, if the task being trained is how to operate a piece of machinery, then some medium will be needed to provide information on how to operate the machine. In addition, either the machine itself or a computerized simulation of the machine will be required for practice, and some medium will be needed to provide feedback during or after the practice. If the task being trained involves stating reasons why a customer should purchase a particular item, then a medium that can provide information about the reasons, and a medium that can facilitate and monitor the practice of communicating these reasons to customers will be needed. Thus, a simple classification of tasks as "doing" versus "stating" does not lead to clear media choices.

Considering each task separately is preferable to classifying the task in order to narrow media choices. Some tasks may have elements that involve using particular senses (i.e., touch, hearing, sight, taste, or smell). For example, when troubleshooting a problem in a car engine, one may have to distinguish among different sounds that might come from the engine; therefore, a medium capable of reproducing those sounds may be required during information presentation and during practice to facilitate transfer to the real situation. On the other hand, if the task requires a trainee to handle customer complaints in a telephone company, it may not be necessary to present visual and auditory representations of the customer. The text of the customer's verbal responses may be substituted during both demonstration and practice. Thus, the range of media for presenting information and providing opportunity to practice is extended for this particular task.

Matching media to individual differences among trainees. Most media selection models recommend matching media to individual differences among trainees. However, the models differ in the number of individual difference variables they consider important. Only two learner characteristics, reading ability and experience, are considered important in Reiser and Gagne's (1983) model. Certainly, reading ability should determine the amount and level of textual material included in a training program, which in turn may suggest different media. However, the idea of matching media to trainee's "experience" is less clear-cut. Reiser and Gagne defined experience as level of accumulated knowledge and cognitive strategies. Taken together, these probably indicate the extent to which a trainee can learn in a particular domain without external support. That this is what Reiser and Gagne had in mind is evident in their recommendation of more self-instruction via computers, programmed text and interactive TV for trainees with more "experience" and use of a live instructor for trainees with less experience. This assumes that a live trainer can and will provide more of the kind of support required by trainees with less prior knowledge and cognitive strategies than can other media. That may or may not be the case. For example, intelligent tutoring systems may be equally (or more) capable of monitoring individual trainees' performance, and adapting the training accordingly on an individual basis, than a human trainer.

Cantor (1988), like Reiser and Gagne, recommended matching media to the prior knowledge and processing resources of trainees. Cantor suggested that learners with low prior knowledge and/or processing resources require more graphical presentation of information and concrete illustrations. We are not aware of any research to support such a specific recommendation. Research suggest that lower ability students benefit from greater elaboration of information during instruction, and such elaboration can take a number of forms.

Romiszowski (1988) proposed a long list of individual differences that should influence media selection. In addition to "experience with the topic", he included IQ, motivation, ability to learn from verbal or visual material, mechanical ability, preferences for visual versus verbal information, understanding of particular symbolic language, attention span, and physical disabilities as trainee characteristics that may restrict media choices. From that list, physical disabilities are the only learner characteristics that clearly limit the choice of media. The other variables relate to cognitive and affective differences among learners. The interactions between these "aptitude" variables and any instructional variables are extremely complex, and few, if any, are media-specific. For example, learners with lower general ability learn more in structured learning environments because such environments have been found to reduce the cognitive-processing burden on the learner. However, structure can be provided in any medium.

Romiszowski (1988) acknowledged that we do not know enough to make recommendations about which media are appropriate for different learners. Nevertheless, he made many specific recommendations. First, he suggested that learners with below average IQ or a lack of prior experience related to the topic should be given more realistic representations (e.g., working models or films rather than still visuals) of phenomena than learners with average or above average IQ or learners with relevant prior experience. Romiszowski also suggested offering options so that learners who have preferences for audio or visual presentation can select the medium they prefer. Recent research by Plass, Chun, Mayer, and Leutner (1996) supports Romiszowski's recommendation. Plass et al. found that presentation modes interact with learner preferences to influence both encoding and retrieval processes; only learners with a preference for visual information benefited from having access to visual information in addition to verbal information. This suggests that for information presentation, the choice of media should be reserved for the learner. However, this would increase the cost of development, since more than one representation of the same information would have to be created.

One problem with matching instruction to learner preferences is that a trainee may prefer a particular medium or mode of information representation, but may underestimate the amount of mindful effort required to master the learning goals in that medium.

In general, trainees benefit from instructional presentations and activities that lead them to engage in cognitive activity that is essential to acquisition and application of the knowledge involved in task performance. For example, if one suspects that trainees will not pay attention to critical changes in a system as some operation is performed on the system, then those changes should be highlighted in some way, (e.g, either with verbal or graphic cues). Many media might facilitate such cueing. If a trainee is unlikely to recognize the naivete of a personal theory about the relationship between two variables, (e.g., force and motion), then the trainee should be confronted with evidence to contradict that naive theory as a first step toward acquiring a more accurate theory (White, 1992). Such instructional support for cognitive processing can be provided by a variety of media.

Decisions regarding which trainees need more or less support for cognitive processing in a given program are important because trainees who do not need support may learn less when an attempt is made to replace their idiosyncratic and successful cognitive strategies with less familiar competing strategies. When the strategies employed in instruction match a student's own strategies, then learning is increased (Shute, 1992). Thus, interventions supporting cognitive processing should only be given to those who need them, and should not be in conflict with a student's own strategies. This suggests that one of the key attributes that should be included in any mix of media selected to deliver training will be the capability to monitor performance and adapt interventions to the needs of individual trainees. Research on adaptive instruction indicates that such instruction can (a) reduce training time by up to fifty percent and (b) is more effective and efficient when the adaptation is based on trainees' performance on recent tasks within the training, rather than on global or pre-task estimates of ability.

Matching media to instructional events. The most productive and valid approach to media selection, in our view, is to select media based on their ability to support essential components of training (often called instructional events), which in turn support essential cognitive activities. Various models of instructional events have been suggested, for example, Gagne's (1965) classic nine events of instruction:

- gaining attention,
- informing the learner of the objective,
- stimulating recall of prerequisite learning,
- presenting stimulus material,
- providing learning guidance,
- eliciting performance,
- providing corrective feedback,
- assessing performance, and
- enhancing retention and transfer.

Romiszowski (1988) proposed a simpler distinction among three essential elements of instruction:

- transmission of information about the task to the learner,
- transmission of information about the learner's current state of expertise in relation to the goal back to the system (based on the learners' performance on practice activities), and
- provision of corrective feedback to the learner.

While many authors have recommended matching media to events of instruction, few have elaborated on how that might be done.

The most common events of instruction to be analyzed and matched to media are the presentation of information, and practice activities. Romiszowski (1988) and Cantor (1988) both matched media to type of information, particularly the sensory channels through which information must be encoded during task performance. For example, if sounds were an integral part of the task, then a medium capable of transmitting live or pre-recorded sound would be required. Cantor (1988) distinguished among twenty-one physical characteristics of the information that could be presented during training. He grouped these twenty-one characteristics into six categories: visual form, movement, color, scale, audio, and "other". The "other" category consisted of three characteristics: tactile cues, external stimulus motion cues, and internal stimulus motion cues. In a chart, Cantor indicated which types of media are capable of delivering information with each of the twenty-one physical characteristics. This level of detail seems unnecessary for decisions that are fairly obvious. For example, if you want trainees to view some still pictures of different types of chemical processes, then any medium that can deliver pictures can be used; if color is an important component of the process, then a medium that can display color pictures may be necessary.

As for the aspects of practice that dictate media, both Romiszowski's and Cantor's models suggest matching media to response types. However, they differ in how they classify response types. Romiszowski distinguished among three types of responses: motor responses and perceptions; verbal responses (including naming, identifying, discriminating, and classifying); and complex verbal responses (including induction, problem solving, and deduction). The theoretical basis for this set and classification of response types is not clear. For example, why is problem solving classified as an instance of a complex verbal response? Would a verbal response be the only way to demonstrate problem-solving ability? Why would simple verbal responses require different media than do complex verbal responses?

Cantor distinguished among ten types of response modes during practice that would influence the selection of media. Those response modes are covert response, multiple choice, short answer, free style written, decision indicator, voice, fine movement manipulative, broad movement manipulative, tracking, and procedural manipulative.

It is not clear why one should distinguish between these particular types of responses in order to select appropriate media. Neither is it clear what all of the media recommended as appropriate for different types of responses have in common. For example, the media checked as appropriate for handling decision responses are instructor, telephone conference, interactive television, teaching machines, simulator, computer-assisted instruction, and real environment. It is not clear how these media differ from the media recommended for handling multiple-choice responses: instructor, printed material, audio tape, still film, television, teaching machines, and computer-assisted instruction.

In addition to matching media to types of trainee response during practice, Cantor matched media to the form, content, and timing of feedback. Romiszowski did not offer specific guidelines for matching media to feedback variables. Cantor's finer distinctions among feedback variables are confusing; for example, the difference between diagnostic data and correct response data is not clear. Neither is it clear why "branching printed material" would permit feedback based on "correct response data", but would not permit feedback based on "diagnostic data". Could not correct (and by implication, incorrect) response data serve as diagnostic data?

Romiszowski's and Cantor's models are useful in that they represent a first step toward a new generation of media selection models that will focus on matching media to components of training. What they lack is a theory of cognitive process, instructional method and media attributes that could guide and justify links between media and functions of training.

Selecting media based on cost and other practical considerations. In existing media selection models, the final stage occurs once one has narrowed the options based on the requirements of the tasks, trainees, and training events for a particular training program. A final selection is made from the short-list based on the practicalities of development, delivery, and maintenance — practicalities such as time, resources, and budget. Existing media selection models vary in the level of guidance they give regarding compilation and analysis of information relating to practical factors. Some models merely list questions or factors that should guide final selection. Other models (e.g., Braby, Henry, Parrish, & Swope, 1975; Collins, Hernandez, Ruck, Vaughn, Mitchell, & Rueter, 1987) provide worksheets and computerized tools to aid data compilation and analysis of the relative cost of media mixes on the short-list of candidates. Since monetary value can be attached to development and delivery time as well as resources, the final selection of media boils down to an analysis of the relative cost of each alternative media mix.

Any analysis of practical factors is based on projected rather than actual costs since the analysis occurs before development and implementation. The reliability of estimates of time, resources and costs will increase as an organization gains experience with development and delivery via different media configurations. However, when considering a newer set of media, it is difficult to make reliable estimates, and to make valid comparisons with an older set of media for which mechanisms and facilities are already in place for development and delivery. It is also difficult to provide context-independent guidelines on the relative time and costs of development and delivery of different media mixes. Variables such as the content and design of a particular program, size and location of audience, life span of the program, suitability of existing facilities, experience of personnel, and salaries of developers and trainees will influence the cost for a particular program. The cost of producing and delivering the same training program for the same set of media will vary from company to company. The cost of producing and delivering two different programs with the same set of media within the same company may also vary.

Given that costs must be estimated on an individual case basis, the most useful approach is Levin's (1983) ingredients method. Ingredients are resources required to develop and deliver a particular training program to a designated trainee audience. This method involves identifying all ingredients in the development and delivery of the training, for each alternative media configuration. Then a cost or value is attached to each ingredient (even those that appear to be "free"). Finally, the costs are summed for each media mix. Levin advocates categorizing ingredients as personnel, facilities, equipment, materials and supplies, and all other resources. The "all other resources" category can include maintenance of hardware, updating of materials, and training of personnel. Equipment costs, Levin suggests, should be amortized over their projected lifetime. Lost opportunity costs are also included as ingredients; for example, a value should be placed on classroom space since it could have alternative uses were it not being used for training. In addition, cost of trainees' salaries for the training period should be included as an opportunity cost since trainees are not working during this period.

Head and Buchanan (1981) suggested a method similar to Levin's ingredients method, whereby student costs, instructor costs, facilities costs, administrative costs, and development costs are calculated separately, then totaled to obtain an estimate of the overall cost of a particular training program. One can arrive at a total cost for the program given a particular number of trainees, or one can generate a cost per trainee, as is done by Hewlett Packard in a computerized package that prompts the user to enter development and delivery resource costs for alternative media.

MEDIA FOR USE THROUGHOUT THE FULL SPECTRUM OF CONFLICT

General. In an armed conflict and during military operations involving UK Forces, the Ministry of Defence (MOD) aims to provide the media with a range of facilities to enable reporting on operational and tactical military and Defence-related activity. In addition, the Department will seek to understand editors' and correspondents' requirements and provide an accurate, objective and timely information service.

Conflict Definition. The context in which modern conflict is conducted is wide, varied and complex. In most instances the operational setting will be Joint (combining land, air & maritime forces), usually will be part of a wider coalition and increasingly will include the input of other government agencies or departments. The breadth of operations will vary between peace and war and will change over time in terms of type, scale, complexity and intensity. Referred to generically within military circles as the *Spectrum of Conflict*, the predominant campaign themes and operations UK forces.

General Engagement Principles. At the outset of any developing crisis or conflict, the MOD will seek to provide media engagement opportunities including briefings by ministers, officials and military officers, visits to units and/or facilities as appropriate. The purpose of such facilities will be to explain Defence's role in any broader UK government or alliance response to a developing situation; including detail on and possible access to any UK elements preparing for deployment. The MOD will subsequently seek to provide regular updates on the progress of operations to keep the British public and international audiences informed.

MOD Guiding Principle. All media engagement under the Green Book will be guided by the core principle that the safety and security of British Service personnel should not intentionally, directly or indirectly, be jeopardised by any media activity or engagement.

Alternate Sources. The MOD recognises that correspondents are free to look for information in the area of operations and to communicate it back to the public. However, it is important to understand that this implies no specific obligation on the part of UK forces to protect individuals or installations over and above the rights of all civilians working in conflict zones set out in the Geneva Conventions and their Additional Protocols. The MOD additionally recognises its obligations as a UN signatory to respect the professional independence and rights of journalists, media professionals and associated personnel as civilians.

CONTROL OF INFORMATION RESTRICTIONS ON REPORTING

Correspondents must accept that in the conditions under which they will be operating the appropriate operational commander has the right to restrict what operational information can be reported and when. Correspondents will be advised on current restrictions (which will differ from operation to operation) by the nominated Media Ops officer, acting on behalf of the senior commander. Clearances should be attained from Media Ops staff on the suitability of information to be reported especially if given access to restricted areas, such as operations rooms and communication centres. Subjects that correspondents may not be allowed to include in copy, or radio or television reports without specific approval may include at least some of the following:

a. Composition of the force and the locations of ships, units and aircraft.
b. Details of military movements.
c. Operational orders.
d. Plans or intentions.
e. Casualties.
f. Organisations.
g. Place names.
h. Tactics, details of defensive positions, camouflage methods, weapon capabilities or deployments, force protection measures.
i. Names or numbers of ships, units or aircraft.
j. Names of individual servicemen, Prisoners of War or names of hostages and their families.

CONTROL OF THE RELEASE OF INFORMATION

In the interest of the security of the force and of the individual, correspondents must accept that they may be required to submit all written material, voice items intended for radio or television, films or video recordings produced for television, associated scripts or voice accompaniments, and still photographs for security checking clearance before transmission. Details of how this will be applied and actioned will be given by the nominated Media Ops officer.

The purpose of security checking material is to ensure that no information is inadvertently made public which might be of benefit to an enemy, or would endanger an operation, or the lives of British or allied Service personnel or civilians. It is not to constrain journalistic freedom or expression.

Security checking will be exercised in theatre. It will be an operational function of the UK Force Commander and will be conducted by a senior member of the theatre Media Ops staff. The MOD will not impose a second tier of checking in London. Matters of taste and presentation will be for the media - although the MOD reserves the right to make its views known and make representations to editors where particular sensitivities arise. The aim will be to achieve a system which is fair, enlightened and efficient, and to establish a relationship with the media based on openness and co-operation, leading to understanding of what is and what is not genuinely operationally sensitive.

Wherever possible, Media Ops staff and commanders in London and in the theatre of operations will explain the reasons why information cannot be given, or must be delayed. They will not attempt to deceive journalists or use them in furthering deception plans, although there will be occasions when operations are mounted to deceive the enemy when their true purpose will not be disclosed. The MOD recognises that views on what is and what is not of security value are subjective and that individual checking officers may apply different judgements. However, it will strive to achieve a system which is fair and even-handed. In the field, Media Ops staff will represent the views of correspondents in cases of disagreement, and will liaise with senior officers in theatre, and with the MOD, to ensure that decisions are made for appropriate operational reasons.

In the UK, editors should be aware that analysis of events and capabilities by well-informed specialists, such as academics, or retired officers and officials, could be of assistance to an enemy. They are requested, therefore, to take special care when inviting speculation from such experts.

Embargoes

To preserve operational security and for the convenience of the media, there may be occasions when editors or correspondents are provided with operational information on the understanding that it will be embargoed. This will prevent information being published that would be of value to the enemy but will allow early briefing of the media when it would otherwise not be possible, thereby giving the media time to prepare material, or to plan for an event. The MOD undertakes not to use an embargo unnecessarily or for other than operational reasons. The reasons for its imposition will be explained, wherever possible, at the time it is declared and it will be in force for the minimum amount of time necessary.

It should be understood that this will mean at times that a correspondent in theatre might be entrusted not to communicate information even to his or her editor until the expiry of the embargo. This will be made clear at the outset of the embargo by Media Ops staff. Information supplied under embargo implies considerable trust. Breaches will, therefore, be viewed very seriously and may result in loss of accreditation and withdrawal of all facilities.

CASUALTY REPORTING

The MOD will seek to maintain close co-operation with media organisations during hostile operations on the question of casualties. It recognises that casualty information is of legitimate interest to the media and the public but faces the difficulty that reports of casualties from individual operations could be of intelligence value to an enemy and potentially breach patient confidentiality. Given these sensitivities, casualty reporting might be subject to theatre specific restrictions and therefore embedded correspondents are to take advice from Media Ops staffs on arrival in theatre. The term casualty refers to fatality, injury or illness or personnel accounted missing. There may be occasions when the MOD will be forced to delay the release of fatality information for security reasons; in general it will aim to make announcements of fatalities as soon as possible after they are confirmed and next of kin have been informed.

Non-fatal injuries are not normally reported when linked to a specific incident. In the interests of transparency, the MOD will at regular intervals publish statistics on non-fatal casualties. The rationale for this difference in reporting between fatal and non-fatal casualties is to preserve the medical confidentiality of the sick and wounded. For example, a serviceman who has suffered an injury on operations may wish to withhold the detail in order to avoid causing undue distress to their family at home.

Casualty numbers will be provided by the relevant category e.g. as "killed (died on active service)", "injured", or "missing". It is unlikely that the MOD will be able to give details during the course of operations about the individual circumstances surrounding all casualties.

It may be necessary for the MOD to identify an individual group, unit, or ship which has been lost and to give details of the scale of casualties and/or survivors before next of kin have been informed - either to minimise anxiety which might be caused to families whose loved ones are not involved, or to counter enemy propaganda. The names of fatalities will not be released or confirmed until the next of kin have been told officially and have been given a reasonable further period of time, usually 24 hours, to inform their wider families.

Once the next of kin have been informed and the 24 hour period has elapsed, the names, ages, marital status, units, and home areas (not addresses) of those killed will be announced by the MOD in London. Due to the sensitivities attached, unless specifically authorised by MOD correspondents should not show images of casualties or hospitalised personnel which could allow that individual to be recognised, even if only by close family and friends. As a general principle even long distance shots of wounded personnel or the circumstances in close proximity to a casualty, should not be used without close consultation with media operations staff in theatre.

Journalists may become aware of the names of individual casualties before official announcements are made. Editors are strongly urged not to publish such information, gained from whatever source - even if it comes directly from a family member - until it is released or confirmed by the MOD in order to protect the next of kin. The question of "missing" personnel poses particular problems in this respect. In some circumstances it may be necessary for the MOD to withhold information about missing personnel for a considerable period - e.g. if a rescue operation is planned, or there is the likelihood they will evade capture. Editors should be aware that the simple act of reporting that an individual is missing could be of significant value to an enemy. Similarly, personal information published about a missing serviceman could assist potential interrogators if he were to be taken prisoner.

Access to ill or injured personnel in the operational theatre or returning from theatre will only be permitted in specific circumstances requiring express prior authorisation by a senior clinician who is satisfied that the patient is capable of giving proper informed consent and by the patient giving that consent. Seriously injured patients will generally be judged unable to give such consent at least until the acute phase of their treatment is complete, which will normally be some time after repatriation in the case of UK casualties. The restrictions on reporting on patients being treated by UK medical personnel or in UK facilities apply irrespective of the nationality of the patient.

The MOD's overriding concern is to ensure that the families of those killed, wounded, or missing should not be subjected to undue distress and that the medical confidentiality of patients is preserved. The MOD strongly urges editors not to approach next of kin in the immediate period surrounding a fatality and to be suitably cautious and sensitive when doing so thereafter. It is highly recommended that the first point of contact in all such cases should be the MOD Press Office who can advise as to whether the family are ready and willing to engage with media. Editors are also requested to ensure that their staffs do not approach the welfare organisations and casualty "helpline" services which will be set up to assist the families of servicemen during times of armed conflict. Direct enquiries could seriously hamper the work of these organisations. Casualty information and information about welfare activities will be available from the MOD Press Office. Media facilities with the welfare organisations will be arranged by the MOD Press Office and Media Ops staff in the commands if required.

INTERVIEWS WITH THOSE PRONE TO CAPTURE

Correspondents must be aware of additional sensitivities and operational security issues associated with operational roles that are more prone to capture and therefore must follow guidance and advice provided by Media Ops staff when either conducting interviews or preparing reports. Topics and issues to be avoided might include:

a. Any linkage between names and addresses (either home-base or home-town).

b. Showing aircrew in flying suits which bear names, squadron badges or flying brevets.

c. Film or photographs which reveal constituted crews. Shots of individuals are acceptable, as are shots of crews mixing together.

d. Details of operations - e.g. heights and speeds employed, sortie frequency, time on task, and so on.

If the above guidelines are adhered to, there is no requirement to avoid showing faces; the following areas are perfectly acceptable:

a. Film and photographs of aircrew and ground crew:
   (1) Briefing and debriefing (avoid crew linkage).
   (2) Walking to/from their aircraft.
   (3) Cockpit shots showing strapping in/unstrapping.
   (4) Refuelling and arming aircraft.

b. Film and sound interviews focussed on the stated aim of the detachment, and general information about life on the detachment.

c. Interviews may be given by the detachment commander, aircrew and ground crew, provided that the individual from whom the interview is to be obtained agrees to the request.

PRISONERS OF WAR

The numbers of prisoners of war or detainees and the circumstances under which they are taken is a matter of legitimate public interest - but such publicity is constrained by the terms of the Geneva Conventions. Specifically, Article 13 of the Third Geneva Convention of 1949 protects prisoners of war from insults and public curiosity. In essence, this prohibits the public transmission of images of prisoners of war either as identifiable individuals or which undermine their personal dignity.

The MOD and the UK Armed Forces will, therefore, attempt to provide accurate and up-to-date information and, where possible, will allow filming and photography to illustrate the scale and nature of capture. However, they will not offer any facility, or co-operate in any media activity, which contravenes the Geneva Convention. Interviews with prisoners, or close-up photography which focuses on individual prisoners will not normally be permitted. Media Ops staff will work closely with accredited correspondents to enable them to act prudently and discreetly when reporting on prisoners of war, bearing in mind the effect of publication or transmission of their work on prisoners of war or their families.

The names of enemy prisoners of war and enemy dead held by UK Forces will not be made public by the MOD but will be released to the International Committee of the Red Cross (ICRC) in accordance with the terms of the Geneva Convention. The ICRC will normally divulge names only through official government channels or to the next of kin. The names of UK military prisoners of war, or those killed, whose bodies are held by the enemy, will normally be announced by the MOD once official confirmation has been received from the ICRC. Until that time, either their names will not be released, or they will be listed as "missing."

INITIAL MEETINGS WITH EDITORS AND MEDIA ORGANISATIONS

General. As a crisis evolves and/or when military action/activity is either anticipated or already taking place in the case of enduring operations, the MOD's Head of News will have discussions with editors and media organisations. The dialogue will continue, as necessary, as events develop.

Agenda. Discussions will be in line with provisions outlined in this document and will cover practical and policy issues of mutual concern, including:

a. Assignment opportunities and media facilities.

b. Safety issues; including medical and training.

c. The MOD's security requirements.

d. Practical constraints on numbers and allocation of places for correspondents.

e. Pooling arrangements.

f. Accreditation.

g. Relations with the UK's coalition partners/Allies, where applicable.

h. Communications and emission control.

i. General advice for editors and correspondents to assist their own preparations.

j. Other cross government briefings.

Prior to and during any engagement or assignment, media organisations and their correspondents will be briefed as required so that a regular exchange of information is maintained, with the aims of ensuring that the overall situation, including any operational response, is understood and that the British public and international audiences can be kept abreast of developments and events.

MEDIA OPERATIONS STAFF

General. In the event of a new crisis or conflict, specialist Media Ops staff will be dispatched to the theatre of operations with the first troop deployments to assist with the provision of media facilities and the dissemination of information at UK and Allied/Coalition headquarters, and with units in the field. Their role is to support the military commander in the execution of his mission. The Media Ops staff will endeavour to ensure that correspondents are provided with sufficient information, access and facilities to enable the media to develop a coherent understanding of the key issues involved and to pursue storylines as required. Media Ops staff will continue in this role throughout the subsequent and enduring phases of the operation.

TYPES OF ASSIGNMENT AND MEDIA FACILITIES

A range of media facilities may be offered by MOD/Media Ops staff in either the operational theatre or UK. These may be one or a combination of the following:

a. Press Conferences.

b. Interviews.

c. Briefings.

d. Visits.

e. Unit/sub-unit attachments, which can include:

(1) Embed Assignments: Correspondents who are attached to specific units/sub-units (either as temporary embedded media or War Correspondents).

(2) Centralised Assignments: Correspondents who are assigned to Press Information Centres (PICs)/ Media Ops Teams at centralised/formation locations.

(3) Individual Assignments: Correspondents who are working independently but participate in individual MoD/Media Ops staff arranged facilities.

Safety Advice

General. The MOD recognises and understands the concerns of correspondents working in operational areas and other hostile environments regarding their own safety and protection. Correspondents who gain access to operational areas, other than under the auspices of MOD or Media Operations staffs, do so at their own risk. The MOD and Media Ops staffs can neither be held responsible for their safety nor guarantee to provide assistance.

Risk. Media representatives need to recognise that operations, and particularly those involving war-fighting, create extremely hazardous environments in which lethal force may be employed. In the often challenging situations that this engenders, mistakes resulting from mis-identification, weapons systems failure or mallocation may result. It is also important to understand that UK Forces on operations will not deliberately target individual correspondents.

Liability. Media representatives at all levels need to understand the challenges the military faces in working in often confused and fluid environments, and accept that blanket protection of media personnel will not be possible. Accordingly, correspondents who expect to work in these types of environment should be trained in risk evaluation and the fundamentals of working alongside the military.

There are a number of incidents when correspondents' have put themselves in danger through their own lack of understanding or knowledge. The responsibility rests with the individual and/or the individual's employer to ensure that they are appropriately prepared, physically and mentally fit, trained and insured for the assignment.

Minimum Required Standards. Entry standards of health, fitness and training for those wishing to embed with British forces will differ from theatre to theatre.

For each operation the MOD will conduct an environmental assessment to determine the levels to be attained. Advice on the requirements for a specific theatre should be sought from the MOD at the earliest opportunity since it may take individuals a number of weeks to attain the necessary standard to embed. Details of the minimum standard of health and physical fitness that must be attained for all operational theatres when deploying. Media organisations should maintain close and regular contact with the Media Ops staff in MOD especially if employers or correspondents have concerns about the standards recommended.

Security

The MOD's Head of News will maintain a dialogue with media organisations with respect to security and security checks. If required, written guidance will be issued on security matters. This document sets out the principles governing the activities and conduct of correspondents attached to UK Forces.

In addition, if required, a 24-hour advisory service will be maintained via the Duty Defence Press Officer, who editors may consult if in any doubt about security issues; such as personal security concerns, OPSEC issues or pre-deployment clearances and vetting questions.

Accreditation

Accredited Correspondents. All correspondents on operational media assignments with UK Forces are to be accredited under the provisions of the MOD's Green Book. Once accredited, correspondents can be embedded to UK forces either on a temporary embed basis or as a War Correspondent.

General Principles. Accreditation will be at the discretion of the MOD, which reserves the right to decide on numbers and to withhold or withdraw accreditation. However, the MOD accepts the importance of accrediting a broad range of media reflecting a variety of opinions. The reasons for any restrictions and/or limitations on numbers will be explained.

Accreditation Numbers. Where it is necessary to cater for mass media access, the MOD will decide on the number of correspondents that can be safely and appropriately supported on any particular operation or facility, taking account of operational and practical constraints in each instance. Where possible, representatives of the UK national and regional press, news agencies, broadcasters, specialist media and international media, will be included in every operation or facility with the aim of ensuring fair and balanced representation from each category of media.

Selection. Having announced how many places are available for each category of media for an operation or facility, the MOD believes that the choice of which titles and individual correspondents should represent each category should be left to editors and media organisations. In the case of the press, the Newspaper Society, the Society of Editors, the Newspaper Publishers' Association and Scottish Daily Newspaper Society, in consultation with editors, will be invited to select which newspapers will be allocated places on each facility. In the case of the broadcast media and agencies, where there are no corresponding associations, representative managements will be asked to reach mutual agreements. Editors of all titles selected will be expected to nominate individual correspondents. The MOD does not intend to be involved in this selection process unless news organisations are unable to reach agreement.

Application Process. For all visits to UK forces deployed on enduring operations, accreditation should be obtained by application to the Media Ops team within the MOD DMC. By exception, application can also be made by correspondents already within the operational theatre directly to the deployed UK Media Ops staff; referred to as embedding by *Passing Trade*. On Coalition/Allied led operations, the accreditation of media representatives may be carried out either through national or Coalition/Allied channels. Alternatively, host nations may insist on registering all media at national centres. All successful applicants will be expected to attend a pre-deployment brief given by Media Ops staff (MOD or within theatre) to discuss details of the assignment and individual suitability to deploy. Waivers to this requirement will only be authorised by the MOD, DMC Media Ops staff.

Fitness Standards. When selecting correspondents for facilities in the front line, editors should have regard to their health, physical fitness, stamina and ability to endure difficult, dangerous and often extreme environments. Commanders on the ground will have the right to refuse access to a unit and the MOD may refuse access to theatre for an individual considered on grounds of fitness to be likely to jeopardise operations or the safety of personnel.

Embed Aims. The purpose of embedding correspondents with units and formation headquarters is to enable the media to gain a deeper understanding of the operation in which they are involved, particularly through access to personnel and commanders. They will be afforded all possible briefings and other facilities, including the opportunity to accompany British troops during war-fighting operations. Their individual requirements will be met wherever possible. In return, they are likely to be subject to some military orders and training, both for their own safety and that of the unit.

Unit Assignment. Once assigned to a particular unit, formation, ship or air base, it will not normally be possible for embedded correspondents to move between units. However, in some circumstances, they or their editors may apply for their representatives to be re-assigned or replaced and, if it is practically possible, the MOD will make every effort to meet this request.

Accreditation Refusal. If accreditation is refused, the MOD will inform the respective media organisation or individual, explaining the reasons for refusal. This also applies in cases where accreditation is withdrawn or where an individual is removed from an embed assignment. None of these occurrences will necessarily prejudice other nominations from the individual's organisation. Legal. Whilst embedded, a correspondent will not be classified as a Civilian Subject to Service Discipline (CSSD) under the Armed Forces Act 2006 (less, exceptionally, when individuals are passengers on a Service ship or aircraft) unless they have been formally designated under Schedule 15 paragraph 7 of that Act. CSSD however can be arranged to cover any period of embed, either by request or stipulation by persons designated by or on behalf of the Defence Council (such as a hosting Commanding Officer) if it is considered in the interests of the person, for the protection of other persons (whether or not members of any of Her Majesty's forces), or for the purposes of maintaining good order and discipline. Embedded correspondents can alternatively voluntarily request CSSD as their preferred choice of jurisdiction in view of local circumstances. Those excluded from the terms of CSSD include local nationals of the deployed theatre and those considered "ordinarily resident" locally

Paragraph 11 to Schedule 15 (Civilians Subject to Service Discipline) to the Armed Forces Act 06: Exclusions from CSSD.

In extreme cases where a non-CSSD designated correspondent's actions are assessed to be in breach of the general terms and guidelines of the Green Book, are affecting or inhibiting operational effectiveness or jeopardising the safety of service personnel, accreditation can be withdrawn/withheld.

FACILITIES IN THE UK

General. The MOD's Head of News will hold detailed discussions with editors and media organisations to ensure adequate practical provision for outside broadcast units, briefing and interview facilities and, wherever possible, to meet individual requirements. A programme of press conferences, briefings and facilities will be organised and individual briefing and interview requirements met when required and deemed appropriate.

Briefings

General. In the UK and dependent on the operational

situation in theatre, the MOD will consider briefings in various forms, depending upon the scale of the operation:

a. High level meetings with editors or senior editorial staff to resolve operational and facility difficulties and as an aid to understanding strategic thinking and the background to events.

b. A 24-hour media enquiry service provided by the MOD Press Office.

c. A 24-hour high-level MOD advisory service for editors.

d. Open Press conferences by ministers, senior officers and/or officials.

e. Background briefings for defence correspondents.

Briefing Release Caveats. MOD and military spokesmen will offer these briefings at various levels under one of the following terms. The conditions of any briefing will be stated in advance:

a. Attributable: The information is for use and can be quoted in full. It will be either "directly attributable" (where the spokesman can be identified by name), or "indirectly attributable" (where the person providing the information cannot be identified by name but can normally be described as "an MOD official ", "a UK military spokesman", etc).

b. Unattributable: The information may be used but may not be attributed to a named source, either an individual or the organisation involved. Hence, for example, "military sources", or "Whitehall sources", but not "Ministry of Defence sources", or "1 Armoured Division sources".

c. Background: the information is given to aid greater understanding. It will be stated at the time whether it may be used but, if used, may not be attributed in any way, except as though from a journalist's own knowledge.

d. Not for Use: The information may not be published and is given only to aid greater understanding. The term "off the record", is sometimes misinterpreted, misunderstood and misused. It should not be employed.

Other Assignments

Additional categories of association with a unit or formation may be covered under the following auspices:

a. Structured Visit. A formal, deliberate programme, most likely by invitation or grouped for specific events or purposes. Structured visits are most likely to be supported once enduring operational status has been achieved. These visits will invariably include significant Other Government Department (OGD) input.

b. PR projects. Assignments principally sponsored by the single Service Public Relations (PR) branches within DMC in support of wider and for longer term MOD initiatives. Individuals deploying will be covered by separate contract arrangements, the Green Book or a combination of the two. This will be decided on a case by case basis.

c. "Passing Trade". Applications made by both international and domestic correspondents already in a theatre of operations under independent means and made through the deployed theatre Media Operations staff. All applications will be subject to the normal practices and procedures concerning the granting of assignment status.

War Correspondents

General. Correspondents accompanying UK Forces during an International Armed Conflict will need to be accredited to the armed forces if they are to attain the special status provided for them by Art. 4A(4) of the Third Geneva Convention. This will mean that as an accredited 'War Correspondent' they will be required to carry an identity card as a means of proof of such authorisation. War Correspondents will also be provided with distinguishing media insignia while working with units in the field. They will not be permitted to carry arms.

Deployment Notice. Prior to deployment, War Correspondents will be placed at a number of days or hours of notice to move. The period of notice will alter as the situation develops. When placed on notice to move, War Correspondents will be expected to prepare themselves so that they are ready in all respects.

Embed Locations. Subject to conditions at the time, the MOD will aim to embed War Correspondents with UK combat units as a multi-discipline group of about five to seven accredited correspondents assigned to an individual combat unit; in ships at sea, with naval taskgroups; or at air bases.

Embed Conditions. Embedded correspondents will live and work alongside soldiers, sailors and airmen, sharing their food, accommodation and basic domestic chores. Within operational constraints, embedded correspondents will be given as many front line facilities as possible.

Hosting. The host unit will be responsible for assisting embedded correspondents with the dispatch of material, subject to the prevailing controls on emission, and for arranging security checking.

Embed Caveats. Whilst the MOD recognises there is an undeniable interest on the part of the public in the progress of an armed conflict involving UK forces, and that War Correspondents should be free to communicate this, there may be exceptional circumstances when it is necessary to place limits on this freedom. War Correspondents will not be 'controlled' by an MOD 'minder'. Nevertheless, there maybe occasion when circumstances necessitate the accompaniment by Media Ops personnel on certain issues and journalists will be required to submit their material for security checking and to undertake not to publish or divulge any operationally sensitive information gained as a member of a unit, without specific permission of commanders. In addition they will have to agree not to cover events from the opposing side at any stage, without the prior agreement of the MOD.

War Correspondent Status. Each correspondent's status as a War Correspondent will be protected by the issue by the MOD of internationally-recognised identity cards. This accords correspondents a specific status under the terms of the Third Geneva Convention and gives them (officer status) prisoner of war protection should they be captured. In other words the War Correspondent must be treated as a prisoner of war when captured, while at the same time keeping the status of civilian when accompanying British Forces on one essential condition; they must carry on them authorisation issued by the UK military authorities.

Pooling

General. Pooling arrangements will apply whenever demand exceeds capacity on a facility. In such cases, the MOD will endeavour to provide as many places as possible, so that all forms of media will be represented.

By making a wide range and number of facilities available and by adopting the pooling system, both in the UK and in theatre, it is intended that editors will be represented fairly and the media will gain a complete overall picture of events from a variety of sources.

Selection. News organisations, editors and correspondents will have to agree among themselves about matters of style and presentation, resolve any differences about selection and representation and establish mutually acceptable working practices for pools and distribution of material. Editors whose representatives accept a pooled facility will be asked to make their own arrangements for making material available to the rest of the media.

Output Sharing. If pooling occurs it will mean that all written material and photographs and unabridged copies of broadcast tapes and film produced by all correspondents resulting from the facility will have to be made available to all media outlets on request.

MOD Adjudication. The MOD does not wish to interfere in matters of working practices or representation and selection, except in cases of unresolved differences among the media, when it may be forced to make the decisions in the greater public interest.

Pool Coordination. Wherever possible, pooling arrangements will be made at news organisation/editor level but, at times, facility opportunities may arise in theatre at short notice. In these circumstances, the MOD would expect that arrangements with the media will be made locally by the Media Ops staff through a "pool co-ordinator" appointed by the media corps in theatre

DEPLOYMENT PREPARATIONS, ASSISTANCE WITH TRAVEL AND LIFE SUPPORT

General. Preparations for deployment, precise travel and life support arrangements, which will apply for each assignment, will be determined by the MOD in consultation with editors, their correspondents and freelance correspondents in advance of each assignment. Supplementary guidance and specific deployment standards/requirements specific/unique to individual theatres will be issued by the MOD as required. The following paragraphs provide general amplification.

Fitness Levels. As a guide, correspondents must possess a standard of medical, dental, physical and mental fitness that equates to MOD civilian personnel or contractors deployed to the operational theatre.

The MOD does however recognise the need to be able to embed correspondents who might not necessarily automatically have comparable standards of fitness and health of those within the military. So long as there is discussion between the individual and the MOD prior to their embed, base standards of fitness and health are able to be modified or even waived on a case by case basis.

Medical Fitness. The details of minimum standards expected for travel to all theatres, including important vaccination and anti-malarial requirements are contain. In all cases, correspondents are expected to seek medical advice from their doctor prior to travel in order to attain appropriate medical judgement on an individual's suitability to deploy. All deploying correspondents must be in possession of an in date medical certificate (valid for 3 years) and personal medical declaration.

Physical Fitness. As a minimum standard, individuals will be expected to be able to complete a 1.5 mile course wearing body armour and carrying a day sack with 6kg weight plus their helmet, in clothing and footwear to be worn in theatre within the following times:

Serial	***Timings***	***Grade***	***Remarks***
1	0-22 mins	Green	Lower risk candidate
2	22-25 mins	Amber	Medium risk candidate
3	25 mins +	Red	High risk candidate; will need to be assessed on a case by case basis

Personal and Public Liability Insurance. All deploying correspondents are strongly advised to possess full health and Public Liability Insurance. In cases of individual liability, the MOD will seek to recover from individuals or their insurers the full costs for any emergency support provided.

Pre-Deployment and In-Theatre Training Requirements. Deploying correspondents will be required to conduct appropriate training. Training requirements and standards will vary according to the environment and theatre to which they will deploy, and importantly, the nature of their programme.

As a guiding principle, those who wish to deploy to the front line and accompany troops on high risk military tasks will be expected to have a higher degree of recognisable training than correspondents who opt to cover events within the confines and lower risk environemnt of a base. Accordingly, there will be two tiers of pre-deployment training and a third tier of embed specific training delivered only to those sponsored to undertake high risk activities :

Tier 1 - Low Risk. Receipt of a generic MOD Safety and Security briefing (through the medium of an MOD issued DVD; 40 minutes home study). This training essentially gains correspondents entry into theatre and allows them to base/ operate at secure locations. All embeds are to receive this brief.

Tier 2 – Medium Risk. Attendance and completion of any recognisable Hostile Environment (HE) Training course (valid for 3 years). This will allow correspondents greater freedom to both travel and accompany military activities within theatre.

Tier 3 – High Risk. Correspondents have to have completed tier 1 and 2 training requirements in order to undertake this High Risk module and the validity of training last only for the duration of the embed. Tier 3 training will be delivered in theatre by the hosting unit and provides an appropriate moment to assess both fitness and suitability of the individual to undertake any planned programme. Early MOD engagement can provide the outline on what the hosting unit both has planned and the levels of fitness needed to get the most from the visit. Attempting to detail and standardise levels is difficult and goes against the MODs aspiration of developing closer working relationships with correspondents.

Certification. Details of training conducted and completed should be recorded on the embedding correspondents Green Book application. There is no pass or fail requirement.

Visas. Correspondents will be responsible for making their own arrangements to obtain any visas that may be required. MOD Media Ops staff will be able to advise.

Travel to Theatre. The MOD will endeavour, if possible, to provide military transport to and from the theatre of operations (normally from the UK) for correspondents on embed and centralised assignments where no reasonable alternative exists.

Transport within Theatre. The MOD will provide transport for correspondents on embed and centralised assignments. Correspondents on independent assignments will be expected to make their own arrangements to get to media facilities, but they may be offered transport between media facilities.

Food and Accommodation. Correspondents on embed and centralised assignments will be provided with food and accommodation by their host formation/unit. However, a charge may be raised for these. Correspondents on independent assignments should expect to be self-sufficient and not rely on the military for support.

Communications Equipment. Correspondents will be expected to provide their own communications and transmission equipment. If absolutely necessary, assistance with communications may be given using military or MOD-controlled civil facilities. However, since the actual act of transmission could endanger an operation, or the safety of a unit under some circumstances, the use of both military and correspondents' own equipment will be at the discretion of commanders. Charges may be raised for the use of Service equipment.

Medical Fitness and Treatment. Correspondents on MOD-arranged assignments are entitled to receive Service medical treatment free in the operational area, but will be charged for such treatment outside the area. In an International Armed Conflict, any sick or wounded correspondent would be entitled to medical treatment under the Geneva Conventions and Additional Protocols, see for example the definition of "wounded" and "sick" under Article 8(a) of Additional Protocol I, in conjunction with Art. 10, or Common Art. 3(2) to the four Geneva Conventions, and Art. 7 of Additional Protocol II.

Casualties. If an accredited correspondent is killed or injured whilst on an MOD-arranged assignment, the MOD will inform his or her employer as soon as the information is confirmed. It will be the employer's responsibility to inform the next of kin. The MOD will assist with arrangements for the repatriation of the dead or injured, however the MOD may seek to recover its costs. If judged appropriate, the MOD, without prejudice, will help with enquiries into the circumstances surrounding a death or injury.

Dress and Equipment. Accredited correspondents embedded with UK forces will be expected to equip themselves with their own personal protective equipment (e.g. body armour, helmet as advised by MOD). Correspondents will wear appropriate civilian clothing as specified by PJHQ instructions, non-military patterned and neutral in any colour (including body armour and helmet covers), that ensures and maintains their status as non-combatants. On occasion, they may be issued with specialist protective clothing (along with any required training in its use) should the environment or situation demand. When accredited as War Correspondents they will be fully clothed and equipped with standard issue military items, and distinguished from combatants by means of distinctive media shoulder titles/armbands.

THE POSITION OF THE NEWS MEDIA IN CONFLICT AND SERENITY

The role of the news media in political conflicts has been a major area of concern in the field of political communication for many years. This interest has grown in recent years, perhaps because the centrality of the news media in terrorism and wars has become increasingly evident to even the most casual of observers. The role of the news media in attempts to resolve conflicts, on the other hand, has received much less attention. The influence of the media in peace processes is more subtle, in part because what is not reported in the press is in some ways even more significant than what is covered.

This article will be devoted to suggesting some basic theoretical principles that can be used to explain the varying role of the news media in both conflicts and peace process. Looking at these two topics together provides a broader understanding about the ongoing interactions between the political leaders and journalists and the ways in which these relations can change over time and circumstance.

The discussion will center on four central claims: 1) The influence of the news media during a conflict or a peace process is best seen in terms of a cycle in which changes in the political environment lead to changes in media performance that often lead to further changes in the political environment. 2) The greater the level of government control over events associated with a conflict or a peace process the more likely the news media will play a supportive role. 3) The greater the ability of a government to mobilize and maintain a high level of political consensus in support of its policies, the more likely the news media will play a supportive role in the process. 4) Due to the nature of news, the ability of governments to mobilize the media in support of wars is far greater than their ability to mobilize the news media in support of a peace process. The first three arguments are intended to show how researchers can use similar theoretical constructs in dealing with both issues while the last claim focuses on where the two models diverge.

Taking Control over Events

Modern governments spend a great deal of time and effort to maintain control over the political environment. Among the most important aspects of control are the ability to initiate and maintain control over events and ability to regulate the flow of information. A good example can be learned from the 1991 Gulf War. The coalition of governments who fought against Saddam Hussein was in an extremely favourable position to take control over the events associated with the war because Iraq was unable to mount much of an opposition. In addition, the fact that the conflict was almost entirely an air campaign and that western journalists were given very little access to the war zone provided the allies with an unusually high level of control over the flow of information. It should also be kept in mind that there was a huge international interest in the story Gulf War story and only the American military and their allies were in a position to supply the needed information.

Most wars however, are much more difficult to control and as governments loose control over the events, they also find it difficult to maintain control over the news. The most recent examples are the ongoing war in Iraq and the Second Lebanese war between Israel and the Hezbollah that took place in the summer of 2006. In both of these conflicts the many losses suffered by the Americans and the Israelis and the ability of the other side to carry out successful attacks seriously undermined the attempts by these governments to convince the news media and the public that they were winning.

The same principles can be applied to governments attempting to promote a peace process. The inability of the Rabin government to prevent Palestinian terrorism during the Oslo process insured that the most important news narrative was being constructed by the Palestinian opposition movements.

A contrast is provided by the two other peace processes: the process leading up the Good Friday agreement in Northern Ireland and the Israeli peace process with Jordan. One of the most important achievements of George Mitchell in the Northern Ireland talks was to insist that any group that resorted to violence would not be allowed to participate in the peace talks. There were also serious sanctions for any party who leaked details of the talks to the press. Similarly, a tight lid was kept on Israel's negotiations with the Jordanians because both sides were concerned about the negative impact of leaks. There was also no violent attacks carried out by those who opposed the Jordan-Israel peace process, and this too meant that there were no dramatic stories to undermine the narrative being promoted by the two governments.

Politics-Media-Politics

It is helpful to begin by putting forth a central principle that explains the cycle of influence between politics and the media. The Politics-Media-Politics (PMP) principles is formulated as follows: The influence of the news media on conflicts and peace process is best seen in terms of a cycle in which changes in the political environment lead to changes in media performance that can lead to further changes in the political environment. It is not a chicken and an egg problem; politics almost always comes first. A useful rule to follow in these matters is to start by looking at a particular political context, attempt to understand how political actors and journalists interact within the situation, and then examine how the resulting news stories influence the process itself.

The major reason for starting with political factors is that there is very little the news media initiate on their own. They react to events and reflect the cultural climate in which they operate. Consider for example the political changes that took place in the United States during the Civil Rights movement. For many years, there was little political support for equal rights and the media mostly ignored the issue. As pointed out in Lee's (2002) important work it was the political activism of grassroots organizations that led to a change in public perceptions concerning the need for change. The American news media did not spontaneously "discover" the issue of civil rights; their willingness to deal with the issue was a reaction to what was happening in both the South and among political elites throughout the country.

This is not meant to suggest that the news media should be considered passive conveyer belts that merely pass on what is happening to the political world. The news media have their own set of interests that determine how they turn various events into news. The influence of these interests can be best identified by examining the norms and routines associated with the production of news. One of the most important examples is the emphasis on drama which means that some parts of an event are more likely to be reported than others. This means that the in order to understand just how the political changes lead to media changes one must take into account both the political *and* the media environment. In addition, this process of translation can often have a major effect in the second stage of the PMP process in which the news media have a subsequent effect on a political process. Thus, in Giltin's (1980) study *The Whole World* is watching he found that the American news media's emphasis on the most radical leaders in the anti-Vietnam War movement increased their status and power within the group and had an important influence on movement's strategy and actions.

The news media often play another important role in this cycle. Although they almost never initiate political change, they can certainly accelerate it. Thus, as the climate of opinion began to change in the U.S. concerning the Iraq War, the fact that there were an increasing number of dissenting voice receiving an increasing amount of time and space probably accelerated the rate of discontent over the war effort. Similarly, once Western news media developed new ways of relating to minorities, women, and gays it was an indication to the general public about what was now considered politically appropriate attitudes and behavior. There can be little doubt that without such widespread publicity such social changes would have taken much longer.

There are some exceptions to this general principle that are worth noting. These exceptions take place when the news media initiate investigative stories that embarrass the government. An example would be the Abu Ghraib prison scandal in which pictures of Americans abusing Iraqi prisoners created a serious problem for the Bush administration. It is not clear whether this incident had any long-term effects on the administrations policies in Iraq, but it certainly made their efforts to promote the war more difficult.

The PMP principle can also be applied to the role of the news media in peace processes. A comparison between the political environment surrounding the early and later stages of the Oslo peace process between the Israel and the Palestinians offers a useful example. In the beginning of the process there was quite a bit of support for the process within the Israeli public. In the first days only marginal attention was given in the Israeli and international media to the Palestinian opposition movements – especially Hamas and the Islamic Jihad movement – who promised to derail the peace process. Once these movements were able to carry out a large number of terrorist attacks however, the Israeli news media covered them using a high degree of sensationalism. At the very least, the extensive and dramatic coverage ensured that Hamas was transformed into a major player in the process. Some would go even further and argue that this coverage was one of the reasons why this movement achieved so many of their political goals.

One way to look at this issue is to focus on a government's ability to take control over the political environment in its attempts to promote any policy. The lower the level of control over the political environment the more likely the news media will exhibit an independent, critical stance towards the government. This provides important opportunities for the oppositional forces regardless if the policy in question has to do with issues concerned with peace or with war. Lack of political control inevitably leads to a lack of control over the news story. In any given situation there are two major indicators of a government's level of control over the political environment:

the ability of the government to maintain control over events associated with the process and the ability to mobilize and maintain elite consensus in support of their policies.

The Significance of Political Consensus

The ability of antagonists to mobilize and maintain political consensus is one of the most important factors in determining the ultimate role of the news media in both conflicts and peace processes. When government policies enjoy a wide level of support the news media reflect and reinforce those views. While the amount of support among the general public is also important, journalists are much more attuned to their routine sources, who are almost all from the elite. Many wars begin with a great deal of public and elite consensus in support of a war and during these early stages the news media are likely to both reflect and reinforce this mood. However, given the fact that wars rarely run smoothly, the level of support often declines as the conflict drags on and this has a direct influence on media coverage.

Hallin (1986) was one of the first to point to this phenomenon in his important study of the role of the media in the Vietnam War. Contrary to popular myth, the U.S. news media were extremely supportive of the war effort in the early stages of the war partly because the "Cold War" frame tended to dominate media discourse. As long as opposition to Vietnam was confined to marginal groups such as college students such activists were mostly framed as deviants. As a growing number of political, military, and economic elites became skeptical about the possibility of winning the war, the news coverage moved into what Hallin referred to as the "sphere of legitimate controversy" in which the debate over the war became an important element in the coverage. A similar claim could be made about the role of the news media in the U.S.-Iraq war that began in 2003.

The same principle helps explain the role of the news media in peace processes. Here too it is helpful to compare the varying effects of elite consensus on three such processes: The Oslo peace process between Israel and the Palestinians, the peace process between Jordan and Israel, and the peace process in Northern Ireland that led to the Good Friday agreement. The Oslo peace process was extremely controversial from the start and as it progressed the Rabin government had a great deal of trouble mobilizing political consensus in support of its policies.

Two years after the initial breakthrough with the PLO the Oslo "B" agreement was signed and then approved by the Knesset by a vote of 48 to 44. The intensive and even violent debate over the peace process became one more element in a steady stream of negative news about Oslo.

The peace processes in Jordan and Northern Ireland illustrate that the news media can play a more supportive role in peace processes when governments are able to mobilize consensus. In contrast to the vote over Oslo, the agreement concerning peace with Jordan was passed by the Israeli Knesset by a vote of 92 to 3. This overwhelming support was reflected in celebratory media coverage of the events associated with the process. While the amount of support for the Good Friday agreement was less than that found in Israel concerning Jordan, the number of political parties supporting the agreement and the results of the referendum both tell us that over seventy percent of the elites and the public were in favour. Interviews with journalists and political actors and content analyses of media coverage provide convincing evidence that the news media in Northern Ireland was enthusiastic about the Good Friday agreement.

While most of the examples have looked at the decline in consensus, there are certainly political processes that run in the opposite direction. The debate over whether or not to use force against Saddam Hussein in the 1991 Gulf war, for example, was extremely intense. The vote in the Senate approving President Bush's proposal barely passed and the American press was full of criticism of the idea. Once the war began however, and especially after it proved so successful, it was difficult to find oppositional sources within the political elite and the American media became extremely supportive of the wear effort. A similar point could be made by comparing the role of the news media in earlier attempts to initiate a peace process in Northern Ireland – which did not enjoy consensus – with the Good Friday agreement.

THE INTRINSIC CONTRADICTION BETWEEN NEWS AND PEACE

The discussion till this point has emphasized the ways in which a similar set of theoretical principles can explain the varying role of the news media in both conflicts and peace processes. There is, however, one major difference between the two situations: it is generally easier for governments to mobilize the domestic news media for war than for peace. While the media will normally play a supportive role in wars – especially in their initial stages – the press is more likely to play a destructive role in attempts to bring an end to enmity.

The reasons for this difference have to do with the inherent contradiction between the "needs of news" and the "needs for peace". A successful peace process requires patience, and the news media demand immediacy. Peace is most likely to develop within a calm environment and the media have an obsessive interest in threats and violence. Peace building is a complex process and the news media deals with simple events. Progress towards peace requires at least a minimal understanding of the needs of the other side, but the news media reinforces ethnocentrism and hostility towards adversaries.

This contradiction may seem surprising given the fact that journalists in many countries are assumed to lean towards the more liberal/dovish end of the political spectrum. However, contrary to popular myth, the construction of news is not primarily motivated by political opinions but rather by commercial interests. It is far more important for journalists to write an interesting story than one that some circles consider political correct. Conflict is the mainstay of news while peace news is the exception. War is exciting and peace is (mostly) boring.

There are four criteria of newsworthiness that helps explain why conflict and war normally make for better stories:

immediacy, drama, simplicity, and ethnocentrism. The first thing to understand is that news deals with immediate events and not long-term processes. Although conflicts and wars are much more complex than suggested by media coverage, it is much easier to divide them into a serious of dramatic events. The course of a peace process, on the other hand, involves a series of secret and complex negotiations punctuated by an occasional breakthrough or crisis. This means that most of the time there is very little of interest to report.

Many of the dramatic events that *are* associated with a peace process are negative, especially when leaders lose control. Thus, during the Oslo peace process the ability of the Palestinian opposition to carry out terrorist attacks and the Israeli opposition's ability to carry out massive demonstrations generated tremendous amounts of negative news coverage. The Rabin and Peres governments, on the other hand, had little to promote to the media during the long negotiations with the Palestinians. A content analysis of newspapers stories that appeared in the first year of Olso reveals that apart from the "peace festival" associated with the first few weeks of the negotiations, every other period was marked by far more negative news than positive.

The domestic news media also employ a multitude of norms and routines that reflect an ethnocentric view of the world. The fact that virtually all of the journalists and sources come from the same national background, the fact the stories are constructed in order to be understood and accepted by the local audience as well as the extensive use of national beliefs and myths all contribute to this bias. This tendency also makes it easier for governments to promote wars. Journalists who do not exhibit sufficient "patriotism" during such conflicts are likely to become extremely unpopular.

This same ethnocentrism makes it extremely difficult for governments to promote a peace process because the willingness of a public to make serious concessions always involves a certain amount of trust in the other side. However, when the news media on both sides of the fence constantly emphasize a nationalist or even nationalistic perspective, the very idea of compromise appears dangerous.

An interesting exception to this general rule demonstrates its importance. A good deal of the news media in Northern Ireland is "shared" between Protestants and Catholics. The television and radio stations not only have a mixed audience but also employ journalists who come from both sides of the fence. While the newspapers are more sectarian, they too make an effort to appeal to as wide an audience as possible. The result is that journalists have little choice but to find a way to construct nonsectarian news that bridges the gap between the two populations.

Despite the contradiction between news and peace, there are certainly cases in which the news media become supportive of peace processes and critical of wars. The differences is that in order to succeed in promoting a peace process to the news media leaders need to be in almost complete control of the political environment. The news media can perhaps best be described as "fair weather friends" when it comes to conflict resolution: the first sign of clouds and journalists' natural preferences for negative news will have them predicting a major thunderstorm. It is also much more difficult for leaders to exploit the news media in order to turn an enemy into a peace partner than to fan the flames of hatred and suspicion that are already in place.

Some Significant Interactions

It is helpful at this juncture to take note of the ways in which the various components of political control interact with one another and how they can be linked to the PMP principle.

When governments loose control over events associated with a conflict or a peace process, it will often have an effect on the level of elite consensus. Thus, as the number of casualties in a war goes up or when a peace process flounders it will give important ammunition to the opposition in their attempts to mobilize against the government. Nevertheless, the higher the level of consensus in support of official policy, the less such problems will have a major impact on the role of the news media. A useful example of this dynamic was demonstrated through a comparison of two terrorist attacks: one in Northern Ireland and the other in Israel. The attack in Northern Ireland took place in the city of Omagh in August of 1998 and took the lives of twenty-nine people. The terrorist attack on the Israeli bus terminal at Beit Lid took place in January of 1995 and killed twenty people. While both attacks were designed to derail the respective peace processes the news media in the two countries adopted completely different ways of framing the two events. Given the fact that the Oslo peace process was already in dispute, the Israeli press framed the Bet Lid as proof that the Palestinians could not be trusted. It was clear to all that this attack provided increased the political resonance of the arguments against any agreement. A completely different frame was adopted by the Northern Ireland press after the attack on Omagh. Leaders from a wide variety of political parties, as well as the journalists themselves argued that this attack provided further proof of the need to *accelerate* the process in order to prevent such horrors from happening again. The intensity and the vehemence of the public outcry was probably one of the major reasons why the Real IRA to announced a cease-fire only 48 hours after the attack.

This suggests that the level of elite consensus is the most important variable to in any analysis based on the PMP principle. The rise or fall of political consensus has a dramatic impact on whether or not the news media adopt a supportive or oppositional position towards government policy. Level of government control over events is also important, but it is the news media is especially sensitive to changes in what they are hearing from their sources about the *meaning* of such events.

SEEING THROUGH THE CONFLICT: MILITARY-MEDIA RELATIONS

As our country moves closer to a forced regime change in Iraq, the Department of Defense should anticipate that the media will cover this next conflict with as much intensity as they displayed during the Gulf War. During the Gulf War, more than 1600 journalists converged on the Joint Information Bureaus in Dhahran and Riyadh, Saudi Arabia. We can expect no less if and when we go to war with Iraq. The question is, however, will the military be up to the task of supporting this massive convergence?

Tensions between the media have been present in our society since the Revolutionary War, but may have reached its peak of hostility during the Vietnam War. By the end of this conflict, a greater distrust and suspicion developed between the military and the media. Many in the military claimed that the news media, with its graphic portrayal of the war's brutality, lost the war for America. Many in the media counter this position by saying it was the military that, by providing falsehoods and propaganda, lost America's confidence in prosecuting the war any further. Although 30 years have gone by since the end of America's involvement in the war in Vietnam, some believe this conflict still is unresolved.

As we enter the 21st century, the world no longer relies on information but on real-time information. Today's media, with its global reach and real-time capability due to satellite technology, dominates this new information age. World leaders are now able to turn to the media for instant access to national and international incidents as they unfold, and they can do so 24-hours per day. This instant access by the media to world events now circumvents wellestablished intelligence activities and as a result, real-time media has become a part of their decision-making.

The former President Bush once told world leaders that he learned more from CNN than he did from the CIA. In addition, many people may recall seeing pictures of the current President Bush watching TV at a Florida elementary school on September 11, 2001, as the World Trade Center burned and eventually collapsed.

At the time of this writing, war is already being fought between the U.S. and Iraq, but it is a war with information. The U.S. has leveraged its use of images of troops deploying while the Iraqis are allowing unprecedented numbers of international media into its country, both sides hoping to shape national and international public perceptions and thus, public opinion. The stakes are high in this information war. What happens now at the tactical level can be leveraged by an adversary to have strategic importance and consequence. It is therefore, critically important that the U.S. military be prepared to fight what former Air Force Chief of Staff General Ronald R. Fogleman once said is now the fifth dimension of warfare...information operations.

The focus of this paper is to address only one of the key enablers to information operations—military public affairs. Former Chief of Army Public Affairs, Major General Charles W. McClain Jr., stated in an article titled "Public Affairs in America's 21st Century Army," that information would be a center of gravity on future battlefields. He added, "On the battlefield, it [public affairs] is as essential an element of mission success, as important a combat multiplier, and as critical a component of building and sustaining combat power as any of the Battlefield Operating Systems, especially when the global media is a significant element of battle space." Numerous articles, books, and even a scattering of academic research have been written during the last 10 years that conclude that there remains much acrimony to the military-media relations debate. Additionally, recent military after action reviews, that when dissected and compared with what journalists have said about the military-media relationship, produce consistent common lessons learned as to why a perceived conflict may remain between the media and the military.

Key to understanding the current debate is to review and appreciate what others have said about military-media relationships and historical events, which have guided military and media relations up to this point. After all, war correspondents for more than 200 years have often shared many of the same challenges that correspondents do today, such as a perceived lack of access, lack of support, and censorship by the military.

Prior to the 1991 Gulf War, scholarly research regarding military public affairs is rather sparse. This is not to say that articles and books have not been written that address military public affairs operations, but these works are predominately anecdotal in context and are mainly written by journalists. Nevertheless, a review of a selection of recent research and literature may provide some useful insight into military public affairs successes, failures, or challenges. In 1996, Pascale Combelles-Siegel conducted a study titled The Troubled Path to the Pentagon's Rules on Media Access to the Battlefield: Grenada to Today. In this study, Combelles-Siegel investigated the perceived military-media conflict and stated that this relationship "exploded like a bomb" during Operation Urgent Fury in Grenada. It is no secret that upon the end of the U.S. involvement in Vietnam, that many in the military harbored ill feelings toward the media. As a result, this Vietnam "baggage" carried by the media may have assured their exclusion from military operations in Grenada for the first three days.

Combelles-Siegel highlights that this exclusion not only outraged the media, but also some in the Department of Defense. Michael Burch, then Assistant Secretary of Defense for Public Affairs, said, "A combination of mistrust, poor planning, and poor execution on the part of the commander who did not realize that it would have helped the image of the operation and helped gather international support for the operation." Additionally, Navy Captain Robert Sims, spokesperson for the National Security Council, said, "Because the press was excluded, the operation received unfavourably reporting, even though it was a staunch success." Combelles-Siegel followed the military public affairs efforts from Grenada through the Gulf War and concluded on a positive note regarding the future of the military-media relationship because of 10 years of military-media compromises. Nevertheless, as hopeful as she was for a better relationship, she believed that the military still had serious shortfalls in its long-term plan to accommodate the media.

Her main concern was that the large numbers of media that cover future conflicts would overwhelm the military. She recommended that the military find some way to limit the numbers of media who cover U.S. military operations in order to provide adequate logistical support to the media. This recommendation, however, may work well in a conflict such as Grenada, where the area of operations was on an island, but it may not be realistic to believe that the U.S. military can control access to a conflict that takes place on a continent. For example, unless the U.S. could seal all the borders with Iraq it is not likely the U.S. could control the flow, if not the flood, of media into Iraq if the U.S. liberates that country.

In the book titled Distorting Defense, Stephen P. Aubin provides an interesting insight to the media's coverage of defense issues. Although Aubin's book does not specifically address the military-media relationship his research does, however, look at how the media has covered defense-related issues.

Aubin conducted a content analysis, in essence a sampling, of the major networks (ABC, NBC, and CBS) evening broadcasts of defense-related issues during the Reagan, Bush, and Clinton Administrations. He claimed that since the colonial times in America, the nation and the nation's media have been suspicious, if not openly hostile, toward defense-related issues. The American people, according to Aubin, have for more than 200 years preferred less expensive routes toward the nation's security.

Additionally, the content analysis Aubin conducted found that nearly 32 percent of the evening news coverage of defense issues was problematic. Aubin defined "problematic coverage as: general lack of balance or context; lack of context as a result of brevity; lack of knowledge on the par of the correspondent; overemphasis on drama or bad news at the expense of substance and context; loaded labeling or advocacy; and bad news judgment. The picture that Aubin paints in his historical review is that it has been and may always be a hard sell for the military to promote to the American people the importance of new weapons systems, an increase in defense spending, or the deployment of U.S. troops into conflict. If one now couples that thought with what Aubin found in his content analysis regarding problematic news coverage of defense issues, the U.S. military's public affairs has some very big hurdles to overcome in telling the military story. The implication for the military may be that the American people, and especially the media, will continue to be very critical of its operations. The military must understand that what they perceive as good news stories may not be perceived as good news by the American people. And, that bad news stories may be perceived as being worse than they actually are due to the more than 200 years of a predisposition by the media and by the American people.

In 2001, LTC Joseph G. Curtin, U.S. Army, conducted a Strategy Research Project titled Strategic Leaders: It's Time to Meet the Press. His research examined the media environment, challenges, and prospects for improving strategic leader relations with the press. After reviewing historical perspectives between the media and the military, Curtin stated, "Despite the lessons learned from one military operation to the next since Vietnam, the military media relationship continues to sour." I, however, do not necessarily agree with Curtin's assessment that the military-media relationship has not improved through the years. One need only watch the weekly Pentagon Press briefings or watch today's reporting of troops deploying to Iraq to see that the military-media relationship has come a long way in its professionalism since the dark days of the Vietnam War.

Despite Curtin's dour opinion of the current military-media relationship, he does believe that there is hope to improving this relationship, but only if strategic leaders take action. He recommended that strategic leaders consider:

- That the Defense Information School at Fort Meade, Maryland, designs and implements a short-course in media relations for senior leaders.
- That strategic leaders establish professional relationships with members of the press.
- That the Defense Department (DoD) reestablishes a public affairs office in Chicago.

- Evidently DoD had earlier closed down this office as part of the military's downsizing, but has kept public affairs offices open in Los Angeles and New York. Curtain saw a gap in the military's ability to reach the major media markets in the mid-West region.
- As senior leaders mentor subordinates, they should include media relations as part of that mentorship.

The Journalists

"We saw an Army public affairs system fashioned as a dead-end job career for officers and staffed with a sprinkling of incompetents put there by media-wary generals, some of whom still blame the media for losing the Vietnam War." — John J. Fialka, Wall Street Journal

The U.S. media arrived home after their stint in the Gulf War only to find that they had something in common with the Iraqi military—both had been soundly defeated by the U.S. military. President George Bush said prior to Gulf War hostilities that "this conflict would not be like Vietnam." For some in the media, President Bush was right. Unlike the war in Vietnam where the media roamed freely over the battlefield, the Gulf War media found themselves subjected to a military public affairs system that restricted their access to the troops. "On a scale unprecedented in our history, politics and propaganda became criteria in news coverage of the U.S. at war. Sensitivities governed access decisions, with the military acting as news assignment editors," said 17 leaders of the U.S. media in a protest letter to Secretary of Defense Richard Cheney in July 1991.16 These leaders condemned the military public affairs system and described the Gulf War as "the most under-covered major conflict in modern American history.

Reporters acknowledge that restrictions are necessary in wartime, but many allege the Pentagon went beyond legitimate security concerns during the Gulf War and attempted to present the American public a sanitized version of war.

John J. Fialka's book titled Hotel Warriors is also an excellent starting point for discussion when reviewing what the media have recently said about working with the military. Fialka, then a reporter for the Wall Street Journal, had covered defense-related issues since the 1970s. In the Gulf War, Fialka was one of the print media pool coordinators who had the awesome responsibility for assigning fellow print reporters to the pool.

Fialka painted a bleak picture of military support, via the military public affairs officers, to the media during the Gulf War. The military's support, according to Fialka, bordered on near collapse. Everything from a military public affairs operation that sorely lacked required resources to media wary generals contributed to what Fialka said "helped bury one of the most positive Army stories since World War II."

In an article titled "Pentagon Hardball," David Lamb, a national correspondent for the Los Angeles Times during the Gulf War, also echoed Fialka's comments. Lamb reported that the military was not able to handle the shear volumes of media who were arriving at a rate of 50 per day. He said that at one point the Joint Information Bureau (JIB) had a backlog of 1,300 requests by reporters to visit units. Because of this poor support, Lamb said that most correspondents could not get out to cover the military units and thus, were relegated to rewriting the Gulf War.

The other area that Lamb highlighted is the perceived non-support from the senior military leadership. For example, he stated that the 24th Infantry Division entered combat without one correspondent and that the unit "might as well not have existed" to Americans back home. "Younger brigade and battalion commanders—most of all, their troops—welcomed us with enthusiasm and looked on us as their link to home, many of the generals viewed us as some alien force that could be detrimental to morale and mission."

HISTORICAL PERSPECTIVES REVOLUTIONARY WAR: IN THE BEGINNING...

"They that give up essential liberty to obtain a little temporary safety deserve neither liberty or safety." —Benjamin

Franklin Colonial newspapers during the Revolutionary period may not have been well written, but they were well read. Newspapers went into about 40,000 homes, but unlike today, every word was read by a public that was thirsting for information about the conflict. Newspapers of the period also enjoyed a long shelf life as they were passed from one household to another, rarely being discarded. In essence, the local paper had become the community bulletin board. Generals fighting for and against independence quickly realized the power of the press. General George Washington, for example, used the press not only to influence public opinion and thus, public support, but also to maintain the fighting spirit of his forces. Realizing the importance of maintaining public support, both Tory and the colonialist used the press extensively for self-serving reasons during America's fight for independence. Both sides, either by force or by persuasion, used the press that was sympathetic to their cause as a tool of propaganda.

Sitting on the fence, so to speak, was not an option for the editors. Printers took unprecedented risk of not only business failure, but also of death to support their cause. Because of this partiality by the editors, Tory and colonial military forces often literally chased many printers out of business. Additionally, if the editors survived the Tory and colonial governments then they still had to deal with public opinion. The public, with strong divided sympathies between the Tory and colonial cause, often turned to mob action as a form of censorship of a printer who did not support their cause. As a result, most newspaper printers at the beginning of the conflict were forced out of business by the end of the Revolutionary War. Given the often biased and at times libelous reporting, it is interesting to note that the framers of the Constitution and the Bill of Rights would still allow journalists in the First Amendment the tremendous freedom of an unrestricted press, fully understanding how the press was used and could be used in the future.

Therefore, to answer the question posed by some in today's military of who gave the press freedom to cover and report to the American public, they earned their right in one of the most trying times in American history. In no small way, the colonial press played a very large part in saving the colonies from British oppression. As a result, the American press was rewarded for its support during the Revolution when Congressional delegates to the Constitutional Convention ratified the First Amendment in 1791.

Civil War: The Not ao Civil Press...

"Come with a sword or musket in your hand, prepared to share with us our fate in sunshine and storm...and I will welcome you as a brother and associate; but come as you now do, expecting me to ally the reputation and honor of my country and my fellow soldiers with you, as a representative of the press, which you yourself say make so slight a difference between the truth and falsehood, and my answer is, NEVER." —General Sherman to the NY Herald

By the time of the South's shelling of Fort Sumpter in April 1861, the news media went through a revolution in media technology and may have been better prepared to cover the war than the military was in executing the war. In the 30 or so years leading up to the American Civil War, the press underwent a revolution in technology and techniques in reporting. Not only did newspapers become affordable to the masses with the penny press, but publishers also became able to print thousands of newspapers per day because of dramatic advances in printing press technology. Additionally, the media led the way leveraging technology, via 50,000 miles of telegraph lines and railroads. Correspondents at the front could now observe a battle and have their story received by their newspaper headquarters within hours. At the beginning of the war, the military had not fully leveraged technology as well as the media. The military, for the most part, relied on trains that could travel at two miles a minute, or carrier pigeons that could reach speeds of 35 miles per hour. Meanwhile, the media used the telegraph that could transmit a story at the speed of light—186,000 miles per second. Despite this revolution in technology, there appeared to be no revolution in the media's professionalism. Newspaper editors found that news of battles could raise circulation five-fold. War reporters often found that "immediacy" of a story was more important than accuracy or even operational security. Both Northern and Southern generals found the media an annoyance that they attempted to control. In 1863, Northern General Joseph Hooker tried to improve the responsibility of reporting by mandating that reporters traveling with him had to use a byline that gave the reporter's name in the article, a practiced still used by today's media. Some generals, such as William Tecumseh Sherman, took a harsher way of dealing with the press by banishing them from his camps. As a result, however, General Sherman's successful operation from Atlanta to the coast went relatively unreported. And, there were some in the military who, for reasons of maintaining public morale, lied to the press. Edwin Stanton, President Lincoln's secretary of war, altered casualty figures so that the numbers looked much better than reality.

By the end of the war, the rise of professional war correspondents also brought about the rise to the military-media conflict and the stage was now set for all future conflicts. The military saw the impact that the media could have on public opinion as well as on the morale of their troops. The military also realized that they began the war unprepared for the media. There were no uniform press guidelines or trained military personnel to deal with the press. Nor, did the military leverage technology as well as the media. The military's lesson was that no matter what restraints that they might impose on the media, media will always find a way to report the war.

Vietnam: Where are the Ernie Pyle's?

"There is a tendency in the military to blame our problems with lack of (American) public support on the media. This is too easy an answer. The majority of the onthe- scene (Vietnam) reporting was factual—that is, the reporters honestly reported what they had seen, firsthand. Much of what they saw was horrible, for that is the nature of war. It was this horror, not the reporting, that so influenced the American people." —Col. (Ret.) Harry Summers

Some would think that after 30 years, the ghosts of the Vietnam military-media relationship would have been silenced by now. Nevertheless, the debate rages on in some circles in the military today just as loudly as it may have back in 1973. Today's U.S. Army War College students were too young to serve during Vietnam, but it has been interesting to observe that in many seminar discussions it seems that the ghosts of the Vietnam still live. In essence, several students often refer to today's media as being anti-military and use Vietnam-era analogies to support their positions. One seminar officer said that he even believes that all media should be under government control because they (media) cannot be trusted.

When reviewing recent articles written by American journalists, such as in CBS.MarketWatch and the Columbia Journalism Review, references to the Vietnam mediamilitary media relations are common. It appears that the media still harbour ghosts, too, because when conflicts arise with the military some in the media reflect to Vietnam. But, Vietnam was different as the U.S. military broke with previous war public affairs efforts by not imposing press censorship. According to William M. Hammond in his The Army and Public Affairs: Enduring Principles, "General William C. Westmoreland, in consultation with agencies in Washington, opted for a policy of voluntary guidelines for the press over censorship because he trusted the good will of the American correspondents reporting the war." It may have been this lack of military censorship that added to the conflict between the military and the media. The press roamed the battlefields in Vietnam with relatively no control by the U.S. military. Very similar to the Civil War press, the media of the '60s leveraged technology as Americans became glued to television for their daily news. This combination of a free press armed with television now brought the horrors of the war into the homes of America. As the war continued year after year, American's became more attuned to the sights and sounds of war and the evening news often told a different story than was being told by President Johnson's administration. This disconnect between reality and the administration's Vietnam public relations strategy may have been the catalyst that caused Americans to turn pessimistic regarding our involvement in Vietnam.

In a 1984 Proceedings article written by Richard L. Upchurch, he said, "Vietnam in the early '70s was portrayed as a war of brutal death, vice a struggle for victory and democracy. Reporters collected all the stench, gore, and never-ending suffering of war on film and brought it into the living rooms of every American who had a television. Tally boards depicting the number killed or wounded for the week kept the public constantly reminded of just how badly the war was going."

But it was more than just the typical American who turned to TV for information about the war—President Johnson had three televisions set up in the Oval Office so that he could watch all three major TV networks at the same time. The affect that television news has on decision makers was now evident at the highest levels of U.S. leadership.

GULF WAR: CENSORSHIP OR POOR PLANNING?

"One of the earliest casualties in America's desert war was the truth. The truth was wounded by an information directorate bent on controlling the words and images that flow from the battlefields and clogged the vital artery leading to America's brain."

Joseph Galloway, U.S. News and World Report - By the time the U.S. entered the Gulf War, lessons learned from the Sidle and Hoffman Commissions were forgotten or ignored by the military. The Pentagon made it quite clear that it would manage the war reporting by establishing completely new guidelines for media coverage.

Until January 1991, the media had relatively free rein in Saudi Arabia to cover U.S. military operations with the only restrictions being the actual location of troops and material. Nevertheless, in January 1991, Pete Williams, Assistant Secretary of Defense for Public Affairs, developed new press guidelines that went into effect once the war broke out in the Gulf Region. The guidelines included the following restrictions:

- All reporters in combat areas had to belong to officially designated media pools and had to be escorted by military public affairs officers.
- All stories on film filed by the pools would be subject to a "security review" by the accompanying public affairs officers.
- Information deemed by the Pentagon to be "unreleasable" for security reasons included the exact locations of U.S. military units, data on troop strength or the number of armaments, and the disclosures of downed U.S. planes or the sinking of U.S. ships.
- Written descriptions of, or broadcasts showing, severely wounded U.S. military personnel would be discouraged, but allowed.
- Impromptu interviews with U.S. military officers could be conducted only in public places and the interviews had to be "on record."
- Journalists considered physically unfit by U.S. commanders would be subject to medical evaluation from the front lines.

The Pentagon saw these rules as essential to ensure the safety of troops and the reporters. But, a well-respected journalist and former CBS News anchorman, Walter Cronkite, wrote in a February 1991, Newsweek article, "The U.S. military is trampling on the American people's right to know...but the fact that we don't know, the fact that the military apparently feels there is something to hide, can only lead eventually to a breakdown in home-front confidence and the very echoes from Vietnam that the Pentagon fears the most. Nevertheless, reporters' anger with the U.S. military may not be solely due to the Department of Defense guidelines or censorship. There are some in the media and military who believe the large numbers of the press simply overwhelmed an unprepared U.S. military public affairs effort.

According to U.S. News & World Report columnist David Gergen, the total number of media personnel in the Gulf exceeded 1,500 by the time the ground war began. All major networks (NBC, CBS, ABC, and CNN) sent their news anchors to the Gulf for on-the-spot reporting. "Experts were hired and budgets wrecked," Gergen wrote. John Fialka of the Wall Street Journal adds, "We were an indigestible lump being fed into a military press-handling system that was woefully short of resources and teetering on the verge of collapse." Pascale Combelles-Siegel states in her study of the media's access to the battlefield that Navy Captain Mike Sherman, who was the Joint Information Bureau [JIB] director in Dhahran, claimed that he not only was not resourced to run the JIB, but also that the U.S. Central Command was slow to direct units to cooperate with the JIB. "We were the bastard children of the operation," Sherman is quoted as saying.

According to LTC Robert Perrich, an Army public affairs officer who participated in Desert Shield and Desert Storm, "The bottom line is that there was no command planning or priority directed to public affairs." As a result, only about 10 percent of the accredited reporters ever made it to the front lines.

MILITARY'S AVERSION TO THE MEDIA

Whereas the first two trends are a matter of providing adequate resources to public affairs operations, the third trend may be more difficult to fix because it deals with the culture of the military. As we all know, culture is tough to change because it involves the hearts and minds of those in service. But, why after so many years since Vietnam is the military still reluctant to engage the media? Perhaps the military, although some senior leaders claim it is not so, is still in a zero-defect mentality where there is no reward for risk takers. After all, what are the gains to engaging the media when engaging the media can certainly have an immediate detrimental effect to one's career?

Many in the military still recall what happened in 1995 to Colonel Gregory Fontenot, the commander who led the first U.S. brigade into Bosnia, when he was quoted by an embedded reporter from the Wall Street Journal. Tom E. Ricks from the Journal quoted Fontenot of warning his African-American soldiers to be wary of what he described as racist Croats. Fontenot also said that the U.S. would not be out of Bosnia in 12 months, which ran counter to what the Clinton Administration was saying at the time. Fontenot was castigated not only by the administration but also by the military for his comments. This, according to Charles C. Moskos, a military sociologist at MIT, had a "chilling effect on military personnel when journalists are around."

A suggestion then, is that today's senior military leaders need to invest time and resources into transforming this media-adverse culture. It will take time, but so will the military's transformation into an Objective Force. The military cannot continue to have senior leaders setting the example by shying away from the media as their way of conducting public affairs. Because information is now global and what happens in the foxhole may now have strategic implications, it is important that we educate the masses to help in this cultural change in the military. All military schools should review their curriculums for instruction at preparing tomorrow's leaders for engaging the media. For example, during the first six months of this War College Class, there has been less than three hours of time directed to military-media relations. The War College does offer an elective for media-military relations, but it is not required. If this is truly the Information Age where the media can project real-time images of the battlefield, thus effecting strategic leaders emotions and decisions, then why is this last bastion of military schooling directing so little toward preparing tomorrow's senior leaders for the media?

As recently as 2001, the U.S. Central Command's public affairs system seems to have initially faired poorly during Operation Enduring Freedom in Afghanistan. In a December 2001 letter to the Pentagon Bureau Chiefs, Ms. Victoria Clark, Assistant Secretary of Defense for Public Affairs, apologized for "severe shortcomings in our [U.S. military] preparedness to support news organizations in their efforts to cover U.S. military operations in Afghanistan." Sifting through a review of an After Action Review provided by one of the first military public affairs units in Afghanistan, the 49th Public Affairs Detachment from the 82nd Airborne Division, may shed some light into why Ms. Clark felt compelled to apologize for the military's shortcomings to support the media during the early stages of conflict. According to the AAR, submitted by U.S. Army Capt. Jimmie E. Cummings, Jr., the detachment's primary mission was to support the media and the secondary mission was to provide command information products. Despite this being the first major ground operation since the Gulf War, the U.S. military may not have done its best to prepare this frontline public affairs unit for what would become one of the largest U.S. military news story since the Gulf War. Capt. Cummings states that the detachment essentially had five significant issues that negatively effected the execution of their mission. He lists the five issues as:

- Lack of a communications package.
- Divergent demands commanding and controlling of public affairs assets.
- Lack of detailed public affairs guidance at the frontlines.
- Institutional mistrust of media extended to Army journalists in executing missions with the 10th Mountain Division and with the U.S. Special Forces.
- Friction in strategic deploying into and redeploying out of theater.

Regarding the lack of a communications package, the detachment did not have the basic tools to communicate. Lack of dedicated phone lines, tactical FM radios, satellite phones, and even the placement of the detachment 90-minutes drive away from where the media were mostly located spelled trouble from the beginning. Not only could the detachment not get their command information products back in a timely manner, but the detachment also could not support the media. Very few of the media were willing to make the extremely dangerous 90-minute drive between Kabul, where most of the media centralized themselves to cover the conflict in Afghanistan, to the detachment's location at the Bagram Airbase. In addition, because the detachment lacked a dedicated phone line and telephone, the media did not have a military contact number to call when they needed information.

The detachment's third observation regarding the lack of public affairs guidance was probably tied to the second observation regarding the chains of command for public affairs. According to the detachment, there initially was no command or control over the public affairs operations during the critical first month of deployment. Later, the detachment was tasked organized under the Joint Special Operations Task Force, JSOTFN. Then later, the detachment operated under the Combined Force Command Land Component Commander at Bagram. These multiple chains of command provided little public affairs guidance to the detachment and when they did, it contributed to confusing the public affairs personnel as the two chains of command often provided conflicting guidance. The detachment's fourth observation may be the most troublesome: institutional mistrust of media extended to Army journalists in the execution of their missions. This comment may be a two-edged sword in that it says something about a systemic mistrust by the U.S. military in Afghanistan toward journalists that spilled over to the U.S. public affairs personnel who were in essence "guilty by association." These ill feelings toward both journalists and military public affairs personnel did nothing to ease the American people's concern of their sons and daughters who were fighting under the harshest of conditions. Just how many stories of heroics or of unprecedented military capability may never be known because of this attitude of mistrust still engrained by some in today's military.

The fifth observation, I would say, is a criticism not unique to this public affairs detachment. There may not be one commander who does not wish that the higher headquarters staff did more to support their unit during a deployment, whether the deployment was to Afghanistan or to the National Training Center. Nevertheless, the point to take away from the detachment's frustration of having to do more than their fare share of coordinating for transportation and administration support is that losing commands need to ensure that every unit, large or small, deploys combat ready. The last thing a gaining commander may want in the heat of battle is to have a unit fall under their organization and be a sponge of critical resources that should have been provided at the unit's home station.

Nevertheless, public affairs support and operations appears to have improved in the following months. By the time the 28th Public Affairs Detachment from Fort Lewis, Washington, hit the ground in Bagram in June of 2002, it seems that many of the issues experienced by the 49th Public Affairs Detachment were solved. During a review of 28th Public Affairs Detachment's AAR, the unit's chain of command was the Combined Joint Task Force-180, under the command of Lieutenant General Dan McNeil of the 18th Airborne Corps. The 28th eventually built up its command information operation to produce a daily paper, six days a week. Unlike the primary mission of the 49th Public Affairs Detachment, the 28th's primary mission was command information. This is not to say that the detachment did not support the media, because they did, but it was not their primary mission. What was not clear in the AAR, however, is if the change in focus away from the media was due to a continued institutional mistrust by the military.

8

Future of Military/Media Relations

The relationship between the United States military and the media has been a complex one for years. Like any relationship, it can be characterized by ebbs and flows, good times and bad from the perspective of both institutions. From Vietnam to Operation Iraqi Freedom (OIF), the military/media relationship's complexity has been the result of a clash of cultures. The glaring philosophical differences between the two institutions make them unlikely bedfellows. The military is a fundamentally closed society; arguably more conservative than most American institutions.

It is accountable to civilian leadership within the United States government and its mission focus is on the protection of American interests. The media by comparison is considerably more liberal. It is, with few exceptions, privately owned and accountable to stockholders with a mission of reporting newsworthy events that will either sell newspapers, magazines or airtime for a monetary profit. The goal of the American media is to write or present an intriguing story. That "attention-getter" translates to money. The military, by contrast, is not a profit making entity. It exists solely because the American public wants it to exist due to a perceived need for protection from those that would do the country harm. It's an institution funded by tax paying Americans that does not provide a service to the country that is easily quantifiable. This places it in a sensitive position: its competence can be proved to the American public only on rare opportunities. Those opportunities, more often than not, come during times of conflict. Furthermore, its success or failure reflects not only on the military as an institution but also on the administration that made the decision to use military force. The irony of this relationship is that one institution is committed to defending the Constitution of the United States, the very document that allows the other institution to ply its trade. Both are fundamental to American democracy. Despite that ironic link, the military and the media continue to have a love-hate relationship. This paper will attempt to explore that relationship, as it has existed from Vietnam through OIF, while identifying the causes for such a relationship and what it means for the future.

VIETNAM

This history of clashing cultures precedes Vietnam, but one could argue that the challenges apparent in the relationship have not changed much. This analysis will address the relationship as it evolved from that period. Additionally, for clarity, the definition of the relationship cannot always be narrowed to the military. Those governmental institutions that provide the military its marching orders; the Executive Branch of government and the Department of Defense (DOD) often affect it. Therefore, any fair assessment of a relationship between the media and the military will include the influence of such governmental institutions.

Although the cultural differences between the media and the military are significant, the relationship is affected at times by tangible and often interpersonal events. In any commitment of military force, the United States Government eventually comes to the crossroads of having to justify, or at least explain, such a commitment to the American people. The avenue for such an explanation inevitably runs through the media. This reality held true during Vietnam when President Lyndon Johnson's administration ordered an increase in American military involvement. As the conflict in Vietnam escalated from the perspective of a greater commitment of manpower, the Johnson administration found itself in a position where it had to justify such escalation. Unfortunately, when it turned to the media to present the administration's part of the story it turned to an institution that was becoming increasingly frustrated with the administration, and its apparent disdain for the media. The perception of the media was that the Johnson administration failed to treat them with respect. This was especially evident in the White House Press Corps where reporters felt they were not treated as human beings, and that there was no consideration for the reporters as people with lives of their own. By relying on routine last minute announcements of press conferences the administration hampered their travel and personal plans. It left them tied to the White House Press Room, unable to make plans of their own. This process bred contempt as the press considered themselves targets of an administration bent on secrecy. This outlook clouded their perception of how the President handled Vietnam. Johnson and his advisors were astute enough to realize they needed the media to tell their side of the story. With 5000 reporters from 60 countries covering the war at different times, they had no choice but to attempt to get their arms around the media, lest the story get told in a less than flattering way.

During the spring of 1967 Johnson made attempts to endear himself to the media, perhaps subscribing to Sun Tzu's theory that, "to know your enemy, you must become your enemy......... keep your friends close and your enemies closer." He became more forthcoming and invited key correspondents to the White House for social gatherings. This tactic appeared to pay dividends for the President as a noted reporter who lost a son in Vietnam in 1966, Merriman Smith, mentioned at a breakfast he was attending that he felt "Johnson had been treated unfairly by the press – worse than he'd seen in 25 years of covering the White House." Unfortunately, the honeymoon was short-lived. Soon Johnson was reported commenting "about sympathizing with those who would chloroform reporters, and that some reporters would rather drink hemlock than accept the truth of some of his statistics." These comments turned the press against him again. Rather than attempt to repair a failing relationship, the President lashed out. "Counted among those doubters and gloom spreaders, in Johnson's tally, were the members of the media. Unfortunately, a student carrying a sign or a protestor wearing a beard, or an attention-seeker burning a draft card in front of a camera can get more attention – and more billing – than all 10,000 of these volunteers" (referring to the military stationed in Vietnam).

This relationship degenerated as time went on, with the administration continuing to present an appearance of secrecy while the media was more aggressively questioning the methodology of the President and his closest advisors. Consequently, Johnson was unable to clearly communicate his vision of victory in Vietnam through the press to the American public. As a result, journalists' support for the war declined and they reflected their dismay in the articles they wrote.

The contentious relationship was not resident solely within the beltway. The President's ranking military officer in Vietnam, General William Westmoreland, had his own struggles with making the media/military relationship work. Despite early attempts to enhance the relationship by improving the flow of information to reporters by frequent press conferences the relationship declined as more reporters arrived in Vietnam as a result of troop increase through 1965. As the involvement of U.S. troops increased, commanders became concerned about the potential for reporters to release sensitive operational information. In the early part of 1965, General Westmoreland explored the possibility of censoring the press. The growing number of reporters in the country made that option remote. It was ultimately decided that any release of sensitive information would result in a correspondent's loss of press credentials. The end result of this "voluntary restraint" was a freedom on the part of the press never before experienced in a war zone.

The press in Vietnam had relatively free access. That access presented a challenge for Westmoreland as the relationship between his civilian leaders and the media deteriorated. As operations began, the relationship was generally strong. When things soured, negative stories made the papers and airwaves. The military and administration, hyper-sensitive about negative war publicity, lost what little trust they had in the media, effectively throwing fuel on a fire that was already beginning to burn out of control.

As the administration wrestled with the challenge of getting its side of the story out through an increasingly suspicious media, the news rolled on with stories influenced less by governmental input. Throughout the decline of the relationship Americans and the media became more aligned in their view of the war. Their shared skepticism was driven by the feeling that they were uninformed; that the United States Government was keeping something from them.

As he addressed the operational issues on the ground, General Westmoreland was undoubtedly influenced by his Commander-In-Chief's view of the media. Evidence of this can be seen in comments made to Westmoreland during a visit to Johnson's ranch after he was out of office. Johnson commented to Westmoreland that "....early in the war he should have proposed press censorship, no matter how complex the problems that might have generated." This is an indicator of how extensively the relationship had degenerated and the real level of distrust that defined the administration's view of the media. Furthermore, the timing of this comment, after Johnson's departure from government service speaks volumes about the emotional impact the strained relationship had on the president.

In the summer of 1967 a Gallup Poll revealed that 65% of Americans felt the administration wasn't telling them all they should know about Vietnam. Vietnam, in essence, became a turning point with regard to press passivity. During previous wars, the press generally deferred to the United States Government with regard to information passed on regarding military issues. As the consensus on foreign policy began to disintegrate during Vietnam, journalists began to question that deference. The media became aware that a government under pressure will not always speak the truth. This issue would have longstanding negative implications for future military/media relations and lies at the very core of the tension that has existed between the media and the military since Vietnam.

As support for the war waned, the Johnson administration's attempt to repair the damage was met with distrust by a media that was engaged in reporting on the ground, often embedded with units. The media was seeing through what they perceived to be the "spin" of the administration since they were seeing a different Vietnam on the ground than the administration was reporting. The TET Offensive of 1968 drove the point home through the media that the Johnson administration was being less than truthful in its claims that the American military was making significant progress towards winning the war.

Westmoreland's many challenges dealing with the press can be seen by comments in his memoirs that Vietnam was "the first war in history lost in the columns of the New York Times". Westmoreland was, in some ways, the recipient of the media's wrath with the administration. Instead of human-interest stories, the focus over time shifted to reports of failures of the service's rifle (the M-16), and poor morale amongst troops, and criticism of the South Vietnamese government.

Those in the military and the media affected by the relationships that were born in the fields of Vietnam often went on to assume more influential positions within their respective institutions. Reporters in the field, like their military counterparts, were elevated to leadership positions within major news bureaus. They carried their experiences with them as they moved up the organization ladder. Those experiences were often based on a significant amount of distrust. Westmoreland's contention, that the war was "lost in the columns of the New York Times" was not a unique opinion among military leaders or the administration that endorsed their involvement in Vietnam. The end result of this dynamic was a relationship built on distrust.

This contentious relationship can be traced to vast cultural differences between the media and the military. It is summed up well by Melissa Healy, a Los Angeles Times reporter that covered the Pentagon. She writes:

> I began to recognize that I was operating, for all practical purposes, as a foreign correspondent: I was dipping into a world with a language of its own, with a society of its own that, in every respect paralleled U.S. civil society. But it paralleled it; it was not part of it. It was separate. It had its own justice system, its own retail system, its own health-care system. Everything was different. It's really important to have reporters who can be on the beat long enough to understand that.......It's a culture of conservatives and of careerism in the military that sees no potential investment in talking to reporters, that truly sees no benefit to one's career. The point is that you can find few, if any, career military people who can conceive that talking to a reporter not only is in the normal line of responsibility to taxpayers, but that it could ever be of any benefit to them. They can only see the possibility that it could hurt their careers. It's a deeply, deeply inbred attitude.

The opinions of Ms. Healy certainly proved prophetic as the United States moved from Vietnam into other conflicts around the globe, namely Grenada, Panama and Desert Storm. The classic clash of cultures stemming from the obvious differences between the media and the military is striking and can be linked to challenges in each of these conflicts. The media as an institution is trained to be skeptical of authority while those in the military are expected to respect authority. Journalists generally relish their individualism, while their military counterparts are so disciplined that they appear to have sacrificed their individuality. The media see eccentricity as having its own utility while those in uniform are more likely to reject "out of the box" behavior. Given these divergent cultural positions, it should be no surprise that the two institutions have had differing opinions through the years.

PANAMA

One unintended result of the DNMP's establishment was that military commanders believed the organization would take care of itself without significant involvement of the military chain of command. This approach proved disastrous for an already strained relationship as the United States planned and executed the invasion of Panama in 1989. The Pentagon delayed sending its "pool" of reporters from Washington. Instead, non-pool reporters made their way to Panama on their own to cover the invasion.

Those chosen for the job, and sanctioned by DoD, arrived late and developed reports off of prepared DoD briefings and CNN reports from those reporters that were independent of the pool. Hence, the invasion of Panama saw the failure of the DNMP.

Left on their own, reporters without the necessary support from commanders required to operate within Panama, were only able to cover the later stages of the operation. The Pentagon did little to demonstrate good will towards the media, and the new CJCS, General Colin Powell, was compelled to put the word out to commanders that he expected their personal involvement with respect to public affairs planning and execution.

A greater emphasis was placed on Public Affairs planning after the CJCS articulated his guidance. However, the propensity of the media to cover less-than-flattering stories would keep the relationship strained up through Desert Storm. Whether it was covering military shortcomings in the way of sex scandals or cost overruns of weapons systems, the media was in search of a story. Unfortunately, that "story" was often at the expense of career military personnel. The result of this unique arrangement was a military that remained distrustful of the media. This was a military that, as Ms. Healy wrote, saw "no potential investment in talking to reporters, that truly sees no benefit to one's career".

The failure of the Pentagon to effectively balance its desire to assuage the media with its need for a coherent media strategy was a nagging thorn in the side of military/media relations. The media was growing increasingly frustrated as it was promised access that was never delivered.

GRENADA

Despite the palpable tension that continued to exist between the media and the military, public affairs personnel were not involved in the planning for Grenada. As the invasion progressed in 1983 the media made multiple attempts to cover the operation. Nearly 600 reporters from various news agencies arrived on Barbados as the operation began, hoping to cover the invasion. Surprised commanders, having not planned for any media intervention, effectively stiff-armed the media, keeping them away from the area of operations for two days. Journalists that were resourceful enough to make it to the island were detained by the military. Unfortunately, from the perspective of military/ media relations, the lack of media access only served to heighten suspicions that the Pentagon was hiding something. Grenada infuriated the press and caused them to exert a great deal of pressure on the DoD in order to preclude a reoccurrence of such an incident. The inability of the press to effectively cover the Grenada invasion, and their subsequent appeal to the Pentagon's leadership, resulted in then Chairman of the Joint Chiefs of Staff, General John Vessey, convening the Sidle Commission to investigate the best way to ensure access is afforded the media in future conflicts. The end result of this commission was the establishment of the DoD National Media Pool (DNMP). On the surface, the commission's recommendations appeared to be a viable first step towards allowing greater, and timelier, media access to military operations. The new arrangement would allow a representative pool of journalists and photographers, representing all aspects of the media, to report back from a given conflicts' area of operations to a centralized military headquarters.

OPERATION IRAQI FREEDOM

In the 13 years between Desert Storm and OIF, the military appears to have come to the conclusion, at least temporarily, that it needs the media. Although the media has no legal right to force its way onto the battlefield, the American people are not likely to tolerate a military that operates under a veil of secrecy. So, despite vast cultural differences, the military, as the controller of access to the battlefield, allowed the media unprecedented access to its operations as it set the stage for overthrowing the Iraqi regime. The interesting dynamic that defined embedded media during OIF reveals a continuing culture clash that will likely forever define the military/media relationship.

The media had unprecedented access to military operations during OIF. The term "embedded", although in existence long before OIF, became the defining word with regard to the media's coverage of the conflict in Iraq. Despite this unfettered access, the future of the relationship between those who fight the nation's battles and those who report on those battles remains in question. Countless articles published before, during and after OIF judged the embedded media program as flawed. Embedding was said to skew the objectivity of the reporters assigned to units; it was called a propaganda ploy on behalf of the Pentagon. Embedded reporters, these commentators said, could not be trusted because they were "inbed" with the military. *Poynteronline* interviewed Chris Hedges, an accomplished war correspondent with experience in El Salvador, Kosovo, and the Persian Gulf just before the ground offensive of OIF. During the interview he identified his perceived flaws with the embedded media program. Some of these point directly to the inexperience of the reporters that were embedded with units. He cited the fact that these reporters would be dependent on the military for everything, and claimed that they would not want to get very near actual combat; which he said was something that the military would "be all too willing to oblige". Part of this statement is true; namely that the majority of embedded reporters had no experience covering combat operations. However, the latter part of Hedge's opinion is flawed.

Despite the lack of the reporters' combat experience, my personal experience with five embedded reporters showed a genuine willingness to cover the most direct combat. In fact, as a battalion commander, I usually tried to appease my five embeds who all wanted to be with the first unit in contact.

Because of their willingness to confront the dangers associated with combat they developed a close relationship with the Marines with whom they moved. This relationship was predictable in that it is no secret that human beings who share a traumatic experience together tend to bond emotionally. All of my embeds developed personal relationships with the Marines of 2d Tank Battalion; relationships that would continue after the war. Despite the new found relationships, two of my embedded reporters, Mike Cerre of ABC News Nightline, and Jim Landers, of the Dallas Morning News were not only able to witness the horrors of war, but were given the "green light" to report about whatever they saw.

Cerre reported at length for ABC on 2d Tank Battalion's involvement in a five-hour firefight and an incident involving civilian casualties during the evening of 4 April 2003. At no time was he ever restrained with regard to reporting on the command, despite the nature of the subject matter. Cerre comments:

On the same day that ammo dump blew, I was involved in probably the worst nightmare for the Department of Defense concerning the embed process because I was right there when this civilian tragedy happened. The incident started when a civilian vehicle tried to come through the checkpoint and ignored the warning shots. The Marines opened fire to try and disable the vehicle – which they did. Two people were killed in that vehicle and in the backseat were women and children who were wounded........I looked up and saw the headlights of a truck. I could hear it accelerating. The Marines opened fire on it and disabled the driver. The truck careened, hit a dirt mound on the side of the road, flipped over on its side, and went right over our heads. It crashed maybe fifty feet beyond us. It was a dump truck that was beige with military painting and had military colored stripes on the radiator. The driver had an AK47 and a set of uniforms in a duffle bag in the back of the truck. But following right behind was an agricultural truck and a minibus filled with civilians. The Marines opened fire on all the vehicles as they came through the checkpoint. They killed three children and two women on the bus. Because I had such an open relationship with the unit, they knew I was going to have to make this report.

The media covering the war for the 2d Tank Battalion were given seamless access to the command's Marines as well as the story of combat as it unfolded, with little influence from the commander. Mike Cerre was the first reporter to transmit live from a ground combat unit as the battalion crossed the border into Iraq from Kuwait during the early evening hours of 19 March 2003. His timely story, portrayed to ABC News' Peter Jennings back in the states, was made possible by a commander that allowed him to report whatever he wanted, as long as it was accurate and did not compromise operational security. Jim Landers and Cheryl Diaz-Meyers, reporter and photographer for the Dallas Morning News, had the same access Cerre had. Landers wrote an article on the incident Cerre described above, and Diaz-Meyers photographed the scene. The article was published on 6 April 2003, describing the incident with the same detail of Cerre.

They carried the bodies of the children out first. There was a girl of about 12, whom the Marines wrapped in her black abaya cloak. Next off the shattered minibus was her brother, a boy of about 4, whom the Marines covered in a sports jacket. A sister, about 6 years old, had fallen between the seats. They placed her beside her siblings on a blanket.

Before releasing the article, Landers asked me to take a look at it, not because he was required to, but as a professional courtesy. I reviewed it without any intent of debating what we knew to be the facts at the time. No Marine, if given the choice, would have wanted to see either Cerre's or Lander's stories get aired or published. The Marines were not proud of what happened that evening, but it was what it was. It was the ugly side of war, and the reporters reported it.

DESERT SHIELD/STORM

As the Pentagon found itself planning to push the Iraqi military from Kuwait in 1990 a concerted effort was made by the Pentagon and the media to facilitate coverage of any developing conflict. In a continuing effort to repair the relationship with the press, the Pentagon activated the seventeen-member DNMP at the beginning of Operation Desert Shield. Despite the Pentagon's good intentions, Saudi restrictions on granting visas to reporters stymied the pool. Faced with another Panama fiasco, many reporters decided to fly into Bahrain and find their own way to Saudi Arabia.

And senior military leaders remained suspicious of the media. These suspicions, coupled with improvements in technology that allowed for more rapid transmission of stories, set the stage for another contentious military/media showdown. The Commander, U.S. Central Command, General Norman Schwarzkopf, was a Vietnam veteran. It is not too much of an intellectual leap to assume that General Schwarzkopf harbored some ill feelings towards the media from his time as a young officer in Vietnam. Evidence of this was his desire for a controlled press rather than a workable pool arrangement. "Veterans of Vietnam, they remembered not that war was messy but that news accounts made the military look inept. They had no intention of letting reporters have a clear view of the battlefield." Retired Lieutenant General Bernard Trainor, U.S. Marine Corps, believes there is some truth to this Vietnam bias. However, he concluded that the real fallout from this passing of the torch was a new generation of military officers that don't trust the media. "It is a legacy of the war, and it takes root soon after they enter service. Like racism, anti-Semitism, and all forms of bigotry, it is irrational but nonetheless real. The credo of the military seems to have become 'duty, honor, country, and hate the media'". It appears to be this credo that permeated the relationship between the media and the military during the Gulf War. As a result, the military in the Gulf was successful at "managing" the media that were sent to Saudi Arabia to cover the war. Ironically, the very way it was managed by different services appears to have redefined the relationship for future conflicts.

It was generally believed by the different services that the Army and Navy eschewed a golden opportunity to tell their story while the Marine Corps could never get enough media people in the field to cover their units. While General Schwarzkopf was restricting interviews to those reporters he liked, and Army commanders were only grudgingly accepting journalists assigned to them, Lieutenant General Walter Boomer, former Marine Corps Public Affairs Officer and the senior Marine Corps commander in the Gulf War, pushed for more journalists even as the war kicked off. John Fialka states; "The differences between the two services' skills at handling public affairs were so vast that reporters sometimes wondered whether they represented different countries".

The Navy also forfeited a big opportunity in the Gulf War by allowing every ship commander the option of deciding whether or not he wanted media coverage. Although the media desired to cover battleship involvement in the war, the commander of the USS Iowa refused to allow media on his ship. Although the Iowa was a significant supporter of the offensive effort through Naval Gunfire support of ground maneuver, its actions and those of its crew never received media coverage.

In contrast, America witnessed many minutes of video provided by the Air Force of precision-guided munitions striking their intended targets as well as Marine Corps units arriving on the outskirts of Kuwait City. What was largely missed were the largest tank battles since World War II because of the Army's reluctance to allow media to go along during 7 Corps' attack. Although never quantified, it could be argued that the inability of Americans to see the relative value of the Army's contribution to the Gulf War could only hurt when the service competes for its share of a limited Defense Department budget.

The military/media relationship has evolved over the years, driven largely by a desire on the part of the media establishment to open the door into a society that it feels is too secretive; a society that they may never truly understand. It is likely that the process of embedding media will continue in future conflicts. The proverbial cat is out of the bag and any attempt to put it back in is likely to result in the Pentagon getting "clawed" by the media. For the Pentagon leadership it has become a "damned if you do, damned if you don't" scenario. After being criticized by the media for not providing enough access to combat, they now find themselves as the subject of criticism for allowing a level of access that is "too close"; so close that it skews the objectivity of journalists that stake their professional reputations on their ability to remain detached from the subjects they cover.

The idea of embedding reporters with combat units must have been seen as a media utopia to those making the decisions within news organizations around the United States. However, criticism of embedded media continues to focus on the lack of objectivity of the reporters that lived with, and reported on, the servicemen with whom they were embedded. A number of renowned journalists have voiced their opinions that the Pentagon is skewing the view of war that Americans are seeing. Both Morley Safer and Andy Rooney, of 60 Minutes fame, are skeptics. "They called Vietnam 'McNamara's War", says Morley Safer in reference the former defense secretary. This is Rumsfeld's war – and he seems to be managing it far better than McNamara did. The operative word is 'managed.'" Mr. Rooney stated, "It's very difficult to write anything critical about a guy you're going to have breakfast with the next morning. Ernie Pyle didn't write any stories about cowards in World War II, even though there were some. We suspect in this war, we're going to get a lot of stories about heroes." These sentiments were not uncommon with regard to discussions about the embedded media program. Despite viewership being up (300 percent for the cable news channels and 10 percent overall) for broadcasts since March 19, skeptics were readily available. Marvin Kalb, a senior fellow at Harvard University's Shorenstein Center on the Press, stated, "If a reporter is with a soldier, sleeps in the same tent, eats the same food, faces roughly the same danger – if the reporter is a human being, it is very difficult to...write critical copy about the guy he just had dinner with." These negative comments on the objectivity of embedded media are ironic. These same commentators would likely have argued for greater access to military operations had there been no embedded media program.

A generation of combat veterans, both military and media, evolved from the experience of OIF. The process of embedding media served to breakdown some of the preconceived notions and prejudices that the military and media industries had towards one another by educating both sides on the duties and responsibilities of the other. The shared experiences of military members, and the reporters embedded with them, should ultimately result in a better understanding of not only why a relationship is necessary but how such a relationship can be mutually beneficial to both camps. It is for this reason that the process of embedding media with military units should continue as a method to allay the natural distrust found between two institutions with such vast cultural differences. Nonetheless, the ongoing debate on the success or failure of the program points to a future relationship that is destined to be fraught with tension, despite the concessions made by both sides.

RETHINKING THE MILITARY-MEDIA RELATIONSHIP

Over the past twenty five years the agenda for thinking about the relationship between the military, media and public opinion has been set by the perceived lessons of Vietnam. This agenda has shaped the approach of policy-makers and academics. From the perspective of the military it has been argued that the US war effort was undermined by critical reporting: a focus on casualties and lack of progress sustained an anti war movement. On the other side of the argument analysts such as Daniel Hallin have challenged this perception arguing that media coverage was in fact largely supportive of the war effort.

In the mid 1990s the debate shifted to focus on the perceived impact of television coverage in influencing US policy towards Kurdistan, Bosnia, Somalia and so on. It was argued that the impact of television pictures 'forced' policy makers into taking action whether it was to intervene in humanitarian crises or to pull out once intervention had actually occurred. As with the discourse about Vietnam the issue has been the extent to which a powerful media operating from outside the policy process has been able to shape that process through its impact on public opinion. As with the earlier conflict an academic literature has developed disputing the initial claims.

It can be argued that the Vietnam-CNN effect literature defines the problem too narrowly. Partly as a consequence of the research methodologies the media are treated as something external to the political process that pushes in to disrupt it. This might be termed an external paradigm of government-media relations. In contrast there is a growing body of work on domestic politics that suggests the media should be seen as an integral part of contemporary governance. This process of mediatization is not confined to the domestic realm. In the international sphere the media serves as a source of information about events, about the activities of other political agents and as way of achieving positive objectives. To demonstrate that the media rarely exerts a determining influence on policy is not to demonstrate that the media are unimportant but to misunderstand what policy makers do with the media. The media can be found deeply entrenched within the policy process. The evidence for this can be found in the development of the modern apparatus of media management, the memoirs of political practitioners and academic studies that draw on interviews almost uniformly give testimony (sometimes unintentionally) to the role of the media in the contemporary political process.

This paper takes up the issue of the relationship between government and media in the context of the War on Terrorism from this 'internal' perspective. I argue that the relationship between government, military and the media are increasingly intertwined. I tackle these issues via the work of Carl Von Clausewitz and his discussion of the relationship between the military and the political. Although Clausewitz has nothing to say about the press he provides a way of placing the issue of government-military-media relations in war time in a broader and more historical perspective than the standard discussion of censorship versus a free press. This paper falls into three main parts we begin by outlining Clausewitz's argument about the military political relationship. I then examine some of the ways in which the changing social and technological environment over the past two centuries has affected this relationship. The third part of the paper illustrates these themes with examples from the Kosovo Conflict and the War on Terrorism drawing in particular on the case of Task Force Jacana to illustrate the relationship between the press and the military

Clausewitz on War

Clausewitz's central claim in On War (1831) is that to understand warfare one must see it as a social phenomenon. War emerges from concrete circumstances and it is this that makes it comprehensible. This position was directed against two popular beliefs at the time; that war was capable of a simple linear solution, for instance that the angle between base and army was the key to victory and that war was essentially chaotic and not subject to rational analysis.

This view gave rise to the oft quoted maxim that war is the continuation of politics with an admixture of other means, that is violence. This simple maxim concealed a considerable complexity.

Firstly war changed over time. As the form of social organization had changed so had the nature of war. The sources of conflict and the methods used reflected the nature of the entities waging it. Secondly, in understanding what was going on in a conflict one needed to look at the military events in a political context. Thirdly, there was a normative aspect to the formula. Clausewitz believed that force was most effective when it was used as a conscious instrument of state policy. Given the suffering caused by war this was the only morally justifiable reason for the employment of violence. Of course a normative failure would not vitiate the analytical strategy.

Analytically and practically the way to understand war was to examine the relationship between military events and the political context of those events. In general there was a linear relationship between the scale of the objective sought and the level of force required to achieve it. In a war that was fought to defeat an opponent that aimed to totally defeat a country and occupy it one would expect major efforts to defeat the attacker. On the other hand where a much more minor objective was sought the scale of effort would be less

Clausewitz understood that events on the battlefield and in the political sphere influenced each other. A decisive battlefield victory might deter other countries from becoming involved in a conflict or it might convince them that the victor was becoming a danger to them. A victory might persuade a country that its opponent was so weak that it should increase its objectives. The knowledge that another country had decided to intervene or withdraw from a conflict would affect the morale of those doing the fighting. Thus, the political-military interaction was not simply about setting the objective and deciding the means: the political environment of the conflict encompassed all the variables that might have an impact on the military situation. Because military activity was merely one aspect of a more complex whole it followed that the narrower (military) instrument must be subordinated to the broader (political) perspective.

Having made this connection Clausewitz is concerned to explain that war is not simply politics. As he puts it do 'political relations between people and between their governments stop when diplomatic notes are no longer exchanged? Is war not just another expression of their thoughts, another form of speech or writing? Its grammar, indeed may be its own, but not its logic.' Military action has its own peculiar requirements. As he commented political 'considerations do not determine the posting of guards or the employment of patrols. But they are the more influential in the planning of war, of the campaign and even of the battle.'

Clausewitz provides a metatheory of war - war is shaped by the political and social environment so this is always the most appropriate axis of analysis -and a specific theory of strategy for the early 19th Century. The times have changed since then and how have the relationships between war and politics changed?

Transformations

Although there is an enormous literature on the transformation of war since the early 19th century I want to focus on two dimensions that have particular resonance for the relationship between war and politics; firstly the emergence of a democratic, mediated political space and secondly the way in which technology has affected the relationship between the political and military spheres.

Clausewitz was writing in an era strongly marked by the impact of the French Revolution. Powerful political forces demanded greater political involvement while others resisted it. Throughout the 19th century European political elites sought to restrict the impact of democratization on political-military decision making. But even as the old elites resisted change they came to recognize that popular sentiment was an important source of military power. Without the active involvement of large sections of the population national military power would be limited. Thus the people came to be more involved in war. This increasing involvement led to total war. Total war in the First and Second World Wars reflected the Clausewitzian point that the day to day impact of politics declines as the scale of the conflict expands. Where two opponents aim at the total defeat of the other the requirements of military operations, mobilization and logistics tends to push political influence into the background. Political debate shrank under the force of mass mobilization and a public sphere that was dominated a consensus that was actively encouraged by the machinery of the state.

Because Cold War conflicts were designated as limited wars there was scope for a greater degree of political questioning of the conflicts and in a public sphere that was less constrained by censorship and governmental publicity that during the earlier conflicts. In the 1980s the aftermath of Vietnam further loosened social and political pressures for consensus. The Gulf War - as the first post cold war military conflict combined the relatively low level of direct threat to the US and its allies – hence a reluctance to impose far reaching controls on the news and comment with a new media environment. There was a growing volume of media coverage through a variety of media channels and a degree of transnationalization of the media. Coverage could come from a broader range of locations, more quickly and be beamed back across the world.

There are at least three sets of technologically driven transformations that affect the relationship between the military and the political sphere. Firstly, changes in the nature of the relationship between field commanders and national command authorities, secondly an expansion in the political context of military action and thirdly, changes in the nature of the public sphere itself.

Transforming the chain of command: The first of these is the development of an integrated global system of command and control that provides decision makers in national capitals with the ability to communicate directly and in real time with military units around the world.

In the American context the origins of such systems were partly technological and partly political. The fear of surprise nuclear attack and the risks of unauthorized use of nuclear weapons were major drivers in creating a global real time communications system. The development of such systems had political and organizational effects. They reinforced the sense of the world as a single space and encouraged a tendency to see isolated events as part of a single pattern. In the Cold War context the fear that isolated events might be part of a global threat along with the fear of horizontal escalation (the geographical spread of conflict) and vertical escalation (increasing levels of violence) encouraged a desire to keep military forces on a short leash facilitated by the new command and control systems.

The emergence of these control systems affected the chain of command. The assumption is that for a military organization to function effectively lines of responsibility should be clearly defined and that patterns of communication should, in general, follow the chain of command. These conventions, in part, grew of the impossibility of doing anything else. The development of improved command and control systems created the temptation for the political leadership to exert direct control over subordinate units and for military commanders to breach the chain of command. It also, apparently, created the possibility for command to be exerted from greater distance (both literally and figuratively).

Despite the benefits of these systems they have their own pathologies. The danger with these systems is that the local knowledge of those on the ground is over ridden by those further back who believe that they are in a better situation to exercise control. Two recent examples illustrate these concerns. At the Battle of Tora Bora the most senior American officer present was reported to be a Lieutenant Colonel. The next highest level of command was at Central Command in Tampa, FLA. Critics of the way that the operation was handled charge that the absence of more senior commanders meant that those on the ground did not have the clout to bring in additional Coalition ground troops and prevent the escape of senior al-Qaeda figures. Similarly helmet or UAV mounted cameras allow senior officers to watch troops in combat from a safe distance with the result that 'you get too focussed on what you can see and neglect what you can't see'.

The arrival of e-mail in military organizations encourages lateral and diagonal communication. While going over a commander's head is not undertaken lightly functional specialists can communicate across unit boundaries in ways that create surprises for their commanders.

What these developments suggest is a compression of the distance between political leadership, senior military commanders and those at the ground. Information about events on the ground flows back more rapidly, in greater volume and through a multiplicity of channels. Those in the field will have a greater awareness of the political requirements and situation and those in the rear will have a greater awareness of ongoing military events and their potential impact.

The expanding political context: If technology has expanded the flow of information within official channels it has also changed the nature of unofficial channels. The flow of information from and to the war zone via news organizations, NGOS and individuals has also expanded. Although the literature tends to place weight on the ability of military and governmental actors to shape news media access to information it should be recognized that these efforts at management are happening in an environment where technology is working against that control. Although the US media has criticised the willingness of the government to provide access for journalists the extent to which global media were able to report on a conflict in the interior of Afghanistan was striking. The widespread adoption of satellite phone technology allowed journalists to report back in real time with eye witness reports and the views of local actors. In the period before the fall of Kabul one striking feature of media coverage (in the UK at least) was running critique of Coalition strategy from the Northern Alliance.

The result of these information flows is to, potentially at least, change the nature of the political context of the conflict. As Schattschneider argued to expand the scope of a conflict is to change who is involved and its outcome. As information flows out of the battlespace more quickly it becomes more feasible for external groups to exert influence through their political response to events. These external groups may be the American public, governments allied or opposed to the cause, allied publics, the Arab 'street'. Reports are events in their own right. Comments are acts. News about responses flows back to theatre commanders and troops as well as to national command authorities. As the degree of scrutiny increases the political consequences of minor activities have to be considered. Events that were so minor that they would not be known outside the immediate area may take great significance via the process of mediation. Isolated events come to stand as signifiers for a broader picture.

The changing public sphere: This expansion of the political environment is connected to a change in the political discourse about war and the sphere within which this discourse takes place.

While commentary on the impact of 24 hour news has tended to focus on its significance in reporting and informational terms it has also had the effect of expanding the scope for comment, speculation, analysis and explanation.

Even where the news outlet is faced with a developing story - like a war - it is faced with the paradox that the coverage is much faster than the action that it covers. It takes only a few moments to report that a bombing raid is taking place but the flight to the target, the return, the planning the evaluation all take hours or days. 24 hour news is confronted with the reality that war is boredom punctuated by fear and that much of what goes on is routine. The result is that the media sphere is filled not with reporting - after all there are limits to how many times a piece of information can repeated -but with commentary and speculation.

From the point of view of policy makers this provides a running critique of the conduct of the conflict. It is a critique governed by the rules of the news cycle rather than by the reality of military and diplomatic activity.

When we bring these transformations together we see a picture where decision makers are more exposed to external criticism and debate. Direct experience combined with the political folk memory of Vietnam leads to great sensitivity to the political consequences of military action. At the same time the military command, even in theatre, are more tightly connected to the political context at home. As information flows out of the battlefield to the military-political connections with the rest of the world become tighter. Because minor activities take on a greater visibility their political consequences have to be considered: politics may come to affect the posting of guards and the movements of patrols. The following hypotheses might apply.

- Field commanders will have declining autonomy: Because of the potential political significance of their actions their superiors will constantly monitor and seek to control these actions.

- As the diversity of media sources grow managing coverage of war will become more important: Leaders will need to shape coverage to attempt to maintain a consensus regarding the conflict even as the ability to do this declines.
- Rather than the military media relationship being simply a matter of how reporting affects public opinion the media discourse comes to have an impact on how the war is waged.

To put it crudely the separation between the political and the military as spheres of activity become blurred. The communicative elements of warfare grow into importance.

EVIDENCE FROM KOSOVO AND THE WAR ON TERROR

The extent to which we can actually test these hypotheses in a systematic way will depend on further research and the availability of a much more developed set of data than can be assembled at present. However, available evidence gives a degree of plausibility to these suggestions.

Kosovo

While aspects of the Kosovo campaign remain obscure - in particular why Serbia finally conceded - it is clear that it was marked by high levels of concern over public perception of the war.

In his study of American decision-making over Vietnam Leslie Gelb put forward the argument that the system worked perfectly - it produced a response that was the maximum politically feasible and the minimum militarily necessary. The problem was that this was insufficient to produce the desired result. The story of the NATO assault on Yugoslavia seems to have a similar logic. There was a minimal political consensus to launch an air campaign against Milosevic but not on the military campaign that would defeat him. There was a distinctly improvised element to the campaign based on an assumption that Belgrade would cave in after two or three days of bombing.

When this did not happen the limits of the consensus became obvious. Some NATO members appear to have favoured a bombing pause and negotiations, the British appear to have been the most aggressive favouring a ground option while most of the members favoured a continuation of bombing with greater or lesser degrees of escalation. The key to being able to sustain the campaign was not military resources or casualties but the ability to sustain political support in the face of the uncertainties and contingencies of war: civilian casualties, targeting errors, the apparent ineffectiveness of air attacks in hitting Serbian units in Kosovo.

The public face of the conflict was seen by those involved as being of extreme importance. Only by convincing Milosevic and his potential supporters of the inevitability of defeat could he be persuaded to back down. This could only happen by demonstrating allied resolve through the continuation of the campaign. Thus the presentation of the conflict became a key battlefield as NATO sought to maintain its minimal consensus. A striking illustration of Trevor Thrall's view that the pressures for constraints on the media tend to come from the political authorities is the way in which Tony Blair's chief spin doctor was instrumental in importing media management techniques from domestic politics into NATO. The representation of the conflict was seen as part of the conflict. Both sides attempted to define the dominant narrative of the conflict.

Shaping actions to minimize political risks led to arguments over what targets were legitimate and over the risks of collateral damage. Targets had to be approved at the highest political level. The arguments over bombing harked back to Lyndon Johnson's insistence on personal control over the bombing of North Vietnam and looked forward to George W. Bush's control over the air war against Afghanistan. Despite the critiques of the conduct of Rolling Thunder the fact that the same practice endures reflects the changing political and technological environment of war.

Wesley Clark's availability at the end of a telephone or a videoconferencing link ensured that he was aware of practically every twist and turn of the policy debate in Washington and led to a kind of management by nuance that would not be feasible in a less wired age. His superiors judged his performance as much by his media appearances and reaction to them as by any military criteria.

In looking at the Afghan element of the War on Terrorism one might expect that the political and presentation concerns that marked the campaign in Kosovo would have disappeared. Here is the greatest global power the victim of a direct attack seeking to deal with its foes. But what we see are many of the same characteristics as in Kosovo. We see a concern with the media consequences of actions and of the importance of foreign public opinion. As in Kosovo there is the creation of an international news management mechanism. We see the same insistence on the approval of targets at the highest levels. However it might be suggested that Kosovo and the War on Terrorism differ in that while both demonstrate a high degree of sensitivity to media coverage the levels of vulnerability is different. Sensitivity can be treated as the degree to which coverage is a concern to be monitored, managed and responded to. Vulnerability can be thought of as the potential for coverage to bring about a change in policy either directly or through its impact on the members of a coalition or those who can exert pressure on them. Because Kosovo depended on a coalition whose leader was only marginally committed to the war the degree of vulnerability was high. In the second case the relatively high level commitment serves to reduce the degree of vulnerability if not sensitivity.

By way of illustration I offer a case study of the interplay between politics, military and the media that suggests that this linkage is not just an American phenomenon.

Task Force Jacana

In the aftermath of September 11 Britain has been the US's most vocal supporter in the War on Terror. Once operations in Afghanistan began it was widely assumed by the media, encouraged by government, that British ground forces were would be deployed in combat operations. After the liberation of Kabul Britain was quick to insert troops into Bagram air base and as part of the International Security Assistance Force. But the lack of combat operations seems to have led to a degree of frustration both in the government and the media. Thus the announcement in March that a force of Royal Marine Commandos was to be deployed on combat operations in southern Afghanistan was a cause for some excitement. The developments that followed certainly provide prima facie evidence that to support that view that between the political and military spheres are becoming ever closer, linked in large part by the news media.

The context for the deployment of Task Force Jacana was the aftermath of the Battle of Tora Bora in early December. It was widely believed that Osama Bin Laden had been able to escape because of the unreliability of allied Afghan forces. This triggered a decision to commit coalition ground forces to similar operations. The most significant of these was Operation Anaconda in early March. In the wake of this operation the US command requested the deployment of a British force. Largely composed of Royal Marine Commandos Task Force Jacana was trained in mountain warfare and it seemed to be a logical reinforcement for the effort on the ground.

The deployment of the task force was accompanied by extensive media coverage assisted by the Ministry of Defence. The commander of the force, Brigadier Roger Lane, rapidly became a familiar face on television. The rhetoric around the force emphasized their capabilities, the dangers of the terrain and the prospects of fighting and casualties. This rhetoric had a priming effect creating expectations for the media.

This expectation was not met. The force was initially deployed on Operation Ptarmigan. This was a sweep through the mountains south of Tora Bora. The media filled with commentary emphasizing the dangers of the job and the inevitability of casualties. A sceptical voice was a Conservative spokesman who pointed out that valley had already been swept by allied forces. After days of patrolling the operation was terminated without contact with the enemy.

In early May the task force was again sent to sweep mountainous territory in Operation Snipe. This failed to come into contact with enemy forces but it did discover a large quantity of ammunition which was found and blown up (literally and figuratively) with suitable publicity. The media described the explosion in hyberbolic terms. Almost immediately local leaders were disputing whether the munitions destroyed belonged to Al-Qaeda at all.

After two operations without a contact Brigadier Lane felt it necessary to downplay the situation commenting that 'the need for offensive operations is beginning to dwindle and they will be completed in a matter of weeks rather than months' a view that was rebutted by Donald Rumsfeld within hours of Lane making it after it was put to him by a reporter. As the troops returned to their base at Bagram members of the personnel of a British Army field hospital were diagnosed with a serious infection. In some quarters this was attributed to a possible biological weapons attack only for the UK media to wheel out public health specialists who attributed the probable cause to poor hygiene. There were comments about the poor living conditions of British forces versus those of the US and German troops in the area.

Rather than the force becoming evidence of British military prowess it was becoming a joke. The British media were becoming frustrated with the lack of stories.

On Friday 17 of May Britain awoke to hear the voice of Brigadier Roger Lane announcing that 'I can confirm that the coalition has made contact with the enemy and that some have been killed'. The Marines were once again aboard their Chinooks and moving to rescue a patrol of the Australian SAS who had been ambushed. The previous afternoon an ASAS patrol had come under fire. A second patrol had moved to its aid under fire but with the support of US AC-130 gunships. Now it was clear that 'our boys' were going in as a quick reaction force to cover the extraction of the Australians and engage the enemy force. It was later reported that within a matter of minutes the Ministry of Defence in London had to deny Brig. Lane's comments. The impression given that British troops were engaging the enemy was wrong.

Across the Friday and the following day the initial reports were being undermined. It was reported that the men killed and injured by the American planes were locals engaged in a feud over access to woodlands (according to one source) or were firing into the air at a wedding (according to another). For the third time the Commandos failed to make contact with the enemy.

The Sunday Telegraph carried a story citing an anonymous source in the MoD claiming that Brig Lane had lost the confidence of both the MoD and his subordinates and arguing for his replacement. The story further suggested that Lane had pressed his American commander to allow his exhausted men to be sent to rescue the Australians rather than an American force. In response the Minister of Defence, Geoff Hoon, rushed onto David Frost's Sunday morning talk show to support Lane. General Julian Thompson who had commanded 3 Commando Brigade in the Falklands Conflict popped up on Radio 4's Broadcasting House programme to support Brig. Lane. His support actually threw an unwanted sidelight on the narrative of the conflict. The failure of the enemy to engage was normal in this kind of 'counter insurgency operation'. Factually correct but nobody in the coalition was using the language of counter insurgency.

Hoon's support for Lane was immediately undercut by the emergence of fact that the MoD had already decided to cut short Lane's tour of duty as commander of 3 Commando Brigade. The MoD then claimed that this decision had been made to free Lane for an important staff job. It then became clear that Lane in fact had no job to go to. The consequence was political criticism of Hoon and the government in general for hyping up expectations of the operations, for damaging the morale of the troops, and for incompetence in not knowing the facts. The Chief of the Defence Staff appeared in public to take responsibility for the confusion. In the following days stories about difficult relations between the Coalition forces at Bagram and the British Media emerged. These helped to explain the critical tone of some of the press coverage. 'Humiliated' was the headline in the Daily Mirror. By Tuesday the men of 3 Bde were reported to be hurt and angered by their coverage. As one Marine was reported as saying 'How can we be humiliated when we are out on patrol and al-Qaeda won't dare to take us on?' Subsequent reports claimed that the arguments over Brigadier Lane had damaged the morale of the forces and that criticisms had emerged from a struggle between the Navy and the Army.

There is nothing new in the saga of Brigadier Lane. Tensions between field commanders and their superiors, between the military and political leadership, between military and media, between allies are not unusual. What is striking here though is the relative seamlessness of the whole field. British and American figures commented on each others statements, the distance between London and Bagram becomes insignificant, journalists ask marines for responses to the day's press coverage, sources in London brief against commanders in the field, local voices emerge to challenge the official account. Journalists were able to challenge the narrative of policy effectively in real time. People on the ground find that their performance is subject to media commentary and interpretation.

The government found the credibility of their policy challenged as a result of these events. By the end of Operation Condor the media were treating the activities of Task Force Jacana as somewhere between a joke and of marginal significance. While there were undoubtedly difficulties in the media-military relationship most of the problems stemmed from the actions of the government and military. It was the government that created the expectations of combat that were not met. It was they who seemed to lack a clear view of what they wanted the journalists to do. The negative stories emerged from conflicts with the military command. Figures within the government were using the techniques of media politics to advance their own positions and attack their opponents. It was the military and political leadership that was unclear about both about the situation on the ground in Afghanistan and the overall policy context. It was the military and political leadership that effectively failed to develop an effective system to coordinate its message.

The activities of Task Force Jacana provide example of what might be termed Gould's Law 'a modern media environment, competence and good communications are inseparable: you cannot have one without the other.' There is no point at being good at your job if you cannot communicate it effectively. The media will define you as a failure anyway. This was coined in the context of British domestic politics but it is increasingly true of international politics.

THE MILITARY-NEWS MEDIA RELATIONSHIP

The Military-News Media Surroundings

It is ironic that much of the disagreement between the military and the news media is based on an element of essential agreement. Both institutions view the information available in operational units to be very important and vitally interesting. But their reactions to this common judgment vary significantly: The military's response has often been to prevent the release of such information because of various concerns ranging from potential embarrassment to operations security, while the news media's response is typically to seek immediate release because of the "public's right to know."

Shortly before the invasion of Normandy, General Dwight D. Eisenhower addressed this tension with reporters: "The first essential in military operations is that no information of value shall be given to the enemy. The first essential in newspaper work and broadcasting is wide-open publicity. It is your job and mine to try to reconcile those sometimes diverse considerations." In these words lie the basis for cooperation through the development of ground rules and procedures which seek to define "information of value" and outline parameters for its reporting. History records that the effort was generally successful. At the entrance to the American Cemetery at St Laurent, France, overlooking Omaha Beach, rests the following plaque: "In memory of General Dwight D. Eisenhower and the forces under his command this sealed capsule containing news reports of the June 6, 1944 Normandy Landings is placed here by the newsmen who were there." This simple remembrance represents a sincere expression of mutual respect and shared experience often seen in the genre of the war correspondent from all conflicts; it is not a reflection of unquestioning support or "cheerleading" for the attack.

General Walter E. Boomer, the commander of Marine Forces during the Persian Gulf War, has said that among commanders there is a "mythology" of mistrust despite the fact that relatively few have ever had sustained contact with the news media. Often this is because the two institutions generally have very little dealings with each other except during crises or war. Aside from reporters who cover the Pentagon, there are very few journalists who specialize in military and national security issues; and their numbers are decreasing as the trend continues toward reporters with "general" expertise. Further, most reporters don't have the time or support to visit and learn about the military, even during exercises.

Interestingly, given this history of unfamiliarity, both the military and the news media expect the other to perform with understanding and efficiency when events bring them together. Further, while reporters on the ground focus immense effort on covering the military unit, their presence is only one of the many variables competing for the attention of the responsible commander. When things don't go well, minor irritants grow into major issues, and, unfortunately, the two institutions often tend to focus on their mutual competition rather than on their shared responsibility to communicate information to the public. Once again, the fact that both institutions speak to a common audience should lead to cooperation based on mutual interest instead of confrontation often based on stereotypes or past disagreements and misunderstandings.

Yet the differences in institutional perspective are important to understand. Increasingly, reporters see themselves as participants in the events they cover, not merely as chroniclers of those experiences. In the post-cold war world, national leaders and agenda setters regularly appear on international television networks like CNN and the BBC to communicate diplomatic messages and warnings. This practice is also true, although perhaps less dramatically, for radio and print media. Additionally, during the Persian Gulf War, one of the "status symbols" among reporters was the number of prisoners of war each was able to "capture." The increasing role of the news media in outlining the public agenda has led to debate over the apparent linkage between news media coverage of events, especially in television and still pictures, and the decision of nations to act in response. Recent examples include international efforts during Operation Provide Comfort in Northern Iraq, humanitarian assistance to the former Soviet Union, Operation Restore Hope in Somalia, and various actions in the former Yugoslavia, as well as the pace of the domestic response to the Hurricane Andrew disaster in Florida.

An unexpected military consequence of this new role involves providing security for reporters covering an operation. While journalists say that their security is not a military concern and DoD policy calls for working with journalists without regard for their safety, events have proven otherwise. Participants in conflicts are becoming increasingly sensitive to the perception that news coverage often leads to unwanted external intervention. Thus what can be interpreted as retaliatory actions have been taken against reporters to include bounties for those covering U.N. operations in the former Yugoslavia. More than 30 journalists have been killed in fighting there since 1991, and four reporters died in Somalia on July 12,1993 in what has been characterized as an act of revenge by an angry mob. News media demands for assistance when reporters were trapped in hotels in Panama City (1989) and Mogadishu (1993) and after the capture of Bob Simon of CBS Television by Iraqi forces (1991) clearly indicate that the security of journalists will remain a persistent, high visibility issue confronting commanders.

While absolute security cannot be guaranteed, those reporters who accept the protection afforded by military units are probably in the best position to cover the story comprehensively and survive. Yet the situations above, especially that of Simon, involved conscious decisions by reporters to function outside of the established news media relations procedures and to conduct reporting entirely on their own. In response to such behavior, commanders who understand that sustained contacts between military forces and the news media result in the most complete and accurate stories about their units should seek to convince reporters that the acceptance of reasonable military ground rules and the integration of journalists into operational units are in the best interests of both institutions. However, it is inevitable that some reporters will choose not to cooperate. In those cases, commanders have no special responsibilities for such individuals and should, instead, focus their attention on the reporters who desire to abide by the procedures outlined for the operation.

Any discussion of contacts between the military and the news media must address the expectations of reporters covering the operation. Logically, journalists are limited by the same factors of terrain, visibility and information flow that affect the forces with which they travel. Yet reporters don't always understand this. In his book on the Persian Gulf War, John MacArthur, the publisher of Harper's Magazine, quotes Molly Moore of The Washington Post as saying, "I had no idea what was going on, and I was right in the middle of the war" (traveling with Marine commander LTG Boomer). Precisely so! A critical step in developing cooperation between the military and the news media is the explanation of the reality that the mere presence of journalists, regardless of background, will not grant special insight not available to the military personnel they are with. Once again, dialogue and explanation improve the quality of the reporters' experience and, inevitably, of their news products.

The Operational Environment

There is a popular view that the often tense relationship between the military and the news media is a recent product of hard feelings and misunderstandings generated during the

Viet Nam War. In contrast, this perspective claims, the contacts between the two institutions during World War II were usually amicable and cooperative. This view of history appears to be overly simplistic and not entirely accurate. Shelley Smith Mydans, a Life magazine war correspondent in the Pacific Theater 50 years ago, suggests that a sense of common purpose at that time (the defeat of America's enemies) should not be misinterpreted as unquestioning news media support of the political decisions and military actions taken in pursuit of that goal.

It is interesting that a survey of the writings of various war correspondents and discussions with others of that era reveal that the issues of concern today were just as important to the journalists covering the military in those earlier years. In addressing this phenomenon, Hodding Carter has said in the case of military-news media relations, "the wheel often gets reinvented, but it travels over very different terrain. Then, as now, the central news media concern involved the fear of censorship. But issues such as access to the forces, communications, operations security, transportation and logistics support also were of interest. In recent years, deficiencies in any of these have been interpreted by many in the news media as attempts by the Department of Defense to impose censorship indirectly. For instance, using news media pools to cover combat units during the Persian Gulf War or relying on slow ground transportation to deliver news media products were seen as deliberate efforts to restrict journalists from covering stories or to delay their reports once produced.

The important realization is that the issues really haven't changed nor, by extension, have the commanders' responsibilities to ensure that their organizations are in the best position to conduct professional news media relations programs appropriately tailored to their assigned missions. Quite simply, the commanders most likely to succeed will be those who have accurately assessed the level of news media interest in their operation and have anticipated and provided the assets necessary to accomplish the news media relations mission. The instinctive military need for control is irrelevant in the face of an institution which can field, depending on the size of the operation, thousands of reporters who are equipped with instantaneous communications capabilities and who often understand alarmingly little about the stories they are covering. Once again, the challenge and the failure to adapt aren't new. In speaking about his experiences at Pearl Harbour on December 7, 1941, Frank Tremaine (United Press) reported that "the military was no more prepared to handle news coverage than for handling the Japanese." Yet it is always important to be selective in reviewing earlier experiences.

Lessons derived from anecdotal discussions about the circumstances surrounding Operation Urgent Fury (Grenada) and Operations Desert Shield/Storm are limited by the fact that they were unique situations not likely to be replicated. Like the British efforts in the Falkland Islands, geographical and political circumstances dictated that the news media had to be imported and matched up with the forces. The challenges presented by reporters during Operations Just Cause (Panama) and Restore Hope (Somalia) are far more relevant for study because of the presence of significant numbers of journalists in place before operations began and their open access to most areas of operation.

Similarly, news coverage of the fighting in the former Yugoslavia has been conducted for several years by numerous independent, well-equipped journalists who move about freely and flood the international news media with their often compelling reports.

Media relations in any operation cannot be left to chance or to a particularly clever public affairs staff. While language like "handling journalists" and "coping with reporter demands" sounds defensive and may appear to revert to attempts at control of the news media, it is useful for understanding the requirements facing field commanders. A carefully-planned, well-resourced and decisively-positioned infrastructure is necessary for communicating through the news media to the American and, increasingly, international publics. This means that organizations need to be "proactively-reactive": reactive to the extent they must be responsive to news media interest; proactive in that knowledgeable assessments, comprehensive planning and advanced preparation will inevitably determine how effectively they will be able to respond.

Unity in the media relations effort is achieved through the development of public affairs guidance which assists the entire chain of command in communicating consistent and credible information. Although the public affairs plans are approved by the Office of the Secretary of Defense, commanders at each level have a role in formulating the policy, news statements, information packages, and media support arrangements which make up the plan.This effort ensures that those most knowledgeable about the operation play a major role in developing the messages to be communicated. Effective command information programs are also important to ensuring that everyone likely to encounter journalists will understand the mission and their role in it, aspects which are always of interest to reporters covering the military.

To succeed, commanders must "think forward" historically, operationally, and geographically. The perpetuation of confrontation and debate over events past is not useful. Attempts to look back and justify specific decisions or actions do help in gaining understanding, but they also serve to reinforce the sense of conflict between the institutions. Continuing to focus on historical events can cause both the military and the news media to appear to be preparing themselves to conduct media relations as they did in the last conflict or deployment. As with any operational task, the only relevant lessons of the past are those which can be applied to improve readiness and performance in the future.

Additionally, the success of the media relations program rests on the ability of the commander and staff to assess the intensity of news media interest in the mission at hand and to anticipate the personnel, communications, transportation, and deployment requirements necessary to communicate through the news media during every stage of the operation.

In the complexity of today's international security environment, this will often require rather creative applications of judgment. This is especially true since the news media will inevitably appear before commanders are fully prepared to accommodate them. Therefore, regardless of mission, commanders should immediately designate an official source of information (normally the public affairs officer) and activate an information center. Taking the early initiative in these efforts will usually serve to channel reporters to those trained to communicate with them, thus reducing their random movement throughout the area of operation and their unplanned, sometimes disruptive visits to units. These outcomes are also desirable for journalists in their efforts to cover the story and will assist in establishing a constructive dialogue.

Finally, the true challenge for the Department of Defense and its military commanders does not reside in the formal briefing room where well-trained spokespersons are prepared to answer news media questions. It lies, instead, in the forward-deployed units where young leaders, inexperienced with the news media and facing a kaleidoscope of important tasks, are confronted by reporters competing with their colleagues for a unique angle on the operation. Guidance and training for the tactical commander should become a regular part of operational preparations.

The education process should begin with a simple orientation to the military—news media relationship in the officer basic course and continue with increasing complexity through the advanced courses and the Combined Arms and Services Staff School to the senior military schools. A similar pattern should become part of the education system for NCOs.

Since news media contacts with the tactical leadership are inevitable, commanders and their public affairs staffs must concentrate on thinking forward in their planning for the media relations mission. From a commander's perspective, the thoughts generated by the discussion of the issues identified in this study should become planning factors for the development of a responsive news media relations infrastructure.

News Media Admission

Major General Paul E. Funk has written that, on returning from the desert, "I was upset to find that people did not know that the 3d Armoured Division (his command) and VII Corps had been in a very heavy fight under great contact with some of the enemy's first-rate units. The story was not told well enough about the people who did the fighting—the companies, platoons and task forces.... Invariably, if you allow the media to look at what you are doing and put them with the soldiers, it comes out fine."

Both the military and the news media share an interest in providing a more complete picture of military operations than is available at a news briefing. This can best be accomplished by ensuring personal contact between the members of the force and reporters covering the story. Such access is important from the news media's perspective because the information available at news conferences communicates only part of the total story. Similarly, for commanders, there is no more effective way to meet their obligations to communicate with the public than through the perspectives and the experiences of the members of their commands. Yet while commanders have a responsibility to assist journalists in gaining access to military forces, the large number of reporters who inevitably appear in an operational area make it impossible to accommodate them all simultaneously.

After the Persian Gulf War, Pete Williams, the Assistant Secretary of Defense for Public Affairs, and his staff met with various news media representatives and developed guidelines for the coverage of DoD operations. The first of these directly addresses the issue of access. In contrast to the news media pools which were necessary in the environment of Operation Desert Storm, the first guideline states that "open and independent reporting will be the principal means of coverage of U.S. military operations." Essentially, this recognizes the practice of individual journalists moving about an area of options and reporting for their own news organizations without sharing their information with their colleagues, a central feature of pool operations. In fact, this principle is an acknowledgement of reality, not an operational objective. As the events on the beach at Mogadishu, Somalia, clearly revealed, the news media have essentially solved the primary issue of access. In most cases, commanders can assume that reporters will be in position to cover any military activity from the earliest stages. In recent history, this has resulted in images of military personnel performing their tasks while surrounded by reporters who often seem to be regarding them as objects of curiosity. These situations can be as harmless as organized visits to forward positions where tactically deployed combat units become overwhelmed by reporters taking advantage of a photo opportunity; or they can be as potentially dangerous as on the beach in Somalia where the cultures of the military and the news media converged in their most dramatic collision.

The more relevant challenge for commanders is to decide how to include reporters within their organizations. This is particularly true for the Army and the Marine Corps because the story resides with those who execute the mission, and reporters will find their way to the widely-dispersed units who are performing various tasks far from the "influence" of the public affairs staff. Air fields and ships are far less accessible without military assistance. Once again, it is clearly not possible to accommodate simultaneously every journalist desiring to cover the operation. During Operation Desert Storm, one assessment called for the inclusion of 13 reporters in an Army division. In future operations, circumstances may allow for more or dictate fewer.

While inclusion represents the most volatile flashpoint in the relationship between the military and the news media, it also offers the best opportunity for the dialogue necessary for the most effective reporting and understanding. Journalists who are assigned to operational units bring to life the dry facts of the news conference by providing the texture, explanation, and context of what is going on. Further, they communicate a human face by telling the stories of those directly involved with the mission. It has become increasingly true that such reporting is often the only contact most Americans have with the men and women who make up their military establishment.

In every case, commanders must address two related questions: How many reporters can I include in my unit without degrading its operational effectiveness? and, How do I accommodate those journalists who merely appear in a unit area with the desire to report on its activities? A credible answer to the first question reduces the complexity of the second. Reporters working outside a unit possess limited utility as they are only able to gather images of what is happening and provide their own interpretations. Those included in the units are valuable to both the news media and the military as they tend to produce more accurate, complete, and informative stories because of their access to those who are performing the mission.

The first hours of Operation Restore Hope (December 1992) provide a useful example. In the wake of the controversy about the landing at Mogadishu, it is important to remember that those reporters on the beach, squinting into the darkness and transmitting shadows, had not coordinated with the joint task force and were essentially outside of the story. In fact, it is probable that the careless use of lights resulted from a basic misunderstanding of military requirements. In contrast, the public affairs plan included more than 20 journalists who spent several days with the Marines in preparation for the operation and actually participated in the amphibious assault.

Once ashore, efforts began to include the "outsiders," such as by arranging interviews with network anchors perched on the roof of the local airport. This action answered the second question by accommodating those who waited for the force to come to them. Thus the complete media relations plan was flexible enough to include, when events permitted, those journalists who were unable or unwilling to join the Marines before coming ashore. For the commander and the public affairs staff, the task is to achieve inclusiveness, not to grant preference.

Thus it would seem that, once an operation begins, the priority effort for the public affairs staff should involve establishing an identifiable information center, appropriate to the situation, to sustain the efforts of those journalists accompanying the units and to communicate with those journalists outside of the operation. Initially, the facility may consist of no more than an officer and NCO with a satellite telephone around which to build a larger structure. That is sufficient as long as reinforcing personnel and resources arrive at a pace to prevent them from being overwhelmed by the information demand. Such a step ensures that a credible media relations infrastructure is in place which increases the efficiency of the reporting process and reduces the chances of having uninformed and uncooperative journalists disrupting the operation.

In any case, commanders should remain sensitive to the fact that all journalists are increasingly capable of employing sophisticated technology to provide real time coverage of military activities. Therefore, it is important to have public affairs and operational personnel available to furnish brief, but effective, explanations to provide context to the transmitted images and reports. Without such command assistance, there is a chance that misperceptions and misunderstandings can result and that efforts to clarify them can seriously detract from the communications objectives for the mission.

For example, a simple survey of TV network newscasts and daily newspapers reveals that most regularly present identical video and still images of the events in the former Yugoslavia. What sets off specific stories as particularly interesting or compelling are those from journalists on the scene. "Raw" video of operational events, without explanation, doesn't inform very effectively. Once again, today's technology often moves images faster than journalists can provide context, possibly distorting the perceptions of those who view them. A commander's deliberate plan to include journalists reduces the chances for misunderstanding and assists in raising the quality of the reporting and the level of public understanding.

The most effective news media relations programs will be those which provide the widest variety of experiences. While the efforts of "frontline" units may appear to be the most dramatic, the news media and, ultimately, the public are best served by gaining an appreciation for the complexity of all the tasks performed by the force. Additionally, the operational story is best told by shedding the "zero defects" mentality and by exposing reporters to every aspect of the mission and letting them appreciate that military operations are tough challenges where the shape of the final outcome is seldom clear. Making it look easy raises news media and public expectations for future successes and establishes standards which may not be possible to meet. Sounding a theme similar to MG Funk's, Molly Moore provides perspective by writing, "to the men and women who fought it and the commanders who directed it, there was nothing easy about the ground war." Arguably, that story about the "doers" is the most important of any operation and the one which commanders can most affect positively.

Another aspect of the discussion of inclusion concerns escorts. The expectation that all journalists will be accompanied by trained public affairs personnel is unrealistic. In the first place, there are not enough to match up with the large numbers of journalists who will cover military operations. This was especially true during the large scale efforts of Operations Desert Shield and Desert Storm; and it was certainly the case in Somalia where the public affairs staff would have had to land before the assault force to ensure a public affairs presence (not a reasonable course of action). Further, public affairs personnel are probably not the most qualified to act as escorts because it is unlikely that they will have the expertise to explain the activities of the diverse units participating in the operation.

The sixth guideline for combat coverage addresses this issue: "Military public affairs officers should act as liaisons but should not interfere with the reporting process." The thrust of this principle is that the responsibility of the public affairs staff is to assist the news media by arranging for their inclusion in operational units and to prepare those units for their arrival. The requirements for navigation, security and logistical support establish the need for escort assistance, but both institutions are best served by having members of the unit serve those functions. These arrangements need not necessarily place special demands on the commander. Reporters can move forward with supply columns or with any transport which inevitably shuttles among organizations in an area of operation. Journalists are there to cover the functioning of the unit, not to impose upon it as visitors or inspectors.

TECHNOLOGY AND MAINTAIN FOR THE NEWS MEDIA RELATIONS ASSIGNMENT

What is more remarkable about reporters than their numbers is their range of technological capabilities, and commanders have become properly wary about the implications of the live reporting of military activities.

In early December 1992, Pete Williams and Dave Bartlett, the president of the Radio and Television News Directors Association, discussed the likelihood of live battlefield or operational coverage before a group of military public affairs officers. While each proposed different timelines, they agreed that such an event was not imminent. Yet it was only one week and one hour later that the lights went on at Mogadishu beach as the Marine Reconnaissance Force came ashore, demonstrating the fast pace and unpredictability of advances in technology.

It seems that technology has always been central to the relationship of the military and the news media. The Civil War brought the telegraph which raised serious concerns about the security of troop movements and operations. Carrier pigeons later added a different dimension to news coverage as reporters sent dispatches tied to pigeons' legs. Today, experience teaches that the news media bring with them sophisticated communications equipment, computers, and television and radio resources. Especially in the earliest stages of an operation, they appear with equipment demonstrating superior capabilities which they can deploy faster and sustain longer than those available to military public affairs staffs. This results in situations in which commanders lag behind the news media in telling the story of their operational efforts.

Legitimate concerns over today's technology recall those expressed about the telegraph 130 years ago. During Operation Desert Storm, controversy arose over the movement of news products, both print and broadcast, from forward deployed reporters to transmission sites in the rear. Current and emerging technologies are no longer tied to arrangements which depend on ground or air transportation. Radio and television signals can be sent over satellite equipment which is increasingly easy to move about the operational area and set up to provide real time coverage. Continuous broadcast transmission capabilities exist using available satellites, and commanders can expect to confront such sophistication today. Emerging technology is resulting in smaller cameras, editing equipment and uplink facilities which will be even easier to deploy, employ and sustain. Cumbersome television satellite equipment which had to be transported on aircraft pallets to Panama and in pickup trucks in the desert soon will be carried in a few small cases by a reporter and photographer. In areas where the infrastructure exists, television images can already be sent over cellular telephones; similar radio capabilities have existed for several years using satellite and cellular telephones.

Immediate reporting capabilities also exist for print reporters who are capable of transmitting news products from their portable computers through satellite telephones to their newsrooms in the United States. Kirk Spitzer of USA Today demonstrated this capability on July 20, 1993, using the satellite telephone assigned to the Department of Defense National Media Pool. Major national and international wire news services also possess and deploy this technology. While print reports may appear to lack the immediate drama of still pictures or video, they are regularly picked up and broadcast by radio and television networks. In fact, a print report, transmitted through a 60 pound satellite telephone uplink, may become the trigger for broader news media coverage. Recall also that CNN's dramatic reports from Baghdad, Iraq, on the first night of

Operation Desert Storm were sent by telephone; the pictures were added days later.

Of particular concern at the operational and strategic levels is the interest the television networks have expressed in acquiring and broadcasting images obtained from satellite overflights. This capability, demonstrated during coverage of the Persian Gulf War, could be a significant factor during sensitive military operations. As with any technological capability, seeking control over the employment of satellite imagery is largely a futile effort. What is necessary is continuous, candid dialogue with individual reporters and news organizations so that they clearly understand the consequences of reporting information which violates operational coverage ground rules and which could jeopardize the outcome of the mission or the safety of the force.

The technological capabilities of the news media are an operational fact of life for the commander and public affairs staff as they prepare for the media relations mission. While it is not always necessary to understand fully the functioning of such technology, it is important to recognize that, even in the most austere conditions, information moves from journalist to medium (wire service bulletin, television report, newspaper story, radio broadcast) at incredible speeds. Therefore, it is often true that the most pressing task of communicating through the news media is to be able to provide timely detail and context so that the ultimate audiences can understand, as nearly as possible, the facts and implications of any story. This means that the military must also field a credible technological capability.

Those responsible for communicating with the news media must possess the freshest public affairs guidance and unclassified operational information to respond effectively. To do so, public affairs staffs should be equipped with satellite and, as appropriate, cellular telephones; facsimile machines; data transmission devices; and secure transmission means. Currently they are not. Without these capabilities, those designated to communicate with reporters could find themselves the least informed about current situations, and commanders could find their operational efforts characterized as uncoordinated and their spokespersons portrayed as confused. Resulting doubts about the effectiveness of military activities can severely limit the commander's ability to communicate effectively and result in intense efforts to regain credibility rather than disciplined programs to sustain it.

The cost of purchasing current technology is severe for both the military and the news media and often prevents commanders from obtaining the necessary equipment. The acquisition process begins with a complete assessment of necessary capabilities and a survey of the technology available to support the news media relations mission. It may be found that the leasing of technology is more practical than the actual purchase. There are several advantages to this approach. First, leasing will generally be less expensive, resulting in lower fixed costs. Additionally, leasing offers flexibility as mixes of necessary technology can be developed to support specific missions. Finally, this approach assures that the most current technology is available. Purchased equipment becomes obsolescent rather quickly; establishing and updating leases for capabilities will ensure that commanders are best able to communicate through the news media.

But technology is merely an aspect of the larger issue of support. Like the other operational functions, those performing news media relations tasks must be able to deploy, concentrate essential resources and communicate in those areas most central to the public's understanding of the military mission. Once the point(s) of maximum news media interest has been identified, the commander should assign a high priority to respond to that interest. To borrow a sports analogy, the effort to engage the news media using a man-to-man, matchup "defense" is futile; there are simply too many of them. By establishing responsive resource "zones," commanders can accommodate reporters who enter their areas of responsibility and then pass them on to other commanders. This approach also provides the flexibility to manage surges of journalists at particular points of interest by shifting assets from less committed areas. This can only be done if commanders are thinking forward and preparing in advance to establish an infrastructure which provides trained public affairs personnel with appropriate communications, transportation, and logistics assets.

This requirement is particularly challenging as no organization, regardless of size, can accomplish this task without reinforcement. Most importantly, all support should be provided on a dedicated basis since it is impractical to rely on those assets deployed for other operational tasks which are often given higher priorities. Thus the planning process must specify the public affairs support requirements, identify the sources (components, supporting CINCs, the Military Departments), and deploy the resources at a pace to meet the information requirements of the journalists on the ground.

To enhance their news media relations plans, commanders, especially those at the operational level, must also have access to timely summaries of print and broadcast reports prepared by the news media. In the earliest stages of an operation, the daily transmission of the Early Bird news summary product from the Pentagon should meet this requirement. As the operation matures, providing this capability will be a major challenge as it requires current technology such as facsimile machines, wire service printers, television and radio sets, and downlink facilities to obtain the necessary reports.

Commanders at every level should be interested in what is being said about their efforts. Those at the tactical level will often learn of these from the reporters integrated with their units or from news summaries several days old. They don't have to like or agree with what is being said about them, but they do have to understand what is being reported. After all, the public obtains its information about the operation from the news media, and those reports help to shape public perceptions and opinion about the command's effectiveness. An efficient media relations program is aware of any differences between what the command knows to be true and what the news media are reporting. Relying on technology, their own assessments, and their news media relations plans, commanders and their public affairs staffs have to work continuously to ensure that the inevitable gap is as narrow as possible.

In an exercise environment, commanders and their public affairs staffs are usually able to establish and operate such complete infrastructures, but that is often after several years of preparation. The track record is not as successful when the planning and deployment time frames are compressed to a few days as in a crisis. To date, for instance, there has never been a consistent solution for establishing communications with public affairs personnel in the earliest stages of an operation. Public affairs staffs have had to rely on borrowing satellite phones from reporters (Somalia) or struggling with undependable indigenous communications systems as in Macedonia where only 12 commercial international telephone lines exist (July 1993). Thus it is necessary that all contingency planning specifically identifies the necessary assets and builds their movement into all deployment schedules. Timeliness is particularly important because, as discussed, reporters will probably be in the area of operations when the forces arrive. Failure to anticipate and respond to this presence will shift the initiative to the news media and distract the commander who then must expend considerable effort to catch up rather than to communicate as an equal partner in the process.

By maximizing their technology, creating their own logistics support, and renting their own vehicles (as witnessed in the desert, the former Yugoslavia, Somalia, and elsewhere), it appears that the news media have met most of their own resource requirements. Yet commanders can always assume that journalists will call upon them to provide specific assistance such as medical care or potable water. Commanders should anticipate these situations and develop response strategies. Such planning will also be a factor when unique requirements evolve such as during those contingencies which call for chemical protection equipment.

Furthermore, while commanders should focus their primary support efforts on their own public affairs infrastructure, a review of the guidelines for the coverage of DoD operations reveals some responsibility for supporting the news media. In those situations in which "open and independent reporting" is the norm, military communications, transportation, and logistical support should be provided on a space-available basis. There are, however, other factors which affect such support. For instance, when transmission security is a factor, commanders may establish a ground rule that reporters will use available military communications to file their stories. If discussed in advance, this arrangement would probably work, but increased priority must be given to those stories to ensure timeliness and reduce suspicion. Similarly, commanders may find it desirable to provide journalists with transportation to avoid having brightly-colored, light-reflective rental vehicles accompany ground forces. Each of these is situationally dependent and will require individual judgments. In those cases when it is necessary to form news media pools, commanders assume full responsibility for news media support. This reality and the demands it would place on limited resources should guide commanders as they assess the need for such pools.

NEWS MEDIA RELATIONS SUPPORT ARRANGEMENT

Organizing for the media relations mission requires the same disciplined planning as any other operational task. As noted earlier, failure to do so limits the response capabilities of the command and can result in underinformed news reports which can misrepresent the direction and effectiveness of the military effort. This lack of preparation serves neither the military forces nor the reporters sent to cover them. Thus it is not unusual to find that reporters are equally interested in ensuring that procedures and facilities exist to facilitate effective news coverage.

Support efforts for both the public affairs staff and the news media merge at the information bureau established by the commander and subordinate to the command's public affairs officer. This will generally be a Joint Information Bureau (JIB) which supports the Joint Task Force commander; component commanders should also set up service-unique facilities to represent their own roles in the larger effort and to assist journalists seeking to visit forward units. In those operations conducted with international coalition or alliance partners, commanders will operate Combined or Allied Press Information Centres (CIB/APIC). Regardless of type, these facilities serve as the primary source of information, transportation, communications, and logistical support for all aspects of the media relations mission.

Reporters entering an area of operations will normally seek out a JIB, CIB, or APIC to obtain information about the developing situation and to request assistance in gaining access to the deployed forces. Contingency planning should set the establishment of the information bureau as a priority mission with the deployment pace of necessary resources tied to the assessed level of news media interest. The size of the public affairs effort should be linked to the anticipated news media presence, not to the size of the military force. Thus in June and July of 1993, the public affairs challenge was to develop a public affairs presence appropriate to the news media coverage of the initial deployment of U.S. forces into Macedonia; the fact that the force of 300 ground troops would not normally require public affairs support was not a factor. The arrival of 20 members of the Berlin Brigade on July 5, 1993 triggered considerable international news coverage, with video images appearing very quickly on CNN. Additionally, each course of action should allow for surges of news media interest at various locations within the area of operation and at specific times in the movement of the force (recall that the coverage from Macedonia faded soon after the arrival of the main body of troops).

Such situations could be addressed with the efficient deployment and employment of whatever support resources are available. For instance, the British media plan for Operation Desert Storm called for the placement of a Forward Transmission Unit (FTU) in the vicinity of their division headquarters. It consisted of processing and uplink capabilities for both still and video products which greatly reduced the transmission time between the FTU and permanent facilities located outside the area of operations. Though often subjected to a system of security review more restrictive than that imposed by U.S. forces, British journalists were able to provide timely and dramatic reports without venturing very far from the units to which they were assigned.

Operations Security (OPSEC)

Logically, technology which allows for the real time reporting of military activities has enormous implications for OPSEC. The December 9, 1992 beach scene in Somalia represented the essence of every commander's fears over the violation of operations security. The news media have since accused the military of overreaction because there were no negative consequences. In fact, one television producer claimed that the use of lights was an act of deterrence because any hostile gunmen could clearly see the imposing nature of the forces coming ashore. This "no harm, no foul" justification is of no solace. That no one was attacked or injured was because of variables beyond the control of both the military and the news media. Quite simply, the event was benign only because no gunman decided to take advantage of the illuminated target area containing both the U.S. Marines and the news media whose coverage had helped to bring them there.

Yet there are other troublesome, though less obvious, examples of OPSEC violations. At 2:30 PM on January 13, 1993, White House spokesman Marlin Fitzwater announced that Allied aircraft had attacked a variety of air defense facilities in Southern Iraq 75 minutes earlier. Little of his information about this classified operation was new. That was because two hours earlier, the Reuters News Service had broken the story that the attack had been launched; this report originated in Washington, DC, not on the U.S.S. Kitty Hawk or from some unidentified airbase. For the next two hours, CNN and others competed to provide details about the attack by calling on their various military experts. They were able to provide disturbingly accurate reports of the numbers of aircraft and the types and locations of targets. After Fitzwater's announcement, the only fresh information about the attack and, most specifically, those who conducted it flowed from journalists embarked on the aircraft carrier. Much of that reporting was quite good, reinforcing the importance of including reporters with the force.

During the "CBS Evening News" on June 16, 1993, National Security Correspondent David Martin, drawing on his well-placed sources, presented a remarkably complete outline of the U.N. operation against a warlord in Mogadishu, Somalia. This action differed from the earlier example because Martin's report aired after the operation began. Under similar conditions several days earlier, Jamie McIntyre, CNN's Military Affairs Correspondent, and the CNN staff delayed the reporting of operational information they had obtained because of concern that to do so could directly warn the target of the U.N. effort. Although perhaps not up to military OPSEC standards, each demonstrates sensitivity to military security concerns.

While most journalists would not compromise OPSEC intentionally, there is always the chance for an inadvertent release of information by inexperienced or careless journalists. It seems inevitable that information will leak, and journalists understandably believe that they are being given information so that it can be reported. It simply makes no sense to provide classified information to journalists and expect that they will secure it for you. There will be cases, especially at the strategic and operational levels, where "senior officials" will provide sensitive information to assist reporters in telling the complete story, but only after they have agreed to withhold its release until after a time specified in the ground rules or provided the reporters will remain with the unit until OPSEC concerns are no longer relevant to the specific situation (operational and tactical levels).

Because of the pervasiveness of news media presence, the speed of technology, and the apparent inevitably of information leaks at the strategic level, traditional efforts at ensuring OPSEC are being overtaken by events beyond the control of commanders. This is especially true at the operational and tactical levels where intelligence and sensitive information are the most perishable. The solution to much of the concern over security of information lies in a comprehensive plan for the inclusion of news media, reinforced by ground rules and supported by procedures for providing explanation and context about the sensitivity and complexity of the military actions. Penalties for OPSEC violations are also important.

In establishing OPSEC parameters and outlining the consequences of reporting sensitive information, both the military and the news media should consider the following questions: Would the release or reporting of specific information assist the enemy in being more prepared than he would have been otherwise? Would it compromise a deception plan? Identify the main effort? Are the facts the military is providing or the news media are gathering merely helpful in understanding the complete story, or are they central to the success of the operation? In other words, would the disclosure of this information affect the course of events?

Applying these standards to the earlier examples, it would appear that the intense coverage before the airstrike in January posed a significant threat to OPSEC, while the release of details once the U.N. operations began was less likely to influence the outcome. That none of the reports apparently affected the course of events is not relevant; a benign result does not justify the reporting of information whose knowledge could have changed the outcome. Prior notification could increase enemy preparedness and should be a matter of common concern for both the news media and the military.

Journalists often argue that some events, such as the launching of aircraft, are clearly visible to any observer and that their reporting could probably be matched by a phone call by an enemy agent. Perhaps, but it is also very likely that the "real time" reporting by radio and television could reach the enemy's decision makers much faster and more efficiently than a phone call, once again confirming the importance of technology.

It is clear that the mere presence of a reporter in an operational area exposes that person to important information.

Further, it is apparent that a journalist can only report the complete story if provided background information to understand the full context. Personal acquaintance and trust may often ensure that sensitive information is not revealed. When such credibility does not exist, it may well be that certain reporters can be told little or nothing in advance. To preclude doubt or the possibility of confusion, specific ground rules should be developed in each situation to identify that information of concern and specify the parameters for its release.

The fourth Guideline For The Coverage of DoD Operations addresses both the establishment of ground rules and the need for sanctions should they be violated. The facts that both institutions have acknowledged that security concerns are important enough to establish reasonable limits on reporting and that suspension and expulsion can be legitimate remedies if these are ignored encourage commanders and their staffs to outline a set of ground rules appropriate to the mission and to make them central to the inclusion arrangements with the news media.

There has been considerable discussion about the need for the "Security Review" of news products to ensure that ground rules are not violated. No mention of this issue is made in the guidelines because the DoD and news media representatives could not agree on wording that was acceptable. Thus there will always be the potential for controversy. In the wake of the Persian Gulf War, to date, there have been no instances of security review. However, commanders have periodically mandated that news stories be embargoed (delayed) as part of the ground rules until an operation has passed its most critical moment. The exceptional reports from those journalists deployed on the U.S.S. Kitty Hawk on January 13, 1993, embargoed until after the White House announcement, represent a classic success story.

There are new standards for OPSEC emerging. For example, the Secretary of Defense and the Chairman of the Joint Chiefs of Staff conducted a detailed operational briefing several days before the Marines arrived in Somalia. That session reflected an awareness that openness or transparency of action were more appropriate than steps to conceal information. Logically, each situation will require commanders to tailor specific ground rules to their assigned mission. Those for a combat operation (Desert Storm) probably won't resemble those for humanitarian assistance (Somalia), and certainly won't look anything like those for disaster relief (Florida).

Education and Training

Both the military and the news media are woefully deficient in their knowledge of the other institution and in their training for those tasks necessary to make and report news during a military operation. What is particularly alarming about this situation is that the personalities of those involved in the relationship have a huge impact on the success of the media relations mission. While the military can only directly affect its own behavior, it has a stake in improving the level of news media understanding and including them in realistic exercise scenarios. With fewer opportunities to serve in the military and the continuing trend in the news media to generalists, the cultural gap between the military and the news media can only widen. It is important to understand, however, that the news media are concerned about their own deficiencies.

Because they want to retain their most experienced reporters at the Pentagon and at the theater headquarters, news media decision makers will send their best qualified nonmilitary experts to cover the troops in the field. Thus commanders and their public affairs staffs must prepare to accommodate reporters with limited expertise in situations of great stress and uncertainty. At other times, such as in educational settings and during exercises, it is in the best interest of both institutions to increase contact, mutual understanding and trust and to decrease suspicion. At the tactical and operational levels, the most likely venues for those least experienced, reporters should understand military organizations and basic military doctrine. As often as possible they should train with military forces to develop their own field skills, determine their personal equipment needs, and come to understand how individuals function together to form effective units which work to achieve assigned objectives.

Of greatest importance to the success of the military's news media relations program is the commander's commitment to be as accepting of close news media scrutiny during an operation as of the favourable publicity available during an exercise. They are dramatically different environments. During an exercise, reporters tend to focus on the efforts of units to perfect their operational skills, and there is more time to explain, educate and inform journalists about what they are experiencing. Further, most stories are features which tend to be favourable in tone. By contrast, the tension and pace associated with operational deployments do not always allow for the cordial relationships typically associated with exercises. Questions and requests for information, normally welcomed by the military during exercises as opportunities to explain, are often legitimately regarded as unwelcome distractions during an operation and can create friction among those involved. Additionally, the uncertainty of operational situations not governed by structured exercise scenarios can result in stories which are not as comfortable or as forgiving as those from exercises.

In an adaptation of a familiar principle, commanders should ensure that exercise scenarios cause their organizations to train as they would communicate in an actual contingency. More specifically, it is imperative that commanders prepare themselves and their units to communicate operationally by exercising those specific tasks most related to the media relations mission. This begins by ensuring that public affairs personnel have roles to play in both command post exercises, which hone assessment, planning, and response skills, and live field training exercises where the logistical support of the news media is a central feature.

Even in the absence of a dedicated public affairs scenario, media relations training is an integral part of any command post exercise. Since virtually every event, issue, plan, and decision contains some public affairs aspects, commanders and their staffs should derive exercise news media "play" from the rest of the exercise flow. Without the need to actually communicate with reporters, commanders and their public affairs staffs can increase their proficiency in assessing the public affairs implications of evolving courses of action, develop and coordinate appropriate guidance, issue exercise news releases, and "establish" and equip information bureaus. A CPX can also assist commanders in becoming comfortable with reviewing and, as appropriate, responding to events and perceptions reported through the news media (an aspect which should be built into every exercise scenario). Additionally, the kind of precise staffing necessary for the development and deployment of public affairs resources can best take place in the CPX environment. The staging of an exercise news conference, to include preparation and rehearsal, would also be useful because, after all, such sessions have become standard features of every operational deployment.

If well-conceived, many of the irritants which appear during actual deployments should reveal themselves during exercises. That they often do not is evidence of the artificiality often seen in public affairs exercise efforts. It is understandable that live exercise planning generally focuses on a few highly-visible and interesting events to attract reporters who may not otherwise have the inclination or the time to attend. Yet the support for journalists who participate should go beyond rehearsed exercise briefings and the observation of those events from areas marked off by white engineer tape. The exercise reliance on elaborate information facilities; numerous telephones, facsimile machines and photocopiers; vans, buses, and on-call helicopters; and full public affairs staffs is often artificial and can create expectations that such support is always appropriate and, more naively, always available. Generally, this is not relevant training because of its artificiality. As with any operational task, exercise organizations, equipment and procedures for news media relations should be adapted to resemble as closely as possible those required for an actual mission. The administrative treatment of reporters should not be confused with the demands of news media relations during an actual deployment.

Journalists attending exercises should be treated as they would when they arrive to cover military forces conducting any mission along the continuum of operations. They should be informed of the activities of all units involved in the exercise; included in the normal functioning of those units to the extent that they actually live with them for several days; transported in organic tactical vehicles; and encouraged to conduct interviews and file stories. To the extent possible, such an approach can yield a sense of common effort which echoes the shared experience of those war correspondents who came ashore at Normandy. Like military forces, those journalists who have experienced rigorous training deployments, such as to the National Training Center, speak coherently and enthusiastically of their new understanding and increased skill proficiency. Such positive response should be reinforced through sustained contacts between the military and journalists.

Various initiatives have sought to assist journalists in understanding the complexities of military life and of military operations. The annual "Media Days" at the various war colleges and the periodic appearance of journalists before military audiences generally result in brief epiphanies of understanding, but they seldom survive the pressures of an actual deployment. Thus a broader agenda of training opportunities like those outlined earlier and detailed background briefings during actual operations will always be needed to ensure that journalists are prepared to the extent possible to cover the story. More accurate, complete and interesting stories will result as reporters learn about and understand the military culture and how it functions.

Additionally, the military can only benefit from increased exposure to journalists. It is vitally important that these experiences are balanced in their presentation and not geared to reinforce stereotypes. An Associated Press story, in May 1993, reported that training in Germany to prepare U.S. troops to deploy to the former Yugoslavia included "'reporters and cameramen' who pop up and try to make the soldiers say something outrageous." The training technique is sound, but its tone could be unnecessarily threatening. While meetings with journalists can be stressful and risky, the vast majority of such encounters will be simple conversations, constrained by OPSEC concerns, designed to obtain information to produce news stories. Efforts to reduce the fear and distrust of journalists are far more useful than those that reinforce the myth that the role of the news media is to undermine the military effort and to discredit the members of the force.

Media relations training, most often emphasizing the principle of "Security at the Source," is necessary for those operating at the strategic, operational and tactical levels, and should be provided in both service schools and exercise environments. The dialogue between the military and the news media is not simply the concern of the public affairs staff. In fact, such dialogue is less important to reporters who are increasingly interested in speaking directly with those making the decisions and performing the tasks of the operation. The early realization and acceptance of that fact argue strongly for a broad-based orientation to the news media and energetic scenarios which develop and exercise skills necessary to sustain the dialogue.

Any training agenda must consider the increasingly international character of security missions and news media coverage. In the wake of the controversy over the beach scene in Mogadishu, one explanation offered by the news media was that it was only the foreign journalists who were using lights. Such explanations are nonsense, and such distinctions are no longer relevant. Commanders and their public affairs staffs must be sensitive to the reality of full international coverage as represented by CNN, the BBC World Service (radio and, now, television), SkyNews (British), and Reuters television. Of course, various wire services (notably Reuters and the Associated Press) have long had international impact, but never to the degree generated by contemporary broadcast news media. Yet Americans in several cities awoke on July 6, 1993 to front page pictures (some in color) of U.S. troops arriving in Macedonia. The source of those photographs emphasized the international nature of news: they were provided by Agence France-Presse.

Recent experience has also taught much about the challenges of working with public information officials (the international term) from other nations. In addition to Coalition efforts in Desert Shield/Storm and Somalia (before and during the U.N. mission), American public affairs personnel have participated with their NATO allies during Operation Southern Guard (the NATO response during the Persian Gulf War), the naval blockade of Serbia and Montenegro, and Operation Deny Flight over Bosnia-Hercegovina. In the past, only the United States and Canada have fielded trained public affairs/public information personnel; that is no longer true. Several NATO nations have developed strong cadres of public information specialists with experience in NATO, U.N., WEU (Western European Union), and other combined operations. This relationship is further complicated by new information initiatives from the Russian Federation and other nations with whom the United States has not maintained traditional contacts. Training programs and exercise scenarios must be developed to ensure the most efficient possible coverage of those international military operations in which the United States will play important roles.

Missions and Messages

Once again, virtually every military activity will have public affairs implications because of news media and public interest; this is true even if OPSEC and other factors dictate that no public discussion is possible other than a standard disclaimer about not discussing security measures or future operations. Regardless of mission, commanders can expect the predeployment and deployment phases to attract considerable news media attention. This fact offers commanders and their public affairs staffs excellent opportunities to take the initiative in the media relations mission. Even if there is no public acknowledgement that specific units have been alerted, there will be enough visible signatures to lead to speculation. During the deployment to Southwest Asia, the presence of large numbers of soldiers in civilian stores purchasing sunscreen and bottled water clearly indicated an alert status. To retain credibility, some explanation should be available when the reporters call.

Most importantly, efforts in these initial stages can allow commanders to achieve some early objectives at a time when commanders can expect reporters to be functioning at full tempo. As appropriate, deployment plans should allocate seats for local and regional journalists to travel with the force into the operational area. First, this step ensures that news media are included with the force, an important initial goal; there is no reason to wait until arrival to accomplish this task. Additionally, those journalists who have covered the organization regularly and perhaps have participated in various exercises are more likely to be familiar with the military in general and with the deploying units in particular; are immediately available for inclusion because they live close to the deployment base; and are particularly helpful to the total public affairs effort because their stories are sent back to the towns and regions in which the force lives and assist in informing those who remain behind, including the families.

In our uncertain international security environment, the military is facing a variety of unfamiliar challenges. Preparations for news media relations will vary significantly depending on the mission, OPSEC concerns, and the tone of the message to be communicated. In addition to familiar combat contingencies, commanders could also find themselves as participants in complex crisis management efforts, humanitarian aid and disaster relief missions, and peacekeeping/peacemaking/peace-enforcement operations. Strict limits on OPSEC which are familiar in combat contingencies give way to transparency in humanitarian aid, disaster relief and peacekeeping operations.

All military missions provide the types of activities and information on which journalists inevitably focus. Regardless of circumstances, the first rule of communicating with the news media is to speak within the limits of one's own expertise and responsibility. A very inefficient approach is to prepare a list of subjects that anyone speaking with a reporter may discuss. In fact, it is usually easier to focus on those issues respondents should not talk about. In general, the relationship between the reporter and the soldier is simple: That which is said is reported. Thus it is important that military personnel understand the concept of "security at the source" which establishes the standard that information known to be classified or sensitive should not be provided to a reporter.

The Way Ahead

Traditionally, one of the functions of the news media has been to provide the first draft of history through the reporting of the events, issues and personalities of their times. While the emerging trend is for journalists to become participants in those events, definers of the issues and some of the most influential personalities, their basic role remains unchanged. In response to the pace and complexity of events and issues and the speed of the reporting process, it will be increasingly important for the military to become active, visible participants in the dialogue leading to the production of news reports. It is no longer sufficient to remain passive in the face of news media scrutiny, reluctantly accept the visit of a reporter, and then complain about the results. The facts are that the age of activist journalism places special demands on the time and resources of the commander and often results in confrontations with the military.

There is a view that the tension between the military and the news media will diminish with the evolution of younger officers, NCOs, and enlisted personnel who have matured, not just watching television, but by having their growth and development recorded on home video cameras. While it is perhaps inevitable that the comfort level of the military with the news media will thus improve, this trend will be matched by ever decreasing levels of familiarity and understanding which young reporters will have for their contemporaries in the military. Further, budget constraints on news coverage have led to the practice of "parachuting" in which reporters are "dropped" into a story with little preparation and are left there only long enough shoot some video, take a few pictures, and record a variety of observations before being extracted and assigned to another story. Such superficial reporting could have a significant impact on public perceptions about the operation. Thus the need for regular contact through educational opportunities, training visits and exercises will remain at least as important as now.

This is especially true as the news media's impact on the public agenda and public discussion continues to grow, but in new ways unfamiliar today. While traditional television and radio networks, newspapers and magazines may become less relevant, emerging computer technology which will enable citizens to select their own print and broadcast stories from an extensive menu of news services will open fresh opportunities to reach the public, but only if the message and the messenger communicate credibility and retain the public's trust. Obviously it is not possible for military leaders to speak personally with each member of the public, domestic or international. Thus the bond of interdependence strengthens between the military as the source of the message and the news media as the messenger.

Traditional concerns about technology will also remain central to the relationship between the military and the news media as will its increasing impact on OPSEC and public understanding. Additionally, because of new capabilities, the public forum for the military will no longer be limited to those local journalists who live around bases or even to the national reporters who cover security issues at the Pentagon. News media coverage has come to rely on a vast international system of electronic images, text and data which ensures that stories about events in the most remote areas can be made quickly available to any interested news organization. The historic arrival of the first NATO aircraft in Baku, Azerbaijan, on February 5, 1992, was covered by a young radio reporter who was employed as a "stringer" for an American radio network. She then produced two sets of reports and interviews: one for her local audience and one for transmission to the United States.

Ultimately, however, technology only affects the speed of the reporting process and not the quality of the stories themselves. Both institutions will continue to share a common interest in ensuring the accuracy and completeness of every report before it is transmitted over a satellite telephone, video uplink or data line. For the military commander, this will involve the development of a comprehensive news media plan and the commitment of knowledgeable personnel and dedicated resources at the earliest stages of the dialogue with journalists, whoever they are and whatever news organization they represent. Chasing a story once it is produced is far less efficient because it requires the correction of misperceptions and the repeated restatement of the military position, distracting commanders from the events and stories which continue to move forward. Typically, a delayed response which focuses on a published news media report sacrifices the initiative to the reporters, confuses the public and contributes to the persistent tension with the news media, thus making the next story more difficult to tell.

In thinking forward about the news media relations mission, commanders should not fear the inevitable news report. What they should be concerned about are those stories which contain factual errors, misrepresent the goals of an operation, or create false expectations for performance. Fortunately, commanders can affect the quality of reporting by preparing a tailored package of public affairs policies, plans and support packages appropriate to each assigned operation. Normally, commanders will find that most journalists are interested in improving the quality of their own reporting even if it means adapting to reasonable ground rules and procedures outlined by the military. Yet commanders, operational staffs and public affairs practitioners can only directly affect their own assessments, policy judgements, planning and news media relations decisions. They cannot control the news media's reactions or behavior and should not waste effort, time and resources to do so.

Thinking forward takes the initiative by seeking confident engagement with the news media rather than uncertain avoidance or defensive conflict. This includes holding reporters to standards of accuracy and completeness and developing strategies to "correct the record" if events or comments are misrepresented. The relationship between the military and the news media can allow for both institutions to act as equal partners in the communications process. From the military's perspective, the effort should be directed toward assessing the levels of news media interest to be expected in any assigned mission; determining how many reporters can be accommodated in the operational units and what procedures are necessary to assist in their inclusion; and identifying what technology is required, and, like all support packages, ensuring that it is available early enough to affect positively the news media relations environment. Central to the entire effort is the need to make certain that the public affairs plan efficiently supports the commander's scheme of manoeuvre to include the requirements of OPSEC.

Ultimately, of course, the goal is that the next time the lights come on, either literally or metaphorically, the situation will be interpreted as an opportunity to tell the military story, and that the soldiers, regardless of position, will be trained well enough to respond candidly, explain effectively, and continue the mission.

Bibliography

Albert, David H. : *Tell the American People: Perspectives on the Iranian Revolution*, Movement for a New Society, Philadelphia, 1980.

Albert, Michael, *What Is to Be Undone: A Modern Revolutionary Discussion of Classical Left Ideologies*, Porter Sargent, Cambridge, Massachusetts, 1974.

Bagdikian, B. H.: *The New Media Monopoly*. Boston: Beacon Press, 2004.

Carey, A.: *Taking the Risk Out of Democracy: Propaganda in the US and Australia*. Sydney: University of New South Wales Press, 1995.

Chang, T.: *The Press and China Policy: The Illusion of Sino-American Relations 1950-1984*. Norwood, New Jersey: Ablex, 1993.

Davis, A.: *Public Relations Democracy: Public Relations, Politics and the Mass Media in Britain*. Manchester: Manchester University Press, 2002.

Davis, R.: *The Press and American Politics*. New York: Longman, 1992.

Edwards, D. & D. Cromwell: *Guardians of Power: The Myth of the Liberal Media*. London: Pluto Press, 2005.

Gowing, N. : *Real Time TV Coverage from War. In Bosnia by Television*. London: British Film Institute, 1996.

Habermas, J.: *The Structural Transformation of the Public Sphere: An Inquiry into a Category of Bourgeois Society*. Cambridge: Polity Press, 1989.

Hallin, D. C.: *The "Uncensored War": The Media and Vietnam*. New York: Oxford University Press, 1986.

Herman, E. S. & N. Chomsky: *Manufacturing Consent: The Political Economy of the Mass Media*. New York: Pantheon Books, 1988.

King-Hall, Stephen, *Defence in the Nuclear Age*, Victor Gollancz, London, 1958.

Lakey, George, *Strategy for a Living Revolution*, Grossman, New York, 1974.

Liebknecht, Karl, *Militarism*, B. W. Huebsch, New York, 1917.

Martin, Brian, *Social Defence, Social Change,* Freedom Press, London, 1993.

Martin, C. R.: *Framed!: Labor and the Corporate Media*. Ithaca: ILR Press/Cornell University Press, 2004.

McChesney, R. W.: *Rich Media, Poor Democracy: Communication Politics in Dubious Times.* Urbana, University of Illinois Press, 1999.

Meyer, T. : *Media Democracy: How the Media Colonize Politics*. Cambridge, England: Polity Press, 2002.

Oppenheimer, Martin, *The Urban Guerilla*, Quadrangle, Chicago, 1969.

Radine, Lawrence B., *The Taming of the Troops: Social Control in the United States Army*, Greenwood, Westport, Connecticut, 1977.

Randle, Michael, *People Power: The Building of a New European Home*, Hawthorn Press, London, 1991.

Rigby, Andrew, *Living the Intifada*, Zed Books, London, 1991.

Semelin, Jacques, *Unarmed Against Hitler: Civilian Resistance in Europe 1939-1943*, Praeger, Westport, Connecticut, 1993.

Sharp, Gene, *The Politics of Nonviolent Action*, Porter Sargent, Boston, 1973.

Shaw, Martin, *Socialism and Militarism: Remaking a Tradition*, Bertrand Russell Peace Foundation, Nottingham, 1981.

Weinstein, Deena, *Bureaucratic Opposition*, Pergamon, New York, 1979.

Index

□□□